W9-BCA-941

Microsoft
PowerPoint® 97

Microsoft®Press

PUBLISHED BY
Microsoft Press
A Division of Microsoft Corporation
One Microsoft Way
Redmond, Washington 98052-6399

Library of Congress Cataloging-in-Publication Data
Microsoft PowerPoint 97 At a Glance / Perspection, Inc.
   p. cm.
  Includes index.
  ISBN 1-57231-368-4
  1. Computer graphics.   2. Microsoft PowerPoint for Windows.
I. Perspection, Inc.
T385.M522 1996
006.6'869--dc20

                                96-36629
                                   CIP

Printed and bound in the United States of America.

    9   QEQE   1 0 9

Distributed in Canada by Penguin Books Canada Limited.

A CIP catalogue record for this book is available from the British Library.

Microsoft Press books are available through booksellers and distributors worldwide. For further information about international editions, contact your local Microsoft Corporation office or contact Microsoft Press International directly at fax (425) 936-7329. Visit our Web site at mspress.microsoft.com.

For Perspection, Inc.
Managing Editor: Steven M. Johnson
Writers: Patrick Carey, Joan Carey
Production Editor: David W. Beskeen
Developmental Editor: Joan Carey
Copy Editor: Jane Pedicini
Technical Editor: Ann-Marie Buconjic

For Microsoft Press
Acquisitions Editors: Lucinda Rowley, Kim Fryer
Project Editor: Lucinda Rowley

Contents

1   **About At a Glance**   **1**

No Computerese! 1

Useful Tasks 2

And the Easiest Way To Do Them 2

A Quick Overview 2

A Final Word (or Two) 3

2   **Getting Started with PowerPoint**   **5**

Starting PowerPoint 6

Creating a New Presentation 7

Generating Ideas Using AutoContent Wizard 8

Choosing a Template 9

Viewing the Window 10

Opening an Existing Presentation 11

The PowerPoint Views 12

Working with Menus 14

Choosing Dialog Box Options 15

Working with Toolbars 16

Getting Help with the Office Assistant 17

Getting Help 18

Saving a Presentation 20

Closing a Presentation and Exiting PowerPoint 21

3   **Developing a Presentation**   **23**

Creating Consistent Slides 24

Manipulating Objects 26

Developing Text 28

Entering Text 30

Editing Text 32

Developing an Outline 34

Indenting Text 36

Setting Tabs 38

Rearranging Slides 40

"How can I get started quickly in PowerPoint?"

see page 6

Get help with the
Office Assistant
see page 17

A B C

Develop Text in
PowerPoint
see page 28

"How can I save time with templates?"

see page 70

Draw AutoShapes
see page 74

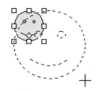

Move and Resize Objects
see page 80

Formatting Text 42

Modifying a Bulleted List 44

Creating a Text Box 46

Correcting Mistakes 48

4 Designing a Look   **51**

Viewing Masters 52

Controlling Slide Appearance with Masters 54

Inserting the Date, Time and Slide Numbering 56

Adding a Header and Footer 58

Understanding Color Schemes 59

Applying a Color Scheme 60

Changing the Color Scheme 62

Applying a Color to an Object 64

Choosing a Fill Effect 66

Saving a Template 68

Applying a Design Template 70

5 Drawing and Modifying Objects   **71**

Creating Line and Arrows 72

Drawing AutoShapes 74

Creating Freeforms 76

Editing Freeforms 78

Moving and Resizing an Object 80

Rotating and Flipping an Object 82

Choosing Object Colors 84

Creating Shadows 86

Creating a 3-D Object 88

Controlling Object Placement 90

Aligning and Distributing Objects 92

Arranging and Grouping Objects 94

Get Clip Art from
the Web
see page 106

Stylize Text with
WordArt
see page 134

Insert a Graph chart
see page 146

6 Adding Multimedia Clips **97**

Inserting Multimedia Objects 98

Inserting Clips 99

Locating Clips 100

Adding and Removing Clips 102

Organizing Clips into Categories 104

Accessing Clip Gallery Live on the Web 106

Editing Clip Art 108

Recoloring an Object 110

Cropping an Image 112

Inserting Sounds 114

Playing and Recording Sounds 116

Using the Custom SoundTrack 118

Inserting and Playing Videos 120

7 Inserting Linked and Embedded Objects **123**

Sharing Information Among Documents 124

Copying and Pasting Objects 125

Embedding and Linking an Object 126

Modifying Links 128

Inserting an Excel Object 130

Inserting a Word Table 132

Creating WordArt Text 134

Editing WordArt Text 136

Applying WordArt Text Effects 138

Creating an Organization Chart 140

Structuring an Organization Chart 142

Formatting an Organization Chart 144

8 Inserting Charts with Microsoft Graph **145**

Inserting a Graph Chart 146

Opening an Existing Chart 147

Entering Graph Data 148

Selecting Graph Data 149

Importing Data 150

Formatting Graph Data 152

Editing Graph Data 154

Moving Graphic Data 156

Hiding and Unhiding Graph Data 157

Selecting a Chart Type 158

Formatting Chart Objects 160

Choosing Advanced Features 162

"How can I select and customize a chart?"

see page 158

E-mailing a presentation
see page 182

Create a slide transition
see page 192

9 Finalizing a Presentation and Its Supplements　　**163**

Finalizing a Presentation in Slide Sorter View 164

Inserting Slides from Other Presentations 166

Inserting Comments 168

Fine-Tuning Text and Its Appearance 170

Setting Page Setup Options 172

Printing a Presentation 174

Preparing Handouts 176

Preparing Speaker Notes 178

Customizing Notes Pages 180

Documenting and E-Mailing a Presentation 182

Exporting Notes and Slides to Word 184

Creating 35-mm Slides 186

Saving Slides in Different Formats 187

10 Preparing a Slide Show　　**189**

Setting Up a Slide Show 190

Creating Slide Transitions 192

Adding Animation 194

Using Specialized Animations 196

Coordinating Multiple Animations 198

Adding Action Buttons 200

Adding Links to Objects 202

Presenting a Show
see page 214

Viewing a presentation
in a browser
see page 232

"How can I record and run a macro?"

see pages 200-202

Creating Hyperlinks to External Objects 204
Timing a Presentation 206
Recording a Narration 208
Creating a Custom Slide Show 210

11 Presenting a Slide Show   **213**
Presenting a Show 214
Accessing Commands During a Show 215
Emphasizing Points 216
Navigating a Slide Show 218
Taking Notes 220
Running a Conference 222
Taking a show on the Road 224
Using Web Templates 226
Creating a Web Page 228
Using the Web Toolbar 230
Viewing a Presentation in a Browser 232
Accessing Information on the Web 234
Accessing PowerPoint Central 235
Accessing the ValuPack 236

12 Customizing PowerPoint   **239**
Setting PowerPoint Options 240
Maximizing Effeciency with Macros 242
Controlling a Macro 244
Assigning a Macro to a Toolbar or Menu 246
Customing PowerPoint Toolbars 248
Customizing Toolbar Buttons 250

Index   **251**

Acknowledgments

The task of creating any book requires the talents of many hard-working people pulling together to meet impossible deadlines and untold stresses. We'd like to thank the outstanding team responsible for making this book possible: the co-writers, Patrick and Joan Carey, the editor, Joan Carey, the copy editor, Jane Pedicini, the technical editor, Ann Marie Buconjic, the production team, Steven Payne, Patrica Young, and Gary Bedard, and the indexer, Michael Brackney.

At Microsoft Press, we'd like to thank Lucinda Rowley for the opportunity to undertake this project and Kim Eggleston for production expertise with the At a Glance series.

Perspection

Perspection

Perspection, Inc. is a technology training company committed to providing information to help people communicate, make decisions, and solve problems. Perspection writes and produces software training books, and develops interactive multimedia applications for Windows-based and Macintosh personal computers.

Microsoft Powerpoint 97 At a Glance incorporates Perspection's training expertise to ensure that you'll receive the maximum return on your time. With this staightforward, easy-to-read reference tool you'll get the information you need when you need it. You'll focus on the skills that increase productivity while working at your own pace and convenience.

We invite you to visit the Perspection World Wide Web site. You can visit us at:

http://www.perspection.com

You'll find a description for all of our books, additional content for our books, information about Perspection, and much more.

About
At a Glance

IN THIS SECTION

No Computerese!

Useful Tasks...

**...And the Easiest Way
To Do Them**

A Quick Overview

A Final Word (or Two)

Microsoft *PowerPoint 97 At a Glance* is for anyone who wants to get the most from their computer and their software with the least amount of time and effort. You'll find this book to be a straightforward, easy-to-read reference tool. With the premise that your computer should work for you, not you for it, this book's purpose is to help you get your work done quickly and efficiently so that you can get away from the computer and live your life.

No Computerese!

Let's face it—when there's a task you don't know how to do but you need to get it done in a hurry, or when you're stuck in the middle of a task and can't figure out what to do next, there's nothing more frustrating than having to read page after page of technical background material. You want the information you need—nothing more, nothing less—and you want it now! And it should be easy to find and understand.

That's what this book is all about. It's written in plain English—no technical jargon and no computerese. There's no single task in the book that takes more than two pages. Just look up the task in the index or the table of contents, turn to the page, and there's the information, laid out step by step and accompanied by a graphic that adds visual clarity. You don't get bogged down by the whys and wherefores; just follow the steps, look at the illustrations, and get your work done with a minimum of hassle.

Occasionally you might want to turn to another page if the procedure you're working on has a "See Also" in the left column. That's because there's a lot of overlap among tasks, and we didn't want to keep repeating ourselves. We've also scattered some useful tips here and there, and thrown in a "Try This" once in a while, but by and large we've tried to remain true to the heart and soul of the book, which is that information you need should be available to you at a glance.

Useful Tasks...

Whether you use PowerPoint 97 for work, play, or some of each, we've tried to pack this book with procedures for everything we could think of that you might want to do, from the simplest tasks to some of the more esoteric ones.

...And the Easiest Way To Do Them

Another thing we've tried to do in *PowerPoint 97 At a Glance* is to find and document the easiest way to accomplish a task. PowerPoint often provides many ways to accomplish a single end result, which can be daunting or delightful, depending on the way you like to work. If you tend to stick with one favorite and familiar approach, we think the methods described in this book are the way to go. If you like trying out alternative techniques, go ahead! The intuitiveness of PowerPoint invites exploration, and you're likely to discover ways of doing things that you think are easier or that you like better. If you do, that's great! It's exactly what

the creators of PowerPoint 97 had in mind when they provided so many alternatives.

A Quick Overview

This book isn't meant to be read in any particular order. It's designed so that you can jump in, get the information you need, and then close the book and keep it near your computer until the next time you need it. But that doesn't mean we scattered the information about with wild abandon. If you were to read the book from front to back, you'd find a logical progression from the simple tasks to the more complex ones. Here's a quick overview.

First, we assume that PowerPoint 97 is already installed on your machine. If it's not, the Setup Wizard makes installation so simple that you won't need our help anyway. So, unlike most computer books, this one doesn't start out with installation instructions and a list of system requirements. You've already got that under control.

Sections 2 through 5 of the book cover the basics: starting Microsoft PowerPoint 97; working with menus, toolbars, and dialog boxes; entering text in Slide view and Outline view; rearranging and modifying slides; adding color and special effects to slides; drawing and modifying objects; and saving presentations.

Sections 6 through 8 describe tasks that are useful for enhancing the look of a presentation: inserting multimedia objects (clip art, pictures, sounds, and videos); playing sounds and videos; inserting Microsoft Excel charts, Microsoft Word tables, organization charts, stylized WordArt text, and Microsoft Graph charts.

Section 9 describes tasks that are essential to finalizing a presentation and creating supplements for the speaker and the audience.

Sections 10 through 11 describes tasks that are important to preparing and presenting a slide show:

setting up slide shows; adding slide transitions and animations; and creating hyperlinks to other slides and programs.

Section 12 covers information that isn't vital to using PowerPoint, but will help you work more efficiently, such as setting PowerPoint options, recording and running macros, and customizing toolbars and toolbar buttons.

A Final Word (or Two)

We had three goals in writing this book, and here they are:

- ◆ Whatever you want to do, we want the book to help you get it done.

- ◆ We want the book to help you discover how to do things you *didn't* know you wanted to do.

- ◆ And, finally, if we've achieved the first two goals, we'll be well on the way to the third, which is for our book to help you enjoy doing your work with PowerPoint 97. We think that would be the best gift we could give you as a "thank you" for buying our book.

We hope you'll have as much fun using *PowerPoint 97 At a Glance* as we've had writing it. The best way to learn is by doing, and that's what we hope you'll get from this book.

Jump right in!

Getting Started with PowerPoint

IN THIS SECTION

Starting PowerPoint

Creating a New Presentation

Generating Ideas Using AutoContent Wizard

Choosing a Template

Viewing the Window

Opening an Existing Presentation

The PowerPoint Views

Working with Menus

Choosing Dialog Box Options

Working with Toolbars

Getting Help with the Office Assistant

Getting Help

Saving a Presentation

Closing a Presentation and Exiting PowerPoint

Whether you need to put together a quick presentation of sales figures for your management team or create a polished slide show for your company's stockholders, Microsoft PowerPoint 97 can help you present your information efficiently and professionally.

Introducing PowerPoint

PowerPoint is a *presentation graphics program*: software that helps you create a slide show presentation. PowerPoint makes it easy to generate and organize ideas. It provides tools you can use to create the objects that make up an effective slide show—charts, graphs, bulleted lists, eye-catching text, multimedia video and sound clips, and more. PowerPoint also makes it easy to create slide show supplements, such as handouts, speaker's notes, and transparencies.

When you're ready, you can share your presentation with others, regardless of whether they have installed PowerPoint—in the office or on the Internet, where you can take instant advantage of the power of the World Wide Web from your planning stages right up to showing your presentation. PowerPoint also includes powerful slide show management tools that give you complete control.

Starting PowerPoint

Because Microsoft PowerPoint 97 is an integrated part of the Microsoft family of products, you start and exit it the same way you would any Microsoft program. To start PowerPoint you can use the Start button, or if you have installed PowerPoint as part of the Microsoft Office 97 suite of programs, you can start the program from the New Office Document dialog box.

TIP

Use the Start menu to start PowerPoint. *Your Start menu might look different from the one shown here, but the steps you take to start PowerPoint should be the same.*

Start PowerPoint from the Start Menu

1 Click the Start button on the taskbar.

2 Point to Programs.

3 Click Microsoft PowerPoint.

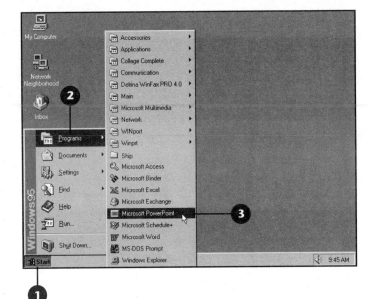

Start PowerPoint as a New Office Document

1 Click the Start button on the Taskbar.

2 Click New Document Office.

3 If necessary, click the General tab.

4 Click Blank Presentation.

5 Click OK.

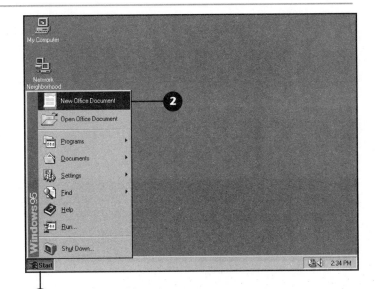

Creating a New Presentation

When you first start PowerPoint, a dialog box opens that provides several presentation type options; the option you choose depends on the requirements of your presentation. You can click the Cancel button to close the dialog box without making a selection. You can also create a new presentation once PowerPoint has started by using the File menu.

TIP

Use the Window menu to switch between presentations. *You can have more than one presentation open at a time—an especially useful feature when you want to copy slides from one presentation into another. To switch between open presentations, click the Window menu, and then click the presentation you want to switch to.*

Start a New Presentation

1. Start PowerPoint.

2. Click the option button you want to use to begin your presentation.

3. Click OK.

4. Follow the instructions that appear. These will vary, depending on the presentation type you chose.

Helps you generate presentation content

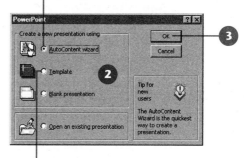

Opens a list of templates, or visual slide designs, from which you preview, and then select the icon representing the design you want.

Start a New Presentation Within PowerPoint

1. Click the File menu, and then click New.

2. Click the tab to display the options you want to use to begin your presentation.

3. Click the icon you want to use as the basis of your presentation.

4. Click OK.

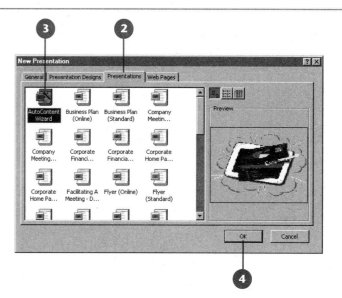

Generating Ideas Using AutoContent Wizard

Often the most difficult part of creating a presentation is knowing where to start. PowerPoint's AutoContent Wizard can help you develop presentation content on a variety of business and personal topics. An AutoContent presentation usually contains 5-10 slides that follow an organized progression of ideas. You edit the text as necessary to meet your needs. Many of the AutoContent presentations are available in Standard or Online formats.

> **TIP**
>
> **Use the AutoContent wizard anytime to create a presentation.** *To use the AutoContent Wizard anytime during a PowerPoint session, click the File menu, click New, click the Presentations tab, click the AutoContent Wizard icon, and then click OK.*

Generate a Presentation Using the AutoContent Wizard

1. Start PowerPoint, click the AutoContent Wizard option button on the PowerPoint dialog box, and then click OK.

2. Read the first wizard dialog box, and then click Next.

3. Click the presentation type you want to use, or to focus on just one set of presentations, click the category option button you want, and then click the presentation you want.

4. Click Next.

5. Click the presentation style option button you want to use, and then click Next.

6. Choose the applicable presentation options—which will vary depending on the topic and style you chose—that you want, and then click Next.

7. Enter information for your title slide, and then click Next.

8. Read the last wizard dialog box, and then click Finish.

Category option buttons

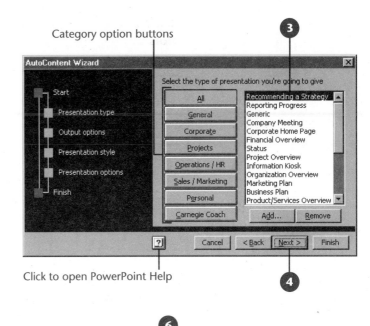

Click to open PowerPoint Help

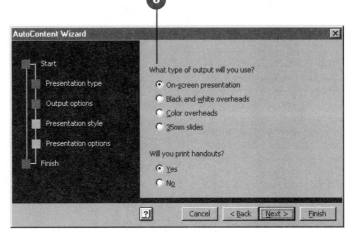

Choosing a Template

PowerPoint provides a collection of professionally designed templates that you can use to create effective presentations. Each template provides a format and color scheme to which you need only add text. You can choose a new template for your presentation at any point: when you first start your presentation or after you've developed the content.

TIP

Use a template anytime to create a presentation. *To use a template anytime during a PowerPoint session, click the File menu, click New, click the Presentation Designs tab, click the presentation design you want to use, and then click OK.*

SEE ALSO

See "Saving a Template" on page 68 for information about modifying a template.

Create a Presentation with a Template

1. Start PowerPoint, click the Template option button on the PowerPoint dialog box, and then click OK.

2. Click the Presentation Designs tab.

3. Click a presentation design icon you want to use.

4. Click OK.

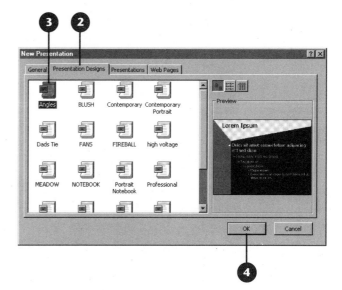

Apply a Template to an Existing Presentation

1. Click the Format menu.

2. Click Apply Design.

3. Click the template you want to apply to your slides.

4. Click Apply.

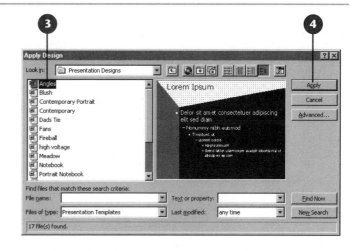

Viewing the Window

The *title bar* displays the program name, Microsoft PowerPoint. If you have a presentation open and maximized, the name of the presentation appears too.

The *Minimize button* shrinks the program window to a button on the taskbar.

The *Maximize button* expands the program window so it fills the entire screen. When you click this button, a Restore button appears in its place that you can click to restore the window to its original size.

The *menu bar* contains the names of the PowerPoint menus that are available. The menus change depending on the task at hand.

The *Close button* closes the program window and exits the program.

The *presentation window* displays the presentation you are currently working on. It has its own Minimize, Maximize, and Close buttons.

The *toolbars* contain buttons you click to carry out commands you use most frequently. You can display additional toolbars as you need them.

Alaska Breeders Marketing Plan

Kita Collins

Slide 1 of 18   Zesty

The *view buttons* let you switch from one view to another.

The *status bar* indicates information about the current presentation. For example, it displays which slide is visible and which template is in use.

Opening an Existing Presentation

You can open an existing presentation from the first PowerPoint dialog box that appears when you start the program. You can also open an existing presentation after you have already started your PowerPoint session using the Open dialog box. If you are not sure where a file is stored, you can search for it.

TIP

Use the Startup dialog box to open a presentation. *To open an existing presentation immediately after starting PowerPoint, click the Open An Existing Presentation option button in the first PowerPoint dialog box that appears.*

Open a File

1. Click the Open button on the Standard toolbar.

2. Click the Look In drop-down arrow, and select the drive or folder containing the file you want to open.

3. If necessary, double-click the folder containing your presentation file.

4. Click the file you want to open.

5. Click Open.

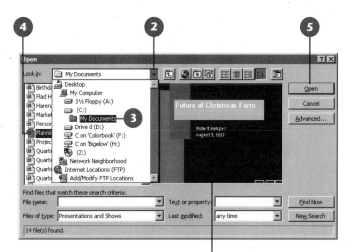

Preview of selected file.

Find a File

1. Click the Open button on the Standard toolbar.

2. Type as much of the filename as you're sure of—even if it's only a few characters. PowerPoint will attempt to match those characters, whether they occur at the beginning, middle, or end of a filename.

3. Click Find Now.

4. Click the file you want to open.

5. Click Open.

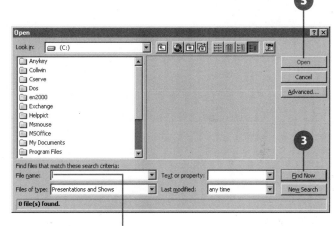

Type all or part of a file name.

The PowerPoint Views

To help you during all aspects of developing a presentation, PowerPoint provides five different views: Slide, Outline, Slide Sorter, Notes Page, and Slide Show. You can switch from one view to another with a single click of one of the view buttons, located next to the horizontal scroll bar.

Slide View

Slide view displays one slide at a time. Use this view to modify individual slides. You can move easily through your slides using the scroll bars or the Previous and Next Slide buttons located at the bottom of the vertical scroll bar. When you drag the scroll box up or down the vertical scroll bar, a label appears that indicates which slide will appear if you release the mouse button.

Slide View

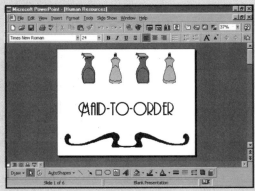

Outline View

Outline view displays a list of the slide titles and their contents in outline format. Use this view to develop your presentation's content. In Outline view, a special toolbar appears that helps you organize and enter your outline. A "thumbnail" or miniature of the active slide appears in a corner to give you an idea of its appearance. Individual slides are numbered. A slide icon appears for each slide. Icons for slides featuring shapes or pictures have small graphics on them.

Outline View

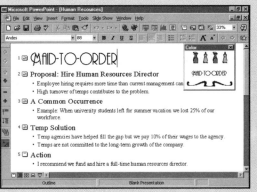

Slide Sorter View

Slide Sorter view displays a thumbnail of each slide in the same window, in the order in which the slides appear in your presentation. Use this view to organize your slides,

Slide Sorter View

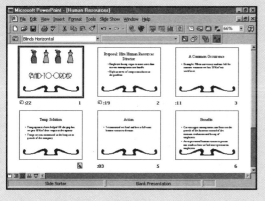

Notes Page View

add actions between slides, called *slide transitions* and other effects to your slide show. In Slide Sorter view, a special toolbar appears that helps you add slide transitions and control other aspects of your presentation. When you add a slide transition, a small icon appears that indicates an action will take place as one slide replaces the previous slide during a show. If you hide a slide, a small icon appears that indicates the slide will not show during the presentation.

Notes Page View

Notes Page view displays a reduced view of a single slide along with a large text box in which you can type notes. You can use these notes as you give your presentation. When you work in Notes Page view you will probably need to use the Zoom drop-down arrow to increase the magnification so you can type more easily. Click the Zoom drop-down arrow and then click the magnification you want.

Slide Show View

Slide Show view presents your slides, one slide at a time. Use this view when you're ready to give your presentation. In Slide Show view, you can click the screen repeatedly or press Enter to move through the show until you've shown all the slides. You can exit Slide Show View at any time by pressing Escape and return to the previous view.

Working with Menus

The PowerPoint commands are organized in menus on the menu bar. Each PowerPoint menu contains a list of related commands. You can also open a *shortcut menu*—a group a related commands that appear when you click the right mouse button on a PowerPoint screen element.

TIP

Use a shortcut key to issue a command. *Press and hold the first key, and then press the second key. For example, press and hold the Ctrl key, and then press S to issue the Save command.*

SEE ALSO

See "Choosing Dialog Box Options" on page 15 for more information on dialog boxes and "Working with Toolbars" on page 16 for more information about using the toolbar buttons.

Issue a Command Using a Menu

1. Click a menu name on the menu bar.

2. Click a menu command you want, or point to a menu command followed by an arrow to open a submenu of related commands, and then click the command.

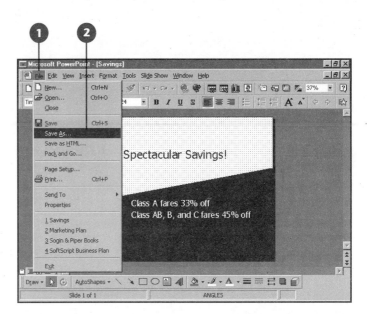

Select a Shortcut Menu Command

1. Right-click an object.

2. Click a command on the shortcut menu, or point to a menu command followed by an arrow to open a submenu, and then click a command.

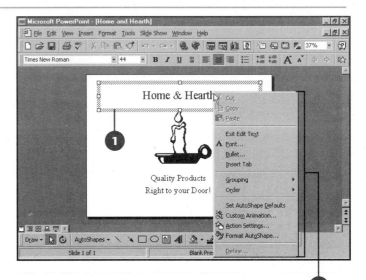

Choosing Dialog Box Options

A *dialog box* is a special window that opens when PowerPoint needs you to provide additional information and specify command-related options in order to complete a task. A dialog box opens when you choose a menu command followed by an ellipsis (...) or click a button whose name is followed by an ellipsis. A dialog box may contain one or more of the following features:

◆ Tabs. *Tabs* organize items into categories for easy access. Click a tab to display its contents.

◆ Option buttons. *Option buttons* precede groups of mutually-exclusive options. You can only click one option button in a group of related option buttons.

◆ Drop-down lists. A *drop-down list* provides available items from which you can choose. Click the drop-down arrow to display the list, and then click the option you want. A scroll bar appears if the list is longer than the box.

◆ Text boxes. You type information directly into a *text box*.

◆ Check boxes. A *check box* precedes an option that has only two possibilities—on or off. If a check box is selected, a check mark is present, and the option is enabled. Clear the check box to turn off the option.

◆ Command buttons. A *command button* carries out an action, or if the button name is followed an ellipsis, another dialog box will open.

After you enter information or make selections in a dialog box, click the OK button to complete the command. Click the Cancel button to close the dialog box without issuing the command. Many dialog boxes also have an Apply button that you can click to apply your changes without closing the dialog box.

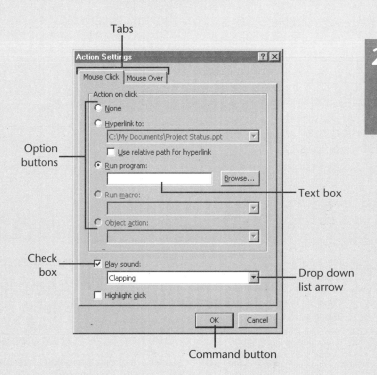

Working with Toolbars

PowerPoint organizes its most common commands into toolbars that contain buttons that you can click to issue a command. When PowerPoint starts, the Standard, Formatting, and Drawing toolbars automatically appear, unless you have changed your PowerPoint settings. You can hide or display any toolbar, and move it around the screen so it's right where you need it.

Select a Toolbar Button

1. Click the button on the toolbar you want.

Some toolbars include drop-down arrows that you click to open a palette of additional options.

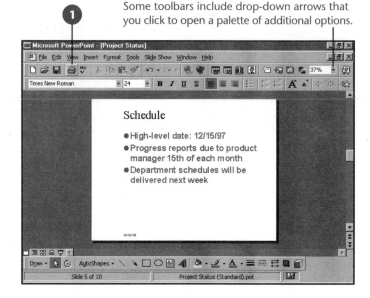

Display or Hide a Toolbar

1. Click the View menu.

2. Point to Toolbars.

3. Click the toolbar you want to display or hide.

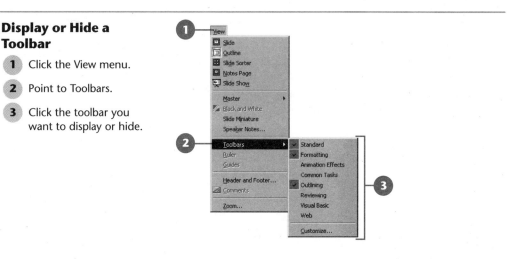

Getting Help with the Office Assistant

You can "ask" the PowerPoint Office Assistant how to accomplish a task—this animated Help feature displays helpful tips while you are working in PowerPoint. PowerPoint also provide access to popular World Wide Web sites that offer assistance and personalized support.

Office Assistant button

TRY THIS

Change the Office Assistant Character. *You can change your "Office Assistant" (the blinking, animated paper clip). Click the Office Assistant, and then click the Options button. Click the Gallery tab and then use the Next and Back buttons to a new Assistant. Click OK when you've found one you like. You might be asked to insert the original installation CD.*

Ask the Office Assistant for Help

1. Click the Office Assistant button on the Standard toolbar (if the Office Assistant is not already displayed). If the Office Assistant is displayed, click the Office Assistant.

2. Type a question in the box.

3. Click Search.

4. Click a topic you want help with.

5. When you're done, click the Close button on the Help window.

6. Click the Close button on the Office Assistant.

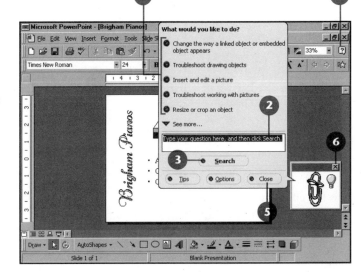

Get Help from Microsoft's World Wide Web Site

1. Make sure you have a modem and Internet access from your computer.

2. Click the Help menu.

3. Point to Microsoft On The Web.

4. Click the page for the Microsoft Web site you want.

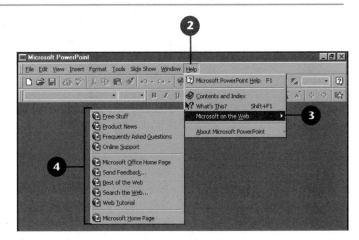

Getting Help

PowerPoint provides several ways to get instantaneous help. You can search for information on a particular topic using PowerPoint's Help topics, or you can use the Help pointer to get information on any PowerPoint object on your screen. To use the Help pointer, click the What's This command on the Help menu or click the Help button on the title bar of a dialog box.

Help button

Locate Information about a Particular Topic

1 Click the Help menu.

2 Click Contents And Index.

3 Click the Contents tab. This tab displays a table of contents. Double-click a Help book icon to open it, and then double-click a question mark icon to open a Help window for that topic.

4 Click the Index tab. This tab displays an index of topics. Type the topic about which you want information. The index list scrolls automatically to match the letters you type. Click the topic you're interested in, and then click Display.

5 Click the Find tab. This tab searches for all topics that pertain to a search word that you specify. Type your search word, and then click one of the words that narrows your search. Click the topic you want to read about from the list of related topics that appears, and then click Display.

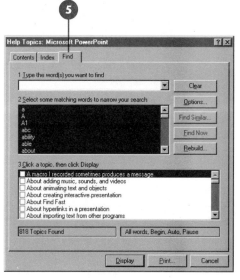

Connect to PowerPoint Central to get more help information. *You can also get help from PowerPoint Central, available via the Internet. PowerPoint Central provides information, tips and tricks, files such as sound and video clips, and tutorials. Click Tools, click PowerPoint Central, and then click on the links that appear on your screen to access and use PowerPoint Central.*

"How do I figure out what a button does?"

Get Help on a PowerPoint Object

1 Click the Help menu.

2 Click What's This?.

3 Click the Help pointer on the object about which you want more information.

4 Click anywhere on the screen to close the Help information box.

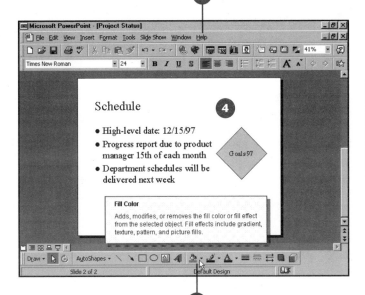

Saving a Presentation

When you create a PowerPoint presentation, you should save it as a file on a disk so you can work with it again later. When you save a presentation for the first time or if you want to save the file with a new name, use the Save As command. When you want to save your changes to an open presentation, use the Save button on the Standard toolbar.

Save a Presentation for the First Time

1 Click the File menu.

2 Click Save As.

3 Click the Save In drop-down arrow, if necessary, and then select the drive and folder that you want to save the presentation file in.

4 Type the new presentation name in the File Name box.

5 Click Save. The new file name appears in the title bar.

Save Changes to an Open Presentation

1 Click the Save button on the Standard toolbar.

Closing a Presentation and Exiting PowerPoint

After you finish working on a presentation, you can close it. Closing a file makes more computer memory available for other processes. Closing a presentation is different from exiting PowerPoint: after you close a presentation, PowerPoint is still running. When you're finished using PowerPoint, you can exit the program. To protect your files, always exit from PowerPoint before turing off the computer.

☒

Close button

SEE ALSO

See "Saving a Presentation" on page 20 for more information about saving your presentation.

Close a Presentation

1 Click the Close button on the presentation window title bar or click the File menu, and then click Close.

2 If you have made changes to the presentation since last saving it, a dialog box opens asking if you want to save changes. Click Yes to save any changes you might have made, or click No to ignore you're changes.

Clicking this button closes the presentation window only. **1**

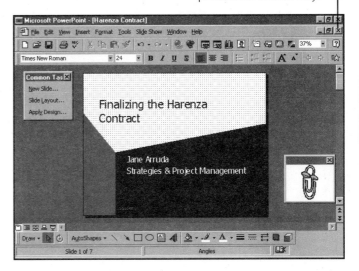

Exit PowerPoint

1 Click the PowerPoint window Close button.

2 If any files are open and you have made any changes since last saving, a dialog box opens asking if you want to save changes. Click Yes to save any changes you've made, or click No to ignore you're changes.

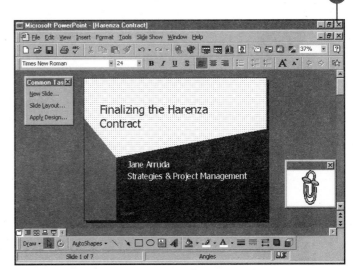

2

3

Developing a Presentation

IN THIS SECTION

Creating Consistent Slides

Manipulating Objects

Developing Text

Entering Text

Editing Text

Developing an Outline

Indenting Text

Setting Tabs

Rearranging Slides

Formatting Text

Modifying a Bulleted List

Creating a Text Box

Correcting Mistakes

Before you can create a slide presentation that includes text, charts, graphs, and pictures, you need to learn a few fundamentals about working with objects in Microsoft PowerPoint 97.

Building A Presentation with Objects

Objects are the fundamental building blocks of a slide. Almost every item you place on your slide is an *object*: an item with characteristics that you can modify. A slide in a presentation is often a combination of text objects, visual objects, and multimedia objects. Text objects include slide titles, subtitles, and bulleted lists. Visual objects include pictures, clip art, charts, and graphs. Multimedia objects include sound and video clips and hypertext links to Internet pages. You manipulate each of these objects using the same basic set of skills:

- Select and deselect an object so that you can work with it

- Resize and move an object

- Delete an object

Once you have mastered these fundamental object manipulation skills, you can apply them to any object on your slides.

Creating Consistent Slides

For a presentation to be understandable, the objects on its slides need to be arranged in a visually meaningful way. PowerPoint's *AutoLayout* feature helps you arrange objects on your slide in a consistent manner. There are 24 AutoLayouts that are designed to accommodate the most common slide arrangements. When you create a new slide, you apply an AutoLayout to the slide. Placeholders for text or other objects on the AutoLayout appear automatically. You can also apply an AutoLayout to an existing slide at any time. When you change the AutoLayout for a slide, you don't lose information that already exists on the slide. PowerPoint applies the new AutoLayout and you can arrange the placeholders the way you want them.

Insert a New Slide

1. Click the Insert New Slide button on the Standard toolbar.

2. Click the AutoLayout that provides the layout you need.

3. Click OK.

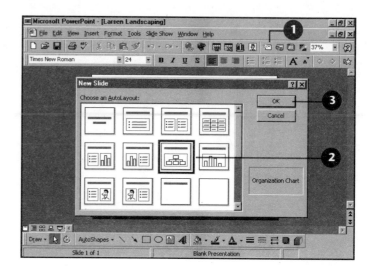

Apply an AutoLayout to an Existing Slide

1. In Slide view, display the slide you want to change.

2. Click the Slide Layout button on the Standard toolbar.

3. Click the AutoLayout you want.

4. Click the Apply button.

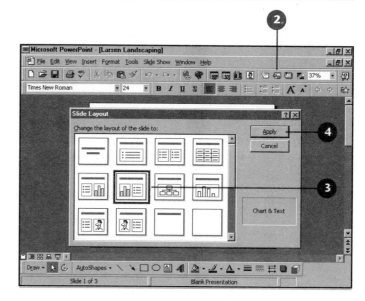

Use placeholder to enter information efficiently.

When you apply an AutoLayout to a slide, an arranged group of placeholders appears—one placeholder for each object on the slide. The placeholders include instructions for entering object contents.

Enter Information into a Placeholder

◆ For text placeholders, click the placeholder and type the necessary text.

◆ For other objects, double-click the placeholder and work with whatever accessory PowerPoint starts.

A placeholder is a border that defines the size and location of an object.

AUTOLAYOUT PLACEHOLDERS	
Placeholder	**Description**
Bulleted List	Displays a short list of related points
Clip Art	Inserts a picture
Chart	Inserts a chart
Organization Chart	Insert an organizational chart
Table	Inserts a table from Microsoft Word
Media Clip	Inserts a music, sound, or video clip
Object	Inserts an object created in another program, such as an Excel spreadsheet or Wordart object

Manipulating Objects

Most of the work you do to develop a presentation involves objects such as the ones provided by the AutoLayouts, but you are not restricted to the layouts they provide. You can add and remove objects to and from your slides at any time, and you can move and resize objects that are already there. To manipulate objects, you use Slide view. To perform any action on an object, you first need to select it.

Select and Deselect an Object

◆ To select an object, click it.

◆ To select multiple objects, press and hold Shift as you click each object.

◆ To deselect an object, click outside its border.

◆ To deselect an object when multiple objects are selected, press and hold Shift and click the object you want to deselect.

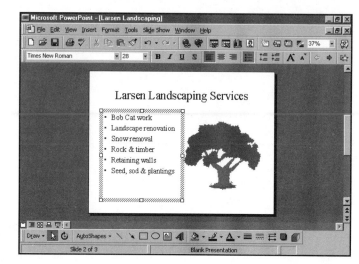

Resize an Object

1 Move the pointer over one of the sizing handles.

2 Drag the sizing handle until the object is the size you want.

3 Release the mouse button.

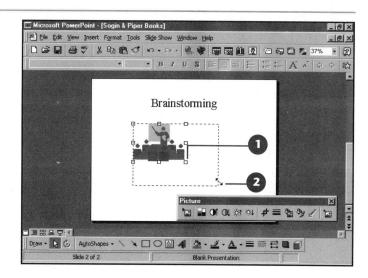

Move an Object

- ◆ Using the mouse, drag the object to the new location. For unfilled objects you need to drag the border. You can move an object in a straight line by pressing Shift as you drag.

- ◆ Using the keyboard, click the object and then press the arrow keys to move the object in the direction you want. This is a handy method when you need to move the object in a straight line.

Delete an Object

1. Click the object you want to delete.

2. Press Delete.

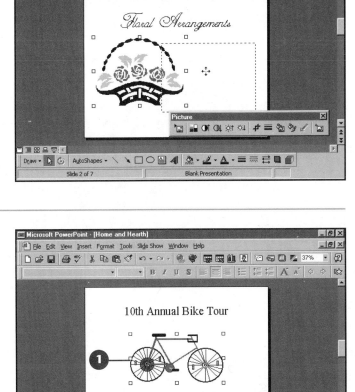

Developing Text

Your presentation's text lays the foundation for the presentation. PowerPoint offers several features that help you organize your text. Slide view lets you work with text and other objects one slide at a time. Outline view lets you work with all the presentation text on all slides in a single window.

PowerPoint offers many of the text formatting features traditionally associated with word processing software. You can apply fonts and text attributes to design the look you want. You can set tabs, indents, and alignment. Finally, you can edit and correct your text using several handy tools, including style, grammar, and spell checkers.

Text exists in PowerPoint in three primary formats:

◆ *Title text objects*. Pre-sized rectangular boxes that appear at the top of each slide—used for slide titles and, if appropriate, subtitles

◆ *Bulleted list objects*. Boxes that accommodate bulleted lists

◆ *Text box objects*. Boxes that contain non-title text that you don't want to format in a bulleted list—often used for captions

The first slide in a presentation typically contains title text and a subtitle. Other slides often have a title accompanied by major points beneath the title organized in a bulleted list. Text boxes are used more rarely—when you need to include annotations or minor points that don't belong in the bulleted list.

When to Enter Text in Slide View

You use Slide view to enter text when you are focusing not on the overall organization and flow of your presentation, but on the text or objects of one slide at a time. Though you have access to the same formatting and editing tools in Slide view as you do in Outline view, it's harder to rearrange the order of your topics in Slide view than it is in Outline view because you see only one slide at a time.

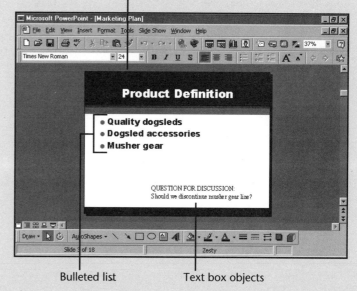

Title text object

Bulleted list

Text box objects

When to Enter Text in Outline View

When you are concentrating primarily on developing presentation content, but not necessarily how the text looks or how it interacts with other objects on the slide, use Outline view. Outline view displays the titles, subtitles, and bulleted text on all your slides at a single glance.

Outline view is particularly useful for reorganizing the content of your presentation and ensuring that topics flow well from one to the next. You can easily move presentation topics up and down the outline.

Title text in Outline view appears next to the slide number and slide icon.

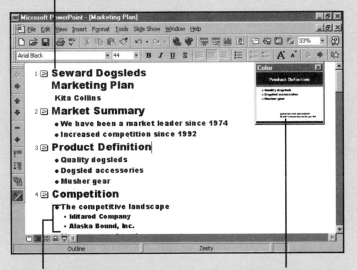

Bulleted lists appear in list format with different levels indented.

Text boxes do not appear in Outline view.

Entering Text

In Slide view, you type text directly into the text place-holders. If you type more text than fits in the placeholder, you might need to adjust the font size of the text you are typing or resize the selection box. You can also increase or decrease the vertical distance between two lines of text. The *insertion point* indicates where text will appear when you type. To place the insertion point into your text, move the pointer arrow over the text—the pointer changes to an I-beam to indicate that you could click and then type.

Enter Text into a Placeholder

1 In Slide view, click the text placeholder if it isn't already selected.

2 Type the text you want to enter.

3 Click outside the text object to deselect the object.

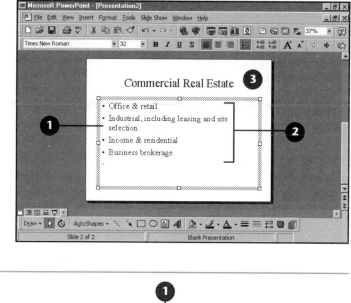

Insert Text

1 To insert text between two existing words, click between the words.

2 Type the text.

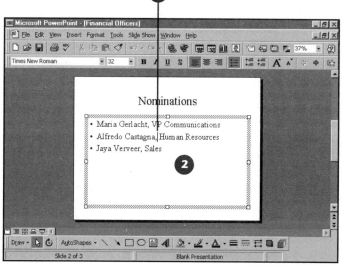

Use the insertion point to determine text location.
When entering bulleted text, be sure the insertion point is at the beginning of the line, press Tab to indent a level and press Shift+Tab to move back out a level.

Expand a bulleted list into a set of slides. *If you decide that the bulleted items in a bulleted list should be separate slides, you can click the bulleted list object, click Tools, and then click Expand Slide. PowerPoint automatically creates new slides whose titles correspond to the items in the first level of the bulleted list.*

Use caution when you adjust line spacing. *When you decrease paragraph spacing, make sure you leave enough space for the height of each entire letter, including extenders such as the bottom of "p" and the top of "b."*

Enter Bulleted Text

1. In Slide view, click the bulleted text placeholder.

2. Type the first bulleted item.

3. Press Enter. PowerPoint automatically bullets the next line.

4. Type the next bulleted item, and continue until you have completed the list.

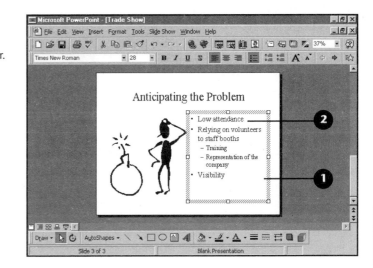

Adjust Paragraph Spacing

1. Click anywhere in the paragraph you want to adjust.

2. Click the Increase Paragraph Spacing or the Decrease Paragraph Spacing buttons on the Formatting toolbar to increase or decrease the vertical distance between paragraphs.

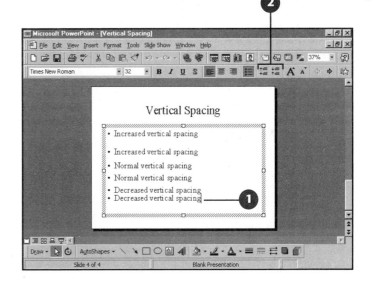

Editing Text

If you are familiar with modern word processing programs, you probably already know how to perform most text editing tasks in PowerPoint. You can delete existing text, replace it with new text, and even undo any changes you just made. Some of the editing methods require that you *highlight*, or select, the text first. You usually highlight text using the mouse, though you can use the keyboard too.

Highlighted Text
Non-highlighted Text

TIP

Different ways to select text. *To highlight the contents of an entire slide, click the Edit menu, and then click Select All. To select a single word, double-click the word. You can also select an object for editing by clicking the object, clicking the Edit menu, and then clicking Object (the Object command will appear as Text Object, Chart Object, and so, depending on the object type).*

Highlight Text Using the Mouse

1. Position the mouse pointer to the left of text you want to highlight.

2. Drag the pointer over the text—just a few words, a few lines, or entire paragraphs.

3. Release the mouse button when you have highlighted all the text you want.

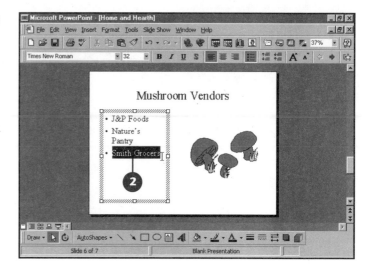

Highlight Text Using the Keyboard

1. Click to the left of the text you want to highlight.

2. Press and hold the Shift key.

   ◆ Press the Right arrow key to highlight one character.

   ◆ Press and hold Shift +Ctrl and press the Right arrow key to highlight text one word at a time.

   ◆ Press and hold Shift+Ctrl and press Right arrow or Down arrow to highlight one line at a time.

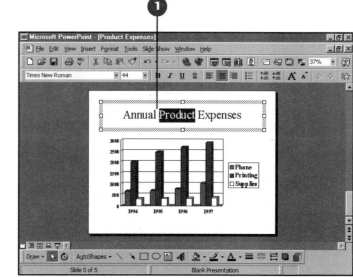

Replace Text

◆ To replace text by typing it, highlight the text you want to replace and type the replacement text.

◆ To replace all occurrences of text in a presentation, click the Edit menu, click Replace, type what you want to replace in the Find What box, type what you want to replace it with in the Replace With box, and then click Replace or Replace All.

Undo and Redo an Action

◆ To undo an action, click the Undo button on the Standard toolbar; click it repeatedly to undo previous actions.

◆ To undo one action without undoing other subsequent actions, click the Undo drop-down arrow on the Standard toolbar to view a list of the most recent changes, and then click the action you want to undo.

◆ To redo an action you just undid, click the Redo button on the Standard toolbar.

Click to replace only the instances of text that match the case of the entry you typed in the Find What box.

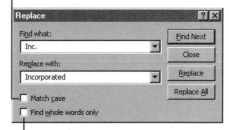

Click to replace only instances of text that are whole words.

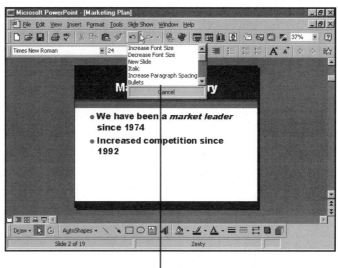

List of actions to undo

Developing an Outline

If you created your presentation using one of the AutoContent Wizards, PowerPoint generates an outline automatically. If you prefer to develop your own outline, you can create a blank presentation, and then switch to Outline view and type in your outline from scratch. If you want to use an existing outline from another document, such as a Microsoft Word document, make sure it is set up using outline heading styles. You can then bring the outline into PowerPoint, and PowerPoint creates slide titles, subtitles, and bulleted lists based on those styles.

Enter Text in Outline View

1. In Outline view, click to position the insertion point where you want the text to appear.

2. Type the text you want to enter, pressing Enter after each line.

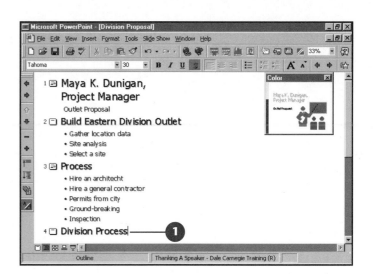

Add a Slide in Outline View

1. In Outline view, click at the end of the previous slide text.

2. Click the Insert New Slide button on the Standard toolbar, or press Ctrl+Enter to insert a slide using the existing slide layout.

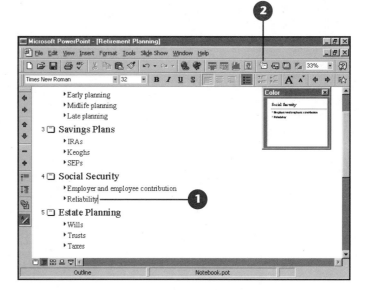

Different ways to delete a Slide. *In Outline or Slide Sorter view, click the slide you want to delete, and then press Delete. In Slide view, move to the slide you want to delete, click the Edit menu, and then click Delete Slide.*

Duplicate a Slide

1 Click the slide you want to duplicate.

2 Click the Insert menu.

3 Click Duplicate Slide.

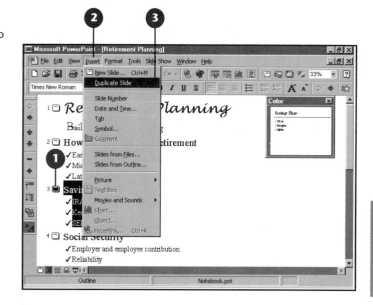

"I have a Word document. I want to create a presentation."

Insert an Outline from Another Application

1 Click the Insert menu.

2 Click Slides From Outline.

3 Locate and then click the file containing the outline you want to insert.

4 Click Insert.

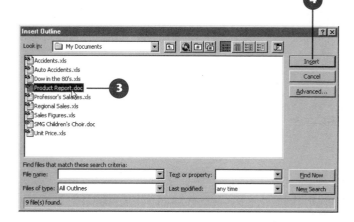

Indenting Text

Title text is usually the most prominent text object on a slide; next is subtitle text, and then body text, which can be indented or bulleted. You can indent paragraphs of body text up to five levels using the Promote and Demote buttons or the Tab and Shift+Tab keys on the keyboard. In Outline view, these tools let you promote or demote text from a title, for example, to bulleted text. You can view and change the locations of the indent markers within a text object using the ruler.

Change the Indent Level

1. In Slide or Outline view, click anywhere in the line you want to indent.

2. Click the Demote button to move the line in one level (to the right).

3. Click the Promote button to move the line out one level (to the left).

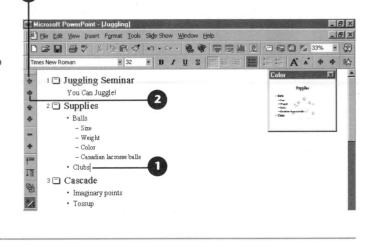

Display the Ruler

1. In Slide view, click the View menu.

2. Click Ruler.

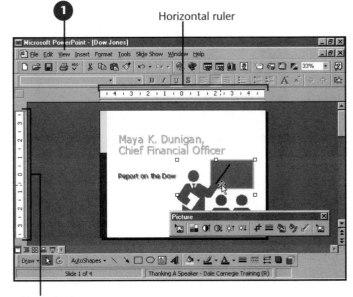

Horizontal ruler

Vertical ruler

Assign indent levels using the keyboard. *Press Tab to indent text one level (demote it) or press Shift+Tab to move it back out (promote it). If the insertion point is at the end of a line of title text, press Enter to insert a new slide. If the insertion point is at the end of a bulleted list item, press Enter to insert another bulleted list item or press Ctrl+Enter to create a new slide. Press Shift+Enter to insert a new line of text at the same level as the current line.*

Change the Indent

① Select the text for which you want to change the indentation.

② Make sure the ruler is visible.

- ◆ To change the indent for the first line of a paragraph, drag the first-line indent marker.

- ◆ To change the indent for the rest of the paragraph, drag the left indent marker.

- ◆ To change the distance between the indents and the left margin but maintain the relative distance between the first line and left indent markers, drag the rectangle below the left indent marker.

First line indent marker   Left indent marker

Rectangle changes first line and left indent marker simultaneously

3

Setting Tabs

PowerPoint includes default tab stops at every inch, and when you press the Tab key, your text moves to the next available tab stop. You can control the location of the tab stops using the ruler. When you set a tab, tab markers appear on the ruler. Tabs apply to an entire paragraph, not a single line within that paragraph.

"How does a tab affect my text?"

Set a Tab

1 Click the paragraph or select the paragraphs whose tabs you want to modify. You can also select a text object to change the tabs for all paragraphs in that object.

2 If necessary, click the View menu, and then click Ruler to display the ruler.

3 Click the Tab button at the left of the horizontal ruler repeatedly until you see the type of tab you want.

4 Click the ruler where you want to set the tab.

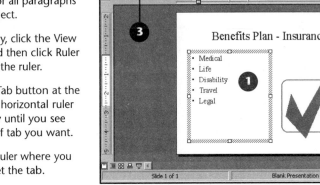

Default tab stops

TAB BUTTON ALIGNMENTS

Tab button	Alignment
L	Left edge of text
⊥	Center of text
⌐	Right edge of text
⊥.	Decimal points in text

"I need to get rid of a tab."

Change the Distance Between Default Tab Stops

1. Make sure your text is selected and the ruler is displayed.

2. Drag any tab marker to a new position.

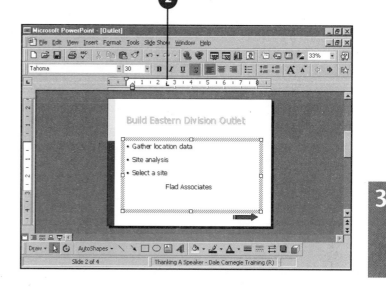

Clear a Tab

1. Drag the tab marker off the ruler.

The tab turns grey when you clear it.

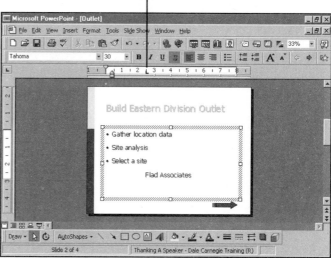

Rearranging Slides

You can instantly rearrange slides in Outline view or Slide Sorter view. You can use the drag and drop method or the Cut and Paste buttons to move slides to a new location. In Outline view, you can use either the Move Up and Move Down buttons to move selected slides up or down through the outline. Outline view also lets you collapse the outline down to its major points so you can more easily see its structure.

Rearrange Slides in Outline View

1 Click the Outline view button.

2 Click the slide icon of the slide or slides you want to move.

3 Click the Move Up button to move the slide up or the Move Down button to move the slide down. Repeat until the slide is where you want it.

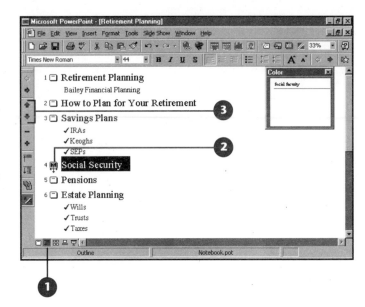

Rearrange Slides in Slide Sorter View

1 Click the Slide Sorter view button.

2 Click the slide you want to move and then drag it to a new location. A vertical bar appears next to the slide you are moving as you drag a slide. It indicates where the slide will drop when you release the mouse button.

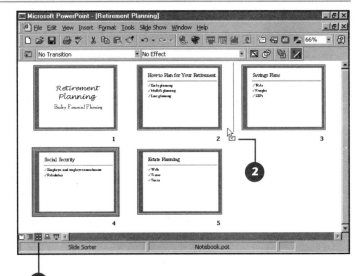

TIP

What happens when you collapse a slide? *A horizontal line appears below a collapsed slide in Outline view.*

Collapse and Expand Slides in Outline View

◆ In Outline view, click the Collapse button to collapse the selected slide or slides.

◆ Click the Expand button to expand the selected slide or slides.

◆ Click the Collapse All button to collapse all slides.

◆ Click the Expand All button to expand all slides.

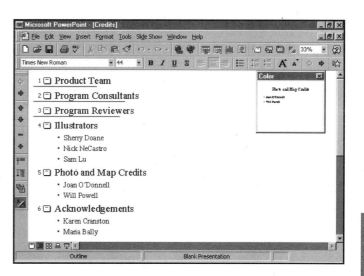

Move a Slide with Cut and Paste

1. In Outline or Slide Sorter view, select the slide or slides you want to move.

2. Click the Cut button on the Standard toolbar.

3. Click the new location.

4. Click the Paste button on the Standard toolbar.

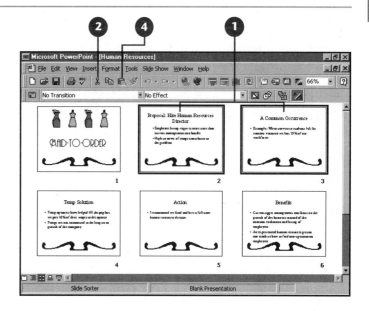

Formatting Text

Although PowerPoint's templates provide preformatted styles for text objects, often you will want to change the existing formatting or add extra emphasis to a word or an entire text object. The four most basic formats you can apply to text are bold, italic, underline, and shadow. Each of these formats has its own button on the Formatting toolbar. You can format a single letter, word, or phrase or all the text in a text object. PowerPoint also offers the Format Painter, a tool that lets you "pick up" the style of one section of text and apply, or "paint," it to another.

TIP

What's the difference between selecting text and selecting object? *When a slanted selection box appears, your changes affect only the highlighted text. When a dotted selection box appears, changes apply to the entire text object.*

Format Text Using the Formatting Toolbar

1. Select the word or words you want to format, or click the selection box of a text object to format all the text in the box.

2. Click one or more of the format buttons on the Formatting toolbar: Bold, Italic, Underline, or Shadow.

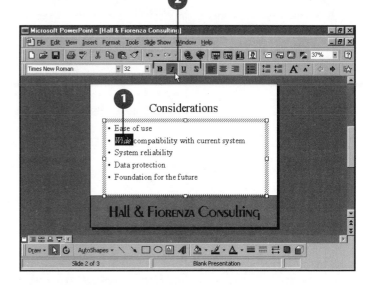

Format the Text Font

1. Select the text whose font you want to format.

2. Right-click the selection and then click Font.

3. Make any changes you want to the font.

4. Click OK.

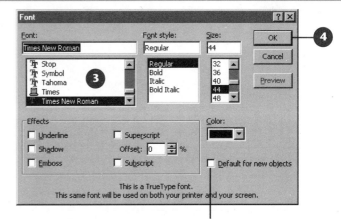

Click to set the current font format as the default for new text objects.

Change the Font Using the Formatting Toolbar

1. Select the text or place-holder whose font you want to change.

2. Click the Font drop-down arrow on the Formatting toolbar.

3. Click the font you want.

4. Click the Font Size drop-down arrow on the Formatting toolbar.

5. Click the font size you want.

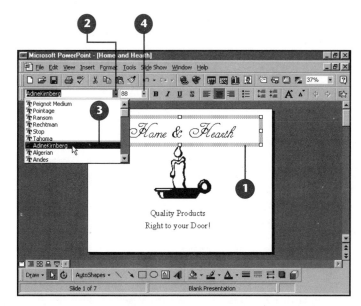

Align Text

1. Select the text you want to align.

2. Click one of the alignment buttons on the Formatting toolbar—Left Alignment, Center Alignment, or Right Alignment—to align the text to the left margin, center, or right margin of the selection box border, respectively.

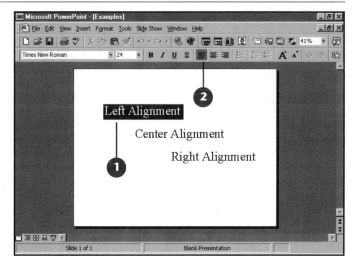

Modifying a Bulleted List

When you create a new slide, you can choose the Bulleted List AutoLayout so that a bulleted list placeholder appears automatically. You can customize the appearance of your bulleted list in a number of ways. You have control over the appearance of your bullets, their size, and their color. You also might want to adjust the distance between a bullet and the text it precedes using the PowerPoint ruler.

Add and Remove Bullets from Text

1. Click anywhere in the paragraph you want to bullet.

2. Click the Bullets button on the Formatting toolbar.

3. Click anywhere in the paragraph from which you want to remove the bullet.

4. Click the Bullets button on the Formatting toolbar.

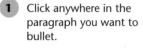

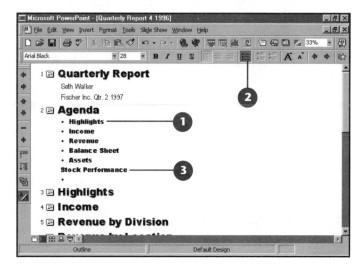

Change the Distance Between Bullets and Text

1. Select the text you want to indent.

2. If the ruler doesn't appear, click the View menu, and then click Ruler.

3. Drag the indent markers on the ruler.

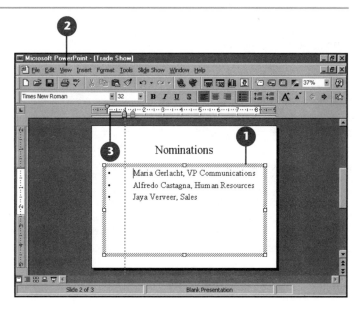

SEE ALSO

See "Understanding Color Schemes" on page 59 for information on working with color schemes.

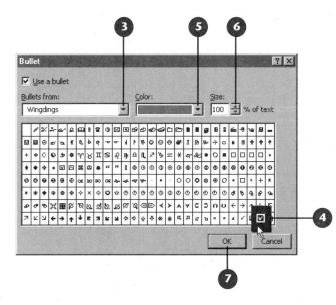

"I want to use a checkmark as my bullet character."

Change the Bullet Character

1. Select the text or text object whose bullet character you want to change.

2. Right-click the object, and then click Bullet.

3. Click the Bullets From drop-down arrow, and then click the font containing the character you want to use.

4. Click the character you want.

5. To change the bullet's color, click the Color drop-down arrow, and then click the color you want.

6. To change the bullet's size, enter a percentage in the Size box.

7. Click OK.

Creating a Text Box

Usually you will use the title, subtitle, and bulleted list placeholders to place text on a slide. However, when you want to add text outside one of the standard placeholders, such as for an annotation to a slide or chart, you can create a text box. Your text box doesn't have to be rectangular—you can also use one of PowerPoint's *AutoShapes*, a collection of shapes that range from rectangles and circles to arrows and stars. When you place text in an AutoShape, the text becomes part of the AutoShape.

Create a Text Box

1. In Slide view, if the Drawing toolbar isn't visible, click the View menu, point to Toolbars, and then click Drawing.

2. Click the Text Box button on the Drawing toolbar.

3. To add text that wraps, drag a box and then start typing, or to add text that doesn't wrap, click and then start typing.

4. Click outside the selection box when you are finished.

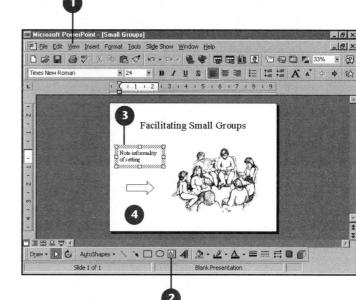

Edit a Text Box

1. Select the text you want to edit.

2. Use PowerPoint's word processing tools to edit your text.

3. Click outside the text box when you are finished.

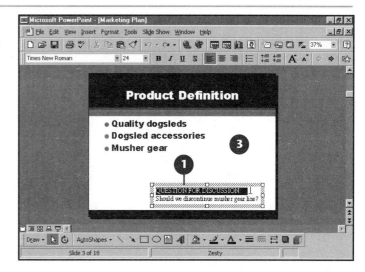

TIP

Use sizing handles to adjust text boxes. *If you create a text box without word wrapping and then find that the text spills over the edge of your slide, use the sizing handles to resize the text box so it fits on your slide. The text will then wrap to the size of the box.*

SEE ALSO

See "Drawing AutoShapes" on page 74 for more information on AutoShapes.

Format a Text Box

1 Right-click the text box.

2 Click Format Text Box.

3 Click the Text Box tab.

4 Select the format options you want.

5 Click OK.

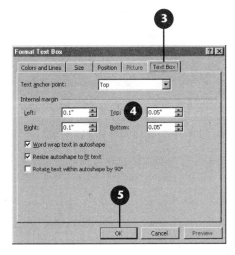

Add Text to an AutoShape

1 Click the AutoShapes button on the Drawing toolbar.

2 Point to the shape category you want.

3 Click the shape you want.

4 Drag the shape on your slide.

5 Type your text.

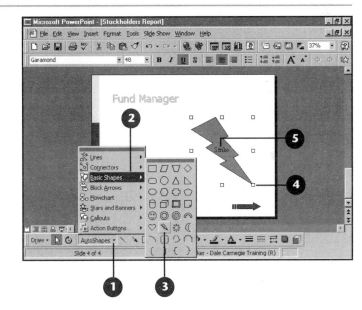

Correcting Mistakes

A slide's textual inaccuracies can distract your audience from your real message, so it's important that your presentation text be error-free. PowerPoint provides several tools that help ensure accuracy. You can check a presentation's style for grammatical errors, and you can control spelling errors in a document in three ways:

♦ AutoCorrect replaces common typing errors with the correct spelling as you type. For example, if you type "ahve," AutoCorrect replaces it with "have."

♦ You can check the spelling in an entire presentation after you've typed it using the Spelling command.

♦ You can enable the Spelling feature to alert you to a potentially misspelled word as you type, which you can correct on the spot.

Correct Common Errors Automatically with AutoCorrect

1 Click the Tools menu, and then click AutoCorrect.

2 Select the check boxes of the AutoCorrect features you want to enable.

3 Click OK.

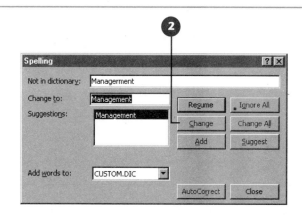

Check Spelling

1 Click the Spelling button on the Standard toolbar.

2 If the Spelling dialog box opens, click Ignore if the word is spelled correctly, or click the correct spelling, and then click Change.

3 Click OK when a message box tells you the spelling checker is complete.

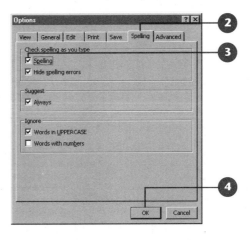

Check the spelling of different language text. *If your presentation includes text in a different language, you can mark it using the Language command on the Tools menu, so that the spell checker will use the appropriate language when spell checking your presentation.*

Correct Spelling as You Type

1 Click the Tools menu, and then click Options.

2 Click the Spelling tab.

3 Select the Spelling check box.

4 Click OK.

5 If a red wavy line appears under a word as you type, right-click it, and then click the correct word.

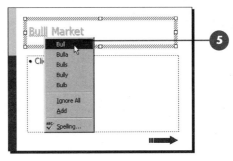

Check a Presentation's Style

1 Click the Tools menu, and then click Style Checker.

2 Click the Start button.

3 Correct any style errors.

4 Click OK when the style checker is finished.

3

Designing a Look

IN THIS SECTION

Viewing Masters

Controlling Slide Appearance with Masters

Inserting the Date, Time, and Slide Numbering

Adding a Header and Footer

Understanding Color Schemes

Applying a Color Scheme

Changing the Color Scheme

Applying a Color to an Object

Choosing a Fill Effect

Saving a Template

Applying a Design Template

The look you create for your presentation depends in part on your content and your audience. A goal-setting session for your company's sales group will look very different from a presentation recommending downsizing. Microsoft PowerPoint 97 gives you control over the look of your presentation in three ways: masters, color schemes, and templates.

Design Features

Masters, available for each component in your presentation—slides, handouts, and speaker's notes—contain the formatting information for your presentation.

A presentation's *color scheme* is a set of eight balanced colors that harmonizes color for your presentation's text, borders, fills, backgrounds, and so on.

PowerPoint features two kinds of templates: design templates and content templates. *Design templates* are professional designs that offer you an array of "looks" to apply to your presentation. *Content templates*, on the other hand, contain both designs and content. They are available through the AutoContent Wizard or on the Presentations tab of the New Presentation dialog box.

Viewing Masters

If you want to make a global change to the look of one or more of the elements on your slides, such as using a different title font than the preset font or giving all your bulleted lists a different bullet character, you don't have to change every slide individually. Instead, you change them all at once using a master. PowerPoint takes care of updating the existing slides, and automatically applies your settings to any slides you add. Which master you open depends on what part of your presentation you want to change.

TIP

Use the scroll bar to change between master views. *Click the vertical scroll bar's up or down arrow to switch between the Slide Master and the Title Master.*

View the Slide Master

1. Click the View menu.

2. Point to Master, and then click Slide Master. The Slide master controls all slides that do not use the Title Slide AutoLayout.

   The changes you make to the slide master do not affect the title slide; nor do changes you make to the title master affect non-title slides.

3. Click the Close button on the Master toolbar.

Dotted lines indicate text placeholders.

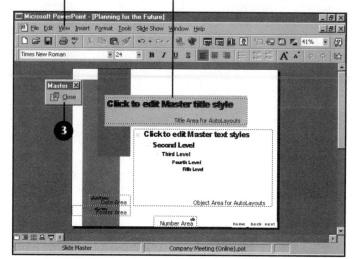

View the Title Master

1. Click the View menu.

2. Point to Master, and then click Title Master. Title master controls the look of your title slide.

3. Click the Close button on the Master toolbar.

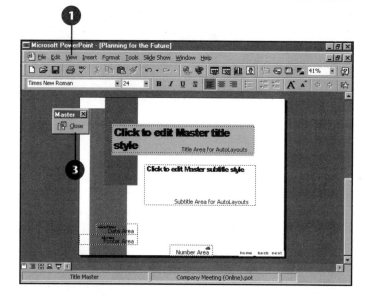

How can you break up a presentation into sections? *To emphasize the sections of a presentation, format the slides that introduce each section with the Title Slide AutoLayout. You can control the look of all your title slides using the title master.*

View the Notes Master

1. Click the View menu.

2. Point to Master, and then click Notes Master. Notes master controls the look of your notes pages.

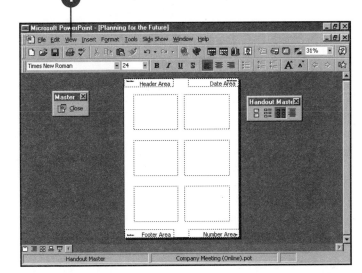

Use the Shift key and the mouse pointer to quickly view a master slide. *To quickly jump to the Slide Master, Handout Master, or Notes Master, press Shift, and then click one of the view buttons.*

View the Handout Master

1. Click the View menu.

2. Point to Master, and then click Handout Master. Handout master controls the look of your handouts.

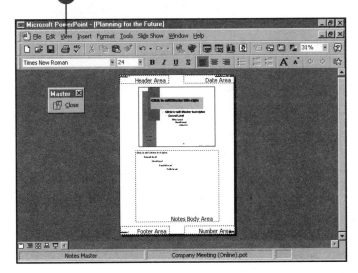

Controlling Slide Appearance with Masters

If you want an object, such as a company logo or clip art, to appear on every slide in your presentation (except the title slide), you place it on the slide master. You can hide the object from any slide you want. You can also create unique slides that don't follow the format of the masters. If you change your mind, you can easily restore a master format to a slide you altered. As you view the master, you might find it helpful to view a sample miniature of the slide, complete with text and graphics, using the Slide Miniature window.

TIP

Use the Slide Master and Title Master to control appearance. *An object you place on the slide master will not appear on the title slide unless you also place it on the title master.*

Include an Object on Every Slide

1 Click the View menu, point to Master, and then click Slide Master.

2 Add the object you want and fine-tune its size and placement.

3 Click Close on the Master toolbar.

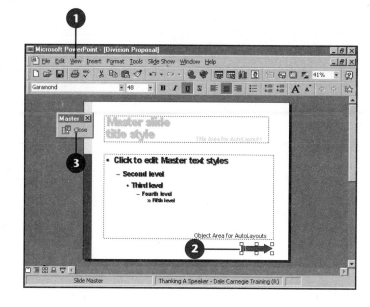

Hide Master Background Objects on a Slide

1 Display the slide whose background object you want to hide.

2 Click the Format menu.

3 Click Background.

4 Click the Omit Background Graphics From Master check box to select it.

5 Click Apply.

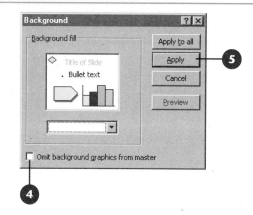

Make a slide format different from the master. *Display the slide you want to change. Make the changes. Your changes now override master formatting, and even if you change the master, this slide will retain the features you changed.*

Make changes to an individual slide. *To apply a change you make to an individual slide to all slides, click Apply To All instead of Apply.*

Reapply the Master to a Changed Slide

1. Right-click the changed slide in Slide view.

2. Click Slide Layout.

3. Click Reapply.

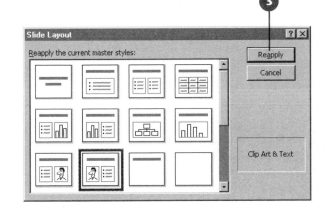

View a Miniature

1. Click the View menu.

2. Click Slide Miniature.

Slide miniature

Inserting the Date, Time, and Slide Numbering

You can insert isolated instances of the date, time, and slide numbering into the text of your presentation. For example, you might want today's date to appear in a stock market quote. Dates and times come in two formats: as a field or as text. If you insert the date as a field, PowerPoint inserts a code for the date and then every time you open the presentation automatically updates the date from your computer's clock. When you insert numbering, PowerPoint keeps track of your slide numbers for you.

TIP

PowerPoint automatically updates slide numbering.
Slide numbering updates automatically, regardless of whether you insert, delete, or reorder the slides in your presentation.

Insert the Date and Time

1. Click the text where you want to insert the date.

2. Click the Insert menu.

3. Click Date And Time.

4. Click the date format you want.

5. Click the OK button.

6. To insert the time, repeat steps 1-5, but this time click a time format instead of a date format.

Insert Slide Numbering

1. Click in the text object where you want to insert the slide number.

2. Click the Insert menu.

3. Click Slide Number.

Available date and time formats

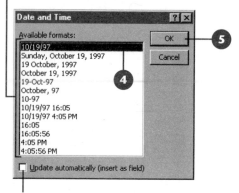

Check if you want the date or time to update automatically whenever you open the presentation

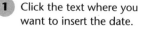

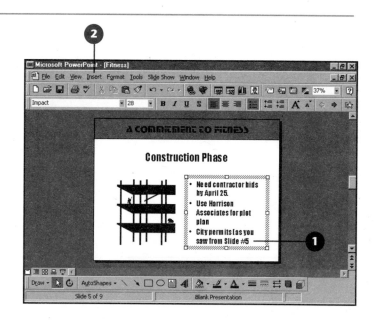

SEE ALSO

See "Adding a Header and Footer" on page 58 for information on adding the date, time, or numbering to every slide in your presentation.

"I want my presentation's slide numbering to start at 15."

Start Numbering with a Different Number

1 Insert the slide number, if one is not present on the slide or slide master.

2 Click the File menu, and then click Page Setup.

3 Click the Number Slides From spin arrows to set the number you want.

4 Click OK.

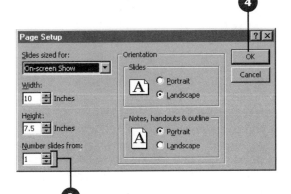

4

Adding a Header and Footer

Header and footer information appears on every slide except the title slide. It often includes information such as the presentation title, slide number, date, and name of the presenter. You use the masters to place header and footer information on your slides, handouts, or notes pages. Make sure your header and footer doesn't make your presentation look cluttered. The default font size of this information is usually small enough to minimize distraction, but you might want to experiment with header and footer font size and placement to make sure.

Add a Header and Footer

1. Click the View menu.

2. Click Header And Footer.

3. Click the tab you want: Slide for slides and Notes And Handouts for notes pages and handouts.

4. Fill in the Header And Footer dialog box to include the information you want.

5. Click Apply to apply to the current slide, or Apply To All to apply to all slides.

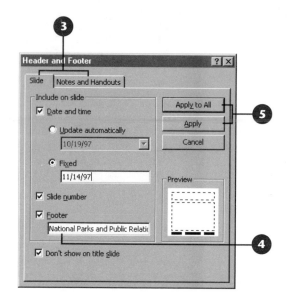

Change the Look of a Header or Footer

1. Click the View menu.

2. Point to Master.

3. Click the master you want to change.

4. Make the necessary changes to the header and footer. You can move it, resize it, or change its text attributes.

5. Click Close on the Master toolbar.

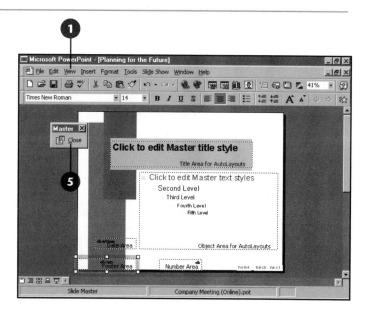

Understanding Color Schemes

If you've created a slide presentation with the AutoContent Wizard or with a presentation template, you've probably noticed that PowerPoint automatically assigns consistent colors to the objects you create.

These colors are chosen from the presentation's color scheme, the collection of eight well-matched colors that are the foundation of a presentation's look and feel.

Title Text
The color of your title text—contrasts with the background color.

Accent & Followed Hyperlink
A color for objects; also the color for a hyperlink you have already chosen.

Accent & Hyperlink
A color for objects; also the color for any hyperlinks you add to your presentation.

Background
The underlying color of a PowerPoint slide. You change the background color using the Background command on the Format menu.

Accent
A color for objects, such as bars on a chart, or objects that make up the template design.

Text & Lines
The color of non-title text and lines—contrasts with the background color. For example, if you type bulleted text, the font uses this color. You change this color using the Line Color and Font Color buttons.

Fills
The color of any object's background. For example, if you drew a circle, the inside of the circle is this color.

Shadows
The color of shadows you create using the Shadow button or 3-D effects. This is usually a darker shade of the fill color.

Microsoft PowerPoint - [Planning for the Future]

File Edit View Insert Format Tools Slide Show Window Help

Times New Roman   24   B I U S

Agenda

Opening Remarks - Mike Burke
Conference Report - Penny Kane
VP Report - Joe Holliday
Pres Report - Kim Wong

home back next

Draw   AutoShapes

Slide 2 of 13   Company Meeting (Online).pot

4

Applying a Color Scheme

You can apply a color scheme to an individual slide or to all the slides in a presentation. Each template offers one or more standard color schemes from which to choose, and you can also create your own color schemes and then save them so you can apply them to other slides and even other presentations.

Choose a Color Scheme

1. Right-click a blank area of a slide.

2. Click Slide Color Scheme.

3. If necessary, click the Standard tab to view the available color schemes.

4. Click the color scheme you want.

5. Click Apply to apply the color scheme to the slide you are viewing, or click Apply To All to apply the color scheme to the entire presentation.

3. Each box represents a different available color scheme.

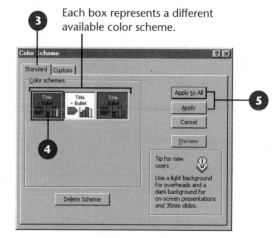

Delete a Color Scheme

1. Open the Color Scheme dialog box.

2. If necessary, click the Standard tab to view the available color schemes.

3. Locate and click the scheme you want to delete.

4. Click Delete Scheme.

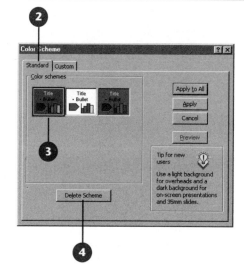

"I really like this color scheme—I'd like to apply it to a different slide."

Apply the Color Scheme of One Slide to Another

1 Click the Slide Sorter View button.

2 Click the slide with the color scheme you want to apply.

3 Click the Format Painter button on the Formatting toolbar once to apply the color scheme to one slide, or double-click to apply the color scheme to multiple slides.

4 Select the slide or slides to which you want to apply the color scheme. This can be in the current presentation or in another open presentation.

5 If you were applying the scheme to more than one slide, press Esc to cancel Format Painter. If you were applying the scheme to only one slide, Format Painter cancels automatically.

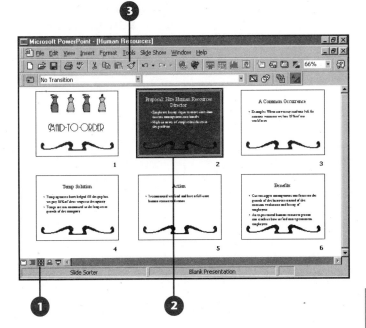

4

Changing the Color Scheme

You might like a certain color scheme, all except for one or two colors. You can change an existing color scheme and apply your changes to the entire presentation or just to a few slides. Once you change a color scheme, you can add it to your collection of color schemes so that you can make it available to any slide in the presentation.

Hue: 170
Sat: 253
Lum: 64

"I need just the right color for this text."

Change a Standard Color Scheme Color

1 In Slide view, right-click a blank area of the slide whose color scheme you want to change, and then click Slide Color Scheme.

2 Click the Custom tab.

3 Click the element you want to change in the Scheme Colors list.

4 Click Change Color.

5 Click a color on the Standard tab.

6 Click OK.

7 Click Apply to apply the changed color scheme to the current slide, or click Apply To All to apply the changed scheme to all slides.

Choose a Nonstandard Color

1 In the Color Scheme dialog box, click the Custom tab.

2 Click the element you want to color in the Scheme Colors list.

3 Click Change Color.

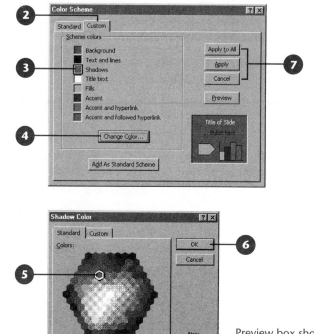

Preview box shows the new color and the current color so you can compose them.

THE PROPERTIES OF COLORS	
Characteristic	**Description**
Hue	The color itself; every color is identified by a number, determined by the number of colors available on your monitor.
Saturation	The intensity of the color. The higher the number the more vivid the color.
Luminosity	The brightness of the color, or how close the color is to black or white. The larger the number, the lighter the color.

SEE ALSO

See "Applying a Color Scheme" on page 60 for information on adding the date, time, or numbering to every slide in your presentation.

4 In the Color dialog box that opens (the name depends on which element you chose), click the Custom tab.

5 Drag across the palette until the pointer is over the color you want, or set the Hue, Sat, Lum, Red, Green, and Blue values manually.

6 Click OK. The color appears in the Scheme Colors list.

7 Click Apply to make the new color part of the color scheme for the current slide, or Apply To All to make it part of the entire presentation.

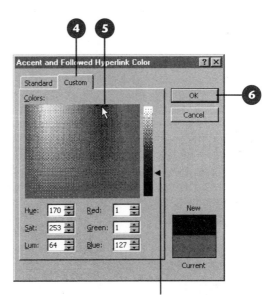

Moving the slider changes the luminosity for the current color.

"I'd like to be able to save this color scheme."

Save a Changed Color Scheme

1 In the Color Scheme dialog box, click the Custom tab.

2 Change the color scheme until all eight colors are as you want them.

3 Click Add As Standard Scheme. Your new scheme now appears on the Standard tab.

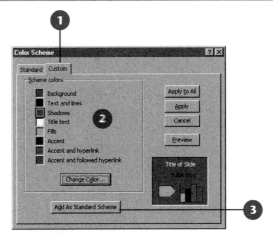

4

Applying a Color to an Object

When you want to change the color of just one element in your presentation on just one slide, you don't need to use the Color Scheme dialog box. Instead you can select the object and then open the color dialog box for the color you want to change—the fill, the border, the line, the text, and so on. The color dialog box that opens looks the same from one element to another. When you work with color, you should keep in mind whether you'll be printing handouts in black and white. PowerPoint makes it easy to preview color presentations in black and white. Note that different formatting effects are affected differently in Black and White view.

Change an Object's Color

1. Click the object whose color you want to change.

2. Click the button on the Drawing toolbar that corresponds to the object you want to change.

3. Select the new color.

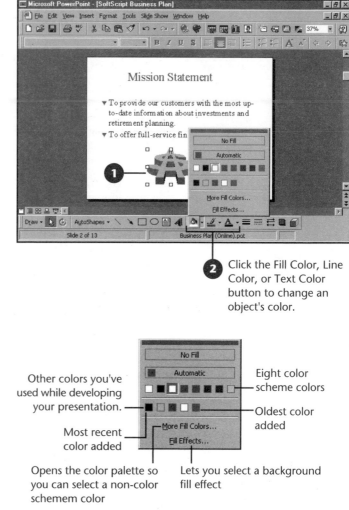

Click the Fill Color, Line Color, or Text Color button to change an object's color.

Other colors you've used while developing your presentation.

Eight color scheme colors

Most recent color added

Oldest color added

Opens the color palette so you can select a non-color schemem color

Lets you select a background fill effect

SEE ALSO

See "Drawing AutoShapes" on page 74 for information on creating drawing objects. See "Choosing Drawing Object Colors" on page 84 for more information about using fill effects.

TIP

PowerPoint remembers when you add colors. *Any time you add a color, PowerPoint adds it to all the color menus—those that appear for text, shadows, bullets, background, and lines. PowerPoint "remembers" up to eight colors that you've added. If you add a ninth, it appears first on the palette and the oldest disappears.*

Choose a Different Slide Background Color

1. Right-click the slide whose background you want to change.

2. Click Background.

3. Click the Background Fill drop-down arrow.

4. Select the color you want.

5. Click Apply to apply the background color to only the current slide, or click Apply To All to apply the background color to the entire presentation.

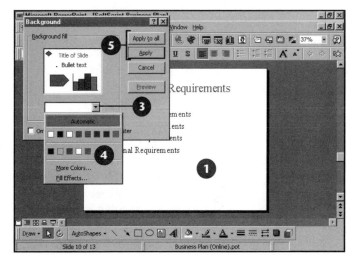

Choosing a Fill Effect

A *fill effect* is the look you give to the fill of an object or the background of your slides. The fill is the inside pattern or color of an object. For example, if you have drawn a square, the fill is the color inside the border. Fill effects are often based on a color or collection of colors that fills the area with an interesting pattern. PowerPoint fill effects are in four categories: gradients, textures, patterns, and pictures. Once you select and apply the fill effect you want, it fills the entire area to which you apply it, be it the fill of an object such as an arrow, or be it the entire slide background.

Select a Background Fill Effect

1 Right-click a blank area of the slide, and then click Background.

2 Click the Background Fill drop-down arrow.

3 Click Fill Effects.

4 Click the Gradient, Texture, Pattern, or Picture tab to display the available fill effects.

5 Click the fill effect you want.

6 Click OK.

7 Click Apply to apply the fill effect to the current slide, or Apply To All to apply the fill effect to all slides.

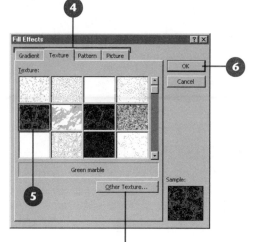

Clicking this button allows you to get other textures off the Microsoft Office 97 CD-ROM.

Apply a Picture Fill

1 In the Effects dialog box, click the Picture tab.

2 Click Select Picture.

3 Navigate your computer's folder structure until you find the picture you want. Double-click the picture.

4 Click OK.

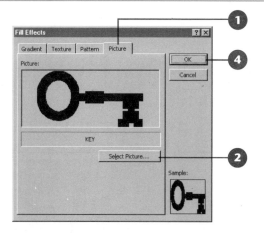

"I'd like to use a pattern as my fill."

Apply a Gradient Fill

1. On the Gradient tab in the Fill Effects dialog box, click the color or color combination you want.

2. Once you have chosen the color or color combination you want, click the Shading Styles option button you want: Horizontal, Vertical, Diagonal Up, and so on.

3. Click the variant you want.

4. Click OK.

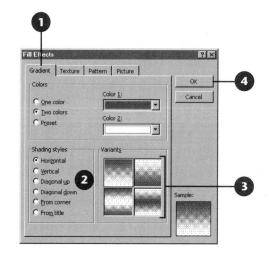

Apply a Pattern Fill

1. In the Effects dialog box, Click the Pattern tab.

2. Click the Foreground drop-down arrow to select the color you want in the foreground.

3. Click the Background drop-down arrow to select the color you want in the background.

4. Click the pattern you want from the grid of available patterns.

5. Click OK.

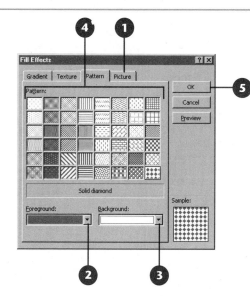

Saving a Template

You can save any presentation as a template. When you create a new presentation from that template, its content and design can form the basis of your next presentation. Although you can store your template anywhere you want, you might find it handy to store it in the folders that PowerPoint uses as the basis for the New Presentation dialog box. Store your design templates in the Presentation Designs folder and your content templates in the Presentations folder, and those templates will appear as options when you choose the New command on the File menu. You can also change existing templates. For example, you might decide to change the Blank Presentation template so that it includes your company's colors or a logo.

Create a Template

1 Start by opening any presentation—a blank one, one created with an existing design template, or even an existing presentation.

2 Select a color scheme and format the placeholders on the masters.

3 Design the title slide if it will be the same for all presentations created with this template, and then place any objects on the masters.

4 Add any footer and header information that you know you'll want to include in every presentation you create from this template.

5 Click the File menu, click Save As, and then enter a name for your template.

6 Click the Save As Type drop-down arrow, and then click Presentation Template.

7 Save the template in the Presentation Designs folder if you want it to appear in the New Presentation dialog box.

8 Click Save.

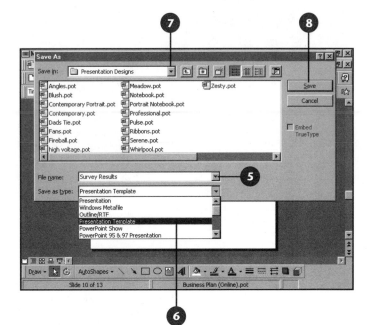

Save an existing presentation as a template. *Open the presentation. Delete anything from the presentation that you don't want to include in the template. Click the File menu. Click Save As. Enter a name for your template. Click the Save As Type drop-down arrow, and then click Presentation Template. Save the template in the Presentation Designs folder if you want it to appear with the other design templates.*

Change an Existing Design Template

1. Open the template you want to change. In the Open dialog box, click the Files Of Type drop-down arrow, and then click Presentation Templates.

2. Locate the template you want to change in one of the subfolders of the Templates folder in the Office folder.

3. Design the template the way you want it.

4. Click the File menu, and then click Save As.

5. Click the Save As Type drop-down arrow, and then click Presentation Template.

6. Select the folder in which you want to save the template.

7. Click Save.

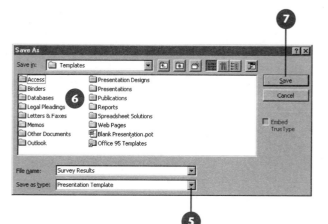

Applying a Design Template

PowerPoint design templates feature customized color schemes, slide and title masters, and fonts that come together to create a particular "look." You can apply a design template to a presentation at any time—even if there is already a template in place. When you apply a design template to a presentation, the masters and color scheme of the new template replace the ones originally in use.

Apply a New Template

1. Right-click a blank area of a slide.

2. Click Apply Design.

3. Click the design template you want.

4. Click Apply.

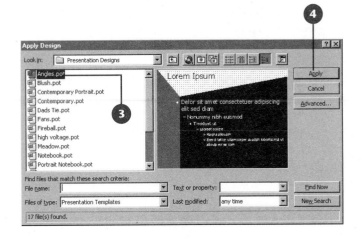

Apply a Design from an Existing Presentation

1. Right-click a blank area of a slide.

2. Click Apply Design.

3. Click the Files Of Type drop-down arrow, and then click Presentation Templates.

4. Locate and select the presentation whose design you want to apply.

5. Click Apply.

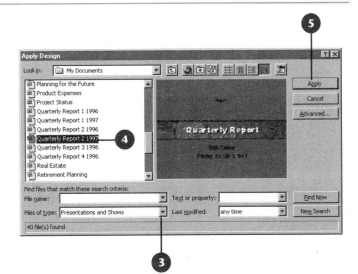

Drawing and Modifying Objects

IN THIS SECTION

Creating Lines and Arrows

Drawing AutoShapes

Creating Freeforms

Editing Freeforms

Moving and Resizing an Object

Rotating and Flipping an Object

Choosing Object Colors

Creating Shadows

Creating a 3-D Object

Controlling Object Placement

Aligning and Distributing Objects

Arranging and Grouping Objects

When you need to be able to create your own pictures, you can use Microsoft PowerPoint 97 as a drawing package. You can choose from a set of predesigned shapes, or you can use tools that allow you to draw and edit your own shapes and forms.

Drawing Objects

Drawing objects can be classified into three categories: lines, AutoShapes, and freeforms. *Lines* are simply the straight or curved lines (arcs) that connect two points. *AutoShapes* are preset shapes, such as stars, circles, or ovals. A *freeform* is an irregular curve or polygon that you can create as a freehand drawing.

Once you have created a drawing object, you can manipulate it in many ways, such as rotating it, coloring it, or changing its style. PowerPoint also provides special effects: drop shadows and 3-D. You can add shadows to any of your images and you can control the shadow's color, location, or angle. You can transform your two dimensional shapes into 3-D surfaces using the 3-D tool. You can rotate, tilt, and revolve the object in three dimensions, you can control the object's perspective, and you can specify the surface texture.

Creating Lines and Arrows

The most basic drawing objects you create on your slides are lines and arrows. PowerPoint includes several tools for this purpose. The Line tool creates line segments. The Drawing toolbar's Line Style and Dash Style tools let you determine the type of line used in any drawing object—be it solid, dashed, or a combination of solid and dashed lines. You can add arrowheads to any lines on your slide. The Arrow tool lets you create arrows that you can use to emphasize key features of your presentation.

Draw a Straight Line

1 In Slide view, click the Line tool on the Drawing toolbar.

2 Drag the pointer to draw a line on your slide. The endpoints of the line are where you started and finished dragging. Sizing handles appear at both ends of the line. Use these handles to resize your line or move an endpoint.

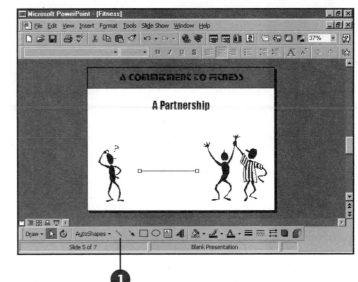

Edit a Line

1 Click the line you want to edit.

2 Click the Line Style button on the Drawing toolbar to select a line thickness.

3 Click the Dash Style button on the Drawing toolbar to select a style.

4 Click the Line Color button on the Drawing toolbar to select a color.

5 Drag the sizing handle at either end to a new location to change the size or angle of the line.

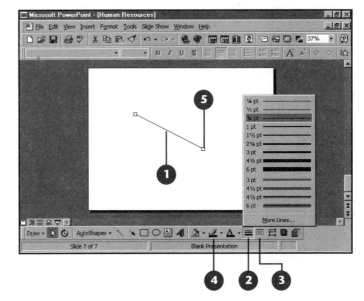

TIP

Shared Drawing toolbar. *If you use other Office 97 products, you might notice that the Drawing toolbar is available in most of them. These shared drawing tools, called Office Art, give superior graphics capabilities to most of your Office documents.*

SEE ALSO

See "Drawing AutoShapes" on page 74 for information on creating block arrows using the AutoShape drawing tools.

TIP

Increase the size of a default arrow. *Because of its size, you might not be able to see the arrow head when you draw a default arrow. To increase the size of the arrow head, click the Arrow Style button, click More Arrows, and then increase the Weight setting or End Size setting.*

Draw an Arrow

1. In Slide view, click the Arrow button on the Drawing toolbar.

2. Drag the pointer from the base of the arrow to the arrow's point.

3. Release the mouse button when the arrow is correct length and angle.

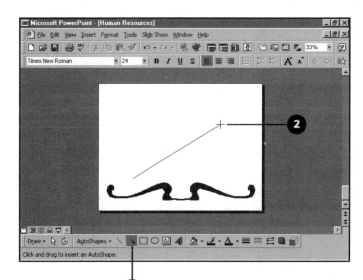

Edit an Arrow

1. Click the arrow you want to edit.

2. Click the Arrow Style button on the Drawing toolbar.

3. Click the arrow type you want to use, or click More Arrows.

4. If you clicked More Arrows, modify the arrow type in the Format AutoShape dialog box as necessary, and click OK when you are finished.

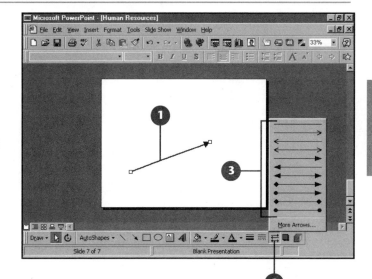

Drawing AutoShapes

PowerPoint supplies 155 different AutoShapes, ranging from hearts to lightening bolts to stars. The two most common AutoShapes, the oval and the rectangle (which you can also use to draw a circle and square), are available directly on the Drawing toolbar. The rest of the AutoShapes are organized into categories that you can view and select from the AutoShapes menu on the Drawing toolbar. Once you have placed an AutoShape on a slide, you can resize it using the sizing handles. Many AutoShapes have an *adjustment handle*, a small yellow diamond, located near a resize handle, that you can drag to alter the shape of the AutoShape.

Draw an Oval or Rectangle

1 Click the Oval or Rectangle tool on the Drawing toolbar.

2 Drag over the slide where you want to place the oval or rectangle. The shape you drew takes on the line color and fill color defined by the presentation's color scheme.

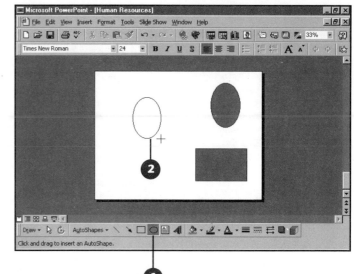

Draw an AutoShape

1 Click the AutoShapes tool on the Drawing toolbar, and then point to the AutoShape category you want to use.

2 Click the symbol you want.

3 Drag the pointer across the slide until the drawing object is the shape and size that you want.

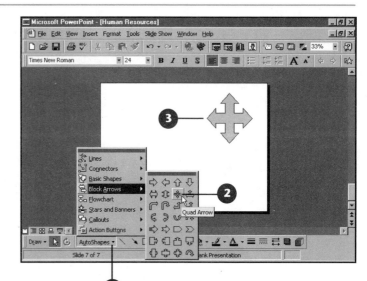

TRY THIS

Replace an AutoShape. *You can replace one AutoShape with another, while retaining the size, color, and orientation of the AutoShape. Click the AutoShape you want replace, click the Draw tool on the Drawing toolbar, point to Change AutoShape, and then select the new AutoShape you want.*

TIP

Draw a circle or square. *To draw a perfect circle or square, click the Oval or Rectangle tool on the Drawing toolbar, and then press and hold the Shift key as you drag the pointer.*

Adjust an AutoShape

1. Click the AutoShape you want to adjust.

2. Click one of the adjustment handles, and then drag the handle to alter the form of the AutoShape.

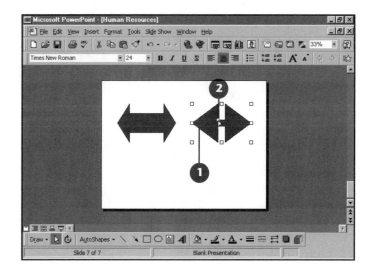

Creating Freeforms

When you need to create a customized shape, you use the PowerPoint freeform tools. They are all located in the Lines category in the list of AutoShapes. Freeforms are like the drawings you make yourself with a pen and paper, except that you have more control over the accuracy and length of the lines you draw. A freeform can either be an open curve or a closed curve.

Draw an Irregular Polygon

1 Click the AutoShape tool on the Drawing toolbar, and then point to Lines.

2 Click the Freeform tool.

3 Click the spot on the slide where you want to place the first vertex of the polygon.

4 Move the pointer to second point of your polygon, and then click the left mouse button. A line joins the two points.

5 Continue moving and clicking the mouse pointer to create additional sides of your polygon.

6 To close the polygon, click near the starting point. PowerPoint automatically closes the polygon for you, although you can specify that the curve be open.

Draw an Irregular Curve

1 Click the AutoShapes tool on the Drawing toolbar, and then point to Lines.

2 Click the Curve tool.

3 Click the spot on the slide where you want to place the curve's starting point.

A vertex is a corner of a polygon.

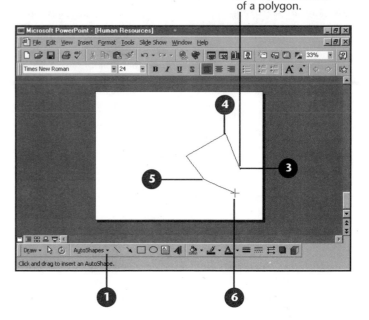

Switch between a closed curve and an open curve. *Right-click the freeform drawing. To switch from an open curve to a closed curve, click Close Curve, or to switch from a closed curve to an open curve, click Open Curve.*

4 Move the pointer to the spot where you want your irregular curve to bend and then click. Repeat this step as often as you need to create bends in your curve.

5 Finish the curve.

◆ For a closed curve, click near the starting point. PowerPoint automatically closes the curve and fills the object with a color.

◆ For an open curve, double-click the last point in the curve.

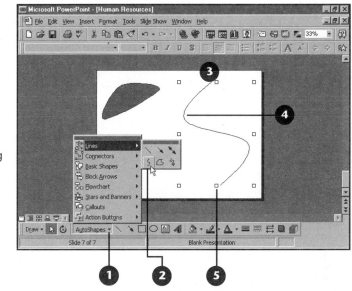

"I want a tool I can use like a pencil—for scribbling."

Scribble

1 Click the AutoShapes tool on the Drawing toolbar, and then point to Lines.

2 Click the Scribble tool.

3 Drag the pointer across the screen to draw freehand.

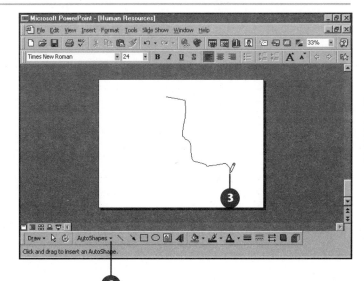

Editing Freeforms

You can edit a freeform by altering the vertices that create the shape using the Edit Points command. Each vertex (a corner in an irregular polygon and a bend in a curve) has two attributes: its position and the angle at which the curve enters and leaves it. You can move the position of each vertex and also control the corner or bend angles. Additionally, you can add or delete vertices. When you delete a vertex, PowerPoint recalculates the freeform and smoothes it among the remaining points. Similarly, if you add a new vertex, PowerPoint adds a corner or bend in your freeform.

Move a Vertex in a Freeform

1. Click the freeform object.

2. Click the Draw tool on the Drawing toolbar, and then click Edit Points.

3. Drag one of the freeform vertices to a new location.

4. Click outside the freeform when you are finished.

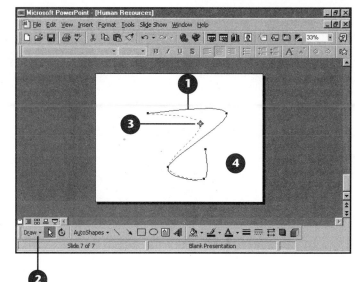

Insert a Freeform Vertex

1. Select the freeform object.

2. Click the Draw tool on the Drawing toolbar, and then click Edit Points.

3. Position the pointer on the curve or polygon border (not on a vertex), and then drag in the direction you want the new vertex.

4. Click outside the freeform to set the new shape.

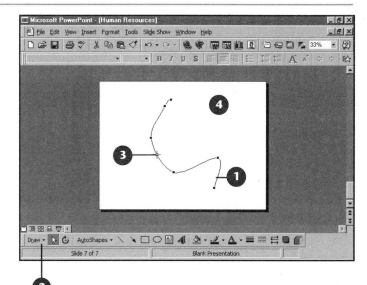

Gain control over your freeform. *After you click Edit Points, right-click a vertex. PowerPoint displays a pop-up menu with options for other types of vertices you can use to refine the shape of the freeform. These commands let you specify, for example, a smooth point, a straight point, or a corner point.*

"How do I change the angle of one of my freeforms?"

Delete a Freeform Vertex

1 Click the freeform object.

2 Click the Draw tool on the Drawing toolbar, and then click Edit Points.

3 Press the Ctrl key while clicking the point you want to delete.

4 Click outside the freeform to set the shape of the freeform.

Modify a Vertex Angle

1 Click the freeform object.

2 Click the Draw tool on the Drawing toolbar, and then click Edit Points.

3 Right-click a vertex and click Smooth Point, Straight Point, or Corner Point. Angle handles appear.

4 Drag one or both of the angle handles to modify the shape of the line segments going into and out of the vertex.

5 Click outside the freeform to set its shape.

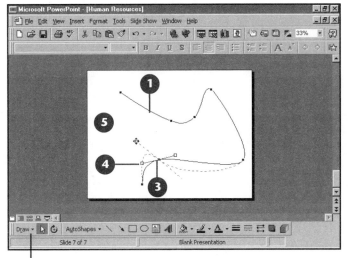

5

Moving and Resizing an Object

After you create a drawing object, you might need to resize it or move it to a different location on your slide. Although you can move and resize objects using the mouse, if you want more precise control over the object's size and position, use PowerPoint's Format command to exactly specify the location and size of the drawing object. You can also use the Nudge command to move drawing objects in tiny increments, up, down, left, or right.

Move a Drawing Object

1. Drag the object to a new location on the slide. Make sure you aren't dragging a sizing handle or adjustment handle. If you are working with a freeform and you are in Edit Points mode, drag the interior of the object, not the border, or you will end up resizing or reshaping the object, not moving it.

Nudge a Drawing Object

1. Click the object you want to nudge.

2. Click the Draw tool on the Drawing toolbar.

3. Point to Nudge and then click the direction: up, down, left, or right.

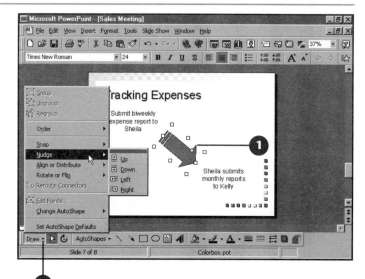

Retain the proportions of an object you're resizing. *Press and hold the Shift key as you drag the pointer to the new size.*

Resize a Drawing Object with the Mouse

1 Click the object to be resized.

2 Drag one of the sizing handles:

♦ To resize the object in the vertical or horizontal direction, drag a sizing handle on the side of the selection box.

♦ To resize the object in both the vertical and horizontal directions, drag a sizing handle on the corner of the selection box.

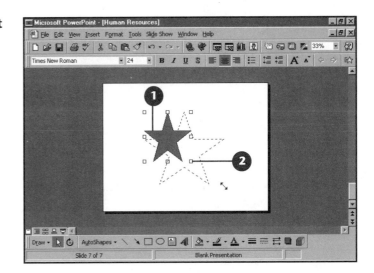

Move or Resize an Object with Precision

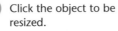

1 Right-click the object you want to move or resize.

2 Click Format AutoShape.

3 Click the Position tab to move the object and change settings as necessary.

4 Click the Size tab to resize the object and change settings as necessary.

5 Click OK.

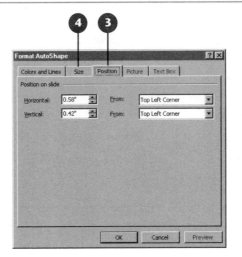

5

Rotating and Flipping an Object

If you need to change the orientation of a drawing object, you can rotate or flip it. For example, if you want to create a mirror image of your object you could flip it or if you want to turn an object on its side you could rotate it 90°. Rotating and flipping tools work with drawing and text objects. You won't usually be able to rotate or flip objects such as charts and pictures.

TIP

Different ways to rotate objects. *To rotate the object 90 degrees to the left, click Rotate Left. To rotate the object 90 degrees to the right, click Rotate Right. To flip the object horizontally, click Flip Horizontal. To flip the object vertically, click Flip Vertical.*

Rotate an Object to any Angle

1 Click the object you want to rotate.

2 Click the Free Rotate button on the Drawing toolbar.

3 Drag a rotation handle to rotate the object.

4 Click outside the object to set the rotation.

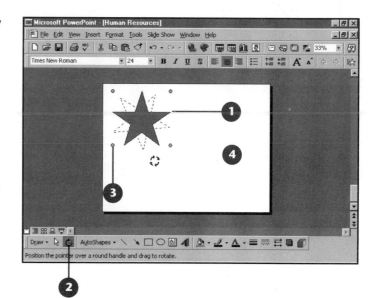

Rotate or Flip a Drawing Using Preset Increments

1 Click the object you want to rotate.

2 Click the Draw tool on the Drawing toolbar.

3 Point to Rotate Or Flip.

4 Click the option you want.

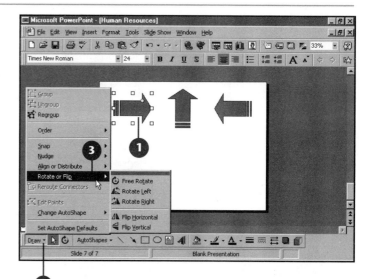

Constrain the rotation to 15-degree increments. *Press and hold the Shift key when rotating the object.*

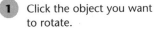

Rotate a Drawing Object Around a Fixed Point

1 Click the object you want to rotate.

2 Click the Free Rotate button on the Drawing toolbar.

3 Click the rotate handle opposite the point you want to rotate, and then press and hold the Ctrl key as you rotate the object.

4 Click outside the object to set the rotation.

5 Click the Free Rotate button again to turn rotation off.

"I want to rotate this arrow by 70°."

Rotate a Drawing Precisely

1 Right-click the object you want to rotate, and then click Format AutoShape.

2 Click the Size tab.

3 Enter the angle of rotation.

4 Click OK.

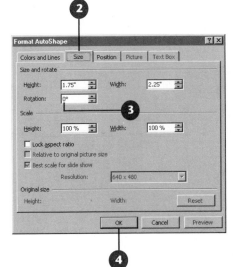

5

Choosing Object Colors

When you create a closed drawing object, it uses two colors from the color scheme: the Fill color and the Line color. When you create a line drawing object, it uses the color scheme Line color. You can change the Fill and Line color settings for drawing objects using the same color tools you use to change a slide's background color or text color. These tools include the ability to use patterns. You can use fill effects as well, including gradients, patterns, and even clip art pictures.

TIP

Apply the current fill color.
An easy way to apply the current fill color to an object is to select the object and then click the Fill Color button.

Change a Drawing Object's Fill Color

1. Click the drawing object whose fill color you want to change.

2. Click the Fill Color drop-down arrow on the Drawing toolbar.

3. Select the fill color or fill effect you want.

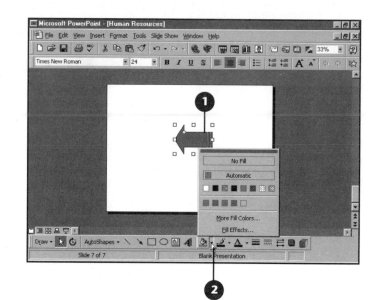

Change Colors and Lines in the Format Dialog Box

1. Right-click the object you want to modify, and then click Format AutoShape.

2. Click the Colors and Lines tab.

3. Set your color, line, and arrow options.

4. Click OK.

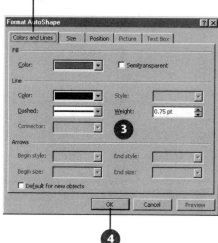

SEE ALSO

See "Apply a Color to an Object" on page 64 for information on selecting and creating customized colors. See "Choosing a Fill Effect" on page 66 for information on using fill effects and patterns.

TIP

Set the color and line style for an object as the default for future drawing objects. *Right-click the object, and then click Set Object Defaults. Any new objects you create will use the same styles.*

Create a Line Pattern

1 Right-click the line you want to change, and then click Format AutoShape.

2 Click the Color drop-down arrow.

3 Click Patterned Lines.

4 Click the Foreground drop-down arrow, and then click the color you want as a foreground.

5 Click the Background drop-down arrow, and then click the color you want as a background.

6 Click the pattern you want in the Pattern grid.

7 Click OK twice.

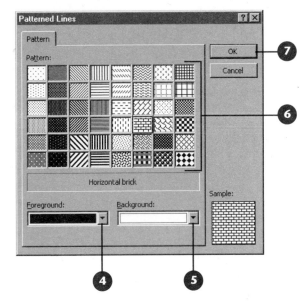

Creating Shadows

You can give objects on your slides the illusion of depth by adding shadows. PowerPoint provides several preset shadowing options, or you can create your own by specifying the location and color of the shadow. If the shadow is falling on another object in your slide, you can create a semitransparent shadow that blends the color of the shadow with the color of the object underneath it.

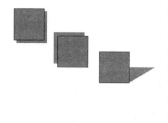

Use a Preset Shadow

1 Click the drawing object.

2 Click the Shadow button on the Drawing toolbar.

3 Click one of the 20 preset shadow styles.

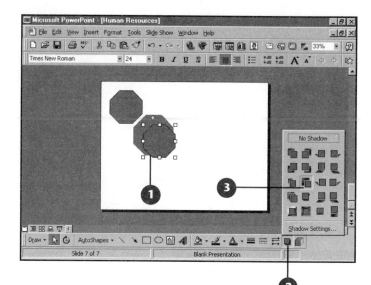

Change the Location of a Shadow

1 Click the drawing object that has the shadow.

2 Click the Shadow button on the Drawing toolbar, and then click Shadow Settings.

3 Click the tool that will give the effect you want. The Nudge buttons move the shadow location slightly up, down, right, or left.

4 Click the Close button on the Shadow Setting toolbar.

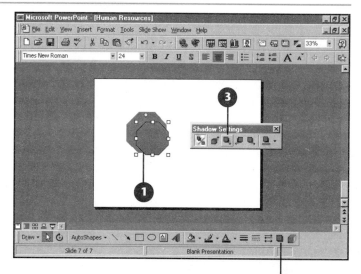

SEE ALSO

See "Choosing Object Colors" on page 84 for information on selecting colors.

ABC

Change the Color of a Shadow

1. Click the drawing object that has the shadow.

2. Click the Shadow button on the Drawing toolbar, and then click Shadow Settings.

3. Click the Shadow Color drop-down arrow on the Shadow Settings toolbar, and then select a new color.

4. Click the Close button on the Shadow Settings toolbar.

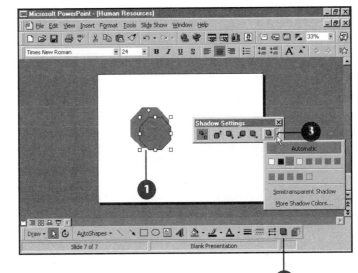

Add a Shadow to Text

1. Select the text.

2. Click the Shadow button on the Formatting toolbar.

Creating a 3-D Object

You can add the illusion of depth to your slides by giving your drawings a three-dimensional appearance using the 3-D tool. Although not all objects can be turned into 3-D objects, most of the AutoShapes can. You can create a 3-D effect using one of the 20 preset 3-D styles supported by PowerPoint, or you can use the 3-D tools to customize your own 3-D style. With the customization tools you can control, among other things, the angle at which the 3-D object is tilted and rotated, the depth of the object, and the direction of light falling upon the object.

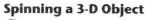

Apply a Preset 3-D Style

1. Click the drawing object.

2. Click the 3-D button on the Drawing toolbar.

3. Click one of the 20 preset 3-D styles

4. Click the Close button on the #-D Settings toolbar.

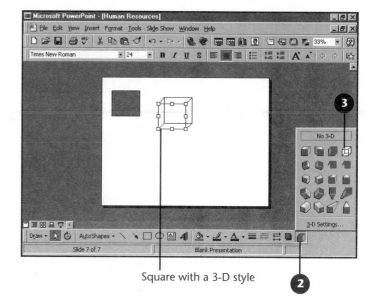

Square with a 3-D style

Spinning a 3-D Object

1. Click the 3-D object.

2. Click the 3-D button on the Drawing toolbar, and then click 3-D Settings.

3. Click the spin setting you want.

4. Click the Close button on the 3-D Settings toolbar.

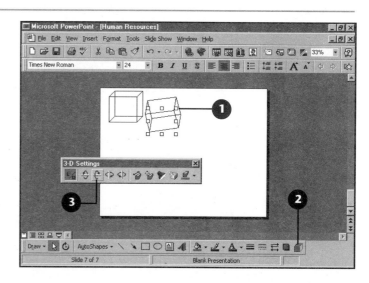

Set Lighting

1 Click the 3-D object, click the 3-D button on the Drawing toolbar, and then click 3-D Settings.

2 Click the Lighting button.

3 Click the spotlight that creates the effect you want.

4 Click the Close button on the 3-D Settings toolbar.

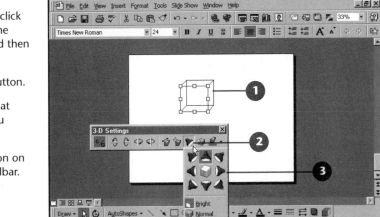

Set 3-D Depth

1 Click the 3-D object, click the 3-D button on the Drawing toolbar, and then click 3-D Settings.

2 Click the Depth button.

3 Click the size of the depth in points, or enter the exact number of points you want in the Custom box.

4 Click the Close button on the 3-D Settings toolbar.

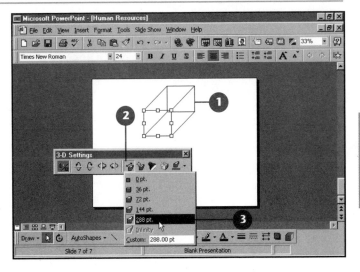

Controlling Object Placement

PowerPoint offers several tools for controlling object placement on the slide. One such tool is the *grid*, an invisible matrix of dots. When the grid is on, an object will "snap" to the nearest point on the grid. PowerPoint also can snap objects to other shapes so that, as new objects, they are placed on the slide they will naturally align themselves with preexisting shapes. Another way of aligning objects is with *alignment guides*, horizontal and vertical lines superimposed on the slide to help manually align objects. When an object is close to a guide, its corner or center, whichever is closer, snaps to the guide.

Set Objects to Snap into Place

1 Click the Draw button on the Drawing toolbar, and then point to Snap.

2 Click To Grid or To Shape.

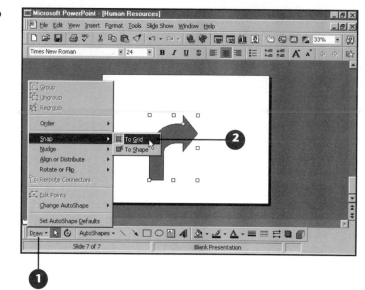

Align an Object to a Guide

1 Click the View menu.

2 Click Guides to display a horizontal and vertical guide.

3 Drag the object's center or edge near the guide. PowerPoint automatically aligns the center or edge to the guide.

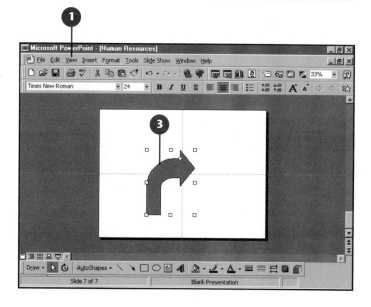

TIP

Use the keyboard to override grid settings. *To temporarily override settings for the grids and guides, press and hold the Alt key as you drag an object.*

SEE ALSO

See "Indenting Text" on page 36 for information on viewing the ruler.

Add, Move, or Remove a Guide

◆ To move a guide, drag it.

◆ To add a new guide, press and hold the Ctrl key and then drag the line to the new location. You can place a guide anywhere on the slide.

◆ To remove a guide, drag the guide off the slide.

A number appears as you drag that indicates the guide's position relative to the ruler.

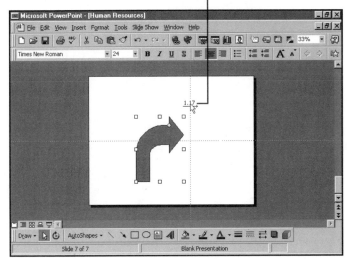

Aligning and Distributing Objects

Often when you work with three similar or identical objects, they look best when aligned in relation to each other. For example, you can align three objects with the leftmost object in the selection so that the tops of all three objects match along an invisible line. Sometimes, your task will not be alignment but to distribute your objects evenly across a space. PowerPoint includes commands to distribute your items horizontally and vertically. You can specify whether the distribution should occur for only the space currently occupied by the objects or across the entire slide.

Align Objects

1 Select the objects that you want to align. You can press Shift to select multiple objects.

2 Click the Draw button on the Drawing toolbar, and point to Align Or Distribute.

3 Decide whether you want the objects to align relative to the slide or relative to each other, and then make sure that Relative To Slide is selected or deselected, based on your decision.

4 Click the alignment option you want.

◆ Click Align Left to line up the objects with the left edge of the selection or slide.

◆ Click Align Center to line up the objects with the center of the selection or slide.

◆ Click Align Right to line up the objects with the right edge of the selection or slide.

◆ Click Align Top to line up the objects with the top edge of the selection or slide.

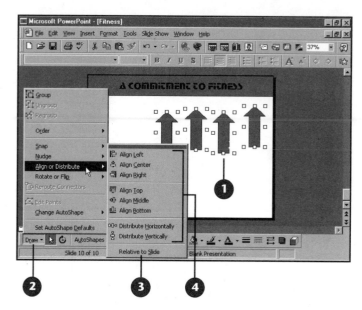

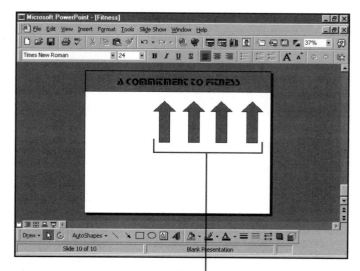

Objects aligned to their top

- ◆ Click Align Middle to line up the objects vertically with the middle of the selection or slide.

- ◆ Click Align Bottom to line up the objects with the bottom of the selection or slide.

Distribute Objects

1 Select the objects that you want to distribute. You can press Shift to select multiple objects.

2 Click the Draw button on the Drawing toolbar, and then point to Align Or Distribute.

3 Click the Distribution option you want.

"How can I ensure these three objects are the same distance apart?"

- ◆ Click Distribute Horizontally to distribute the objects evenly horizontally.

- ◆ Click Distribute Vertically to distribute the objects evenly vertically.

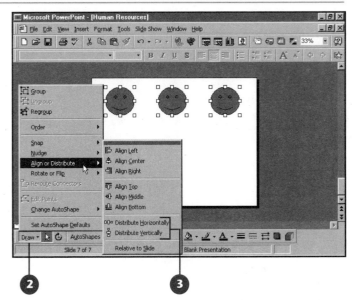

Arranging and Grouping Objects

When a slide contains multiple objects you might need to consider how they interact with each other. If the objects overlap, the most recently-created drawing will be placed on top of older drawings, but you can change how the stack of objects is ordered. If you have created a collection of objects that work together, you might want to group them to create a new drawing object that you can move, resize, or copy as a single unit.

Arrange a Stack of Objects

1 Click the drawing object you want to place.

2 Click the Draw button on the Drawing toolbar, and then point to Order.

3 Click Bring to Front to move the drawing to the top of the stack. Click Send to Back to move a drawing to the bottom of the stack. Click Bring Forward to move a drawing up one location in the stack. Click Send Backward to move a drawing back one location in the stack.

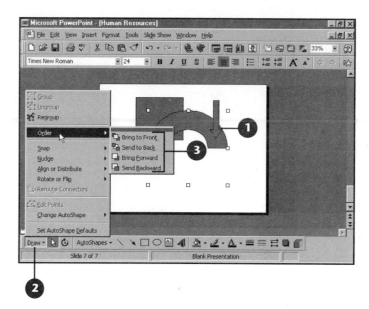

Group Objects Together

1 Select the drawing objects you want to group together. You can press Shift to select multiple objects.

2 Click the Draw button on the Drawing toolbar.

3 Click Group.

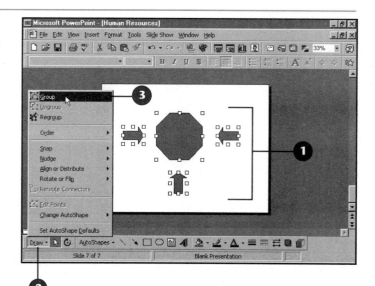

TIP

Use the Tab key to select objects in order. *You can move through the drawing objects on your slide (even those hidden behind other objects) by pressing the Tab key.*

"How can I keep a group of objects together when I move them?"

Ungroup a Drawing

1. Select the object you want to ungroup.

2. Click the Draw button on the Drawing toolbar.

3. Click Ungroup.

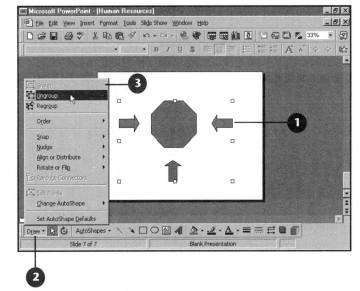

Regroup a Drawing

1. Click the Draw button on the Drawing toolbar.

2. Click Regroup.

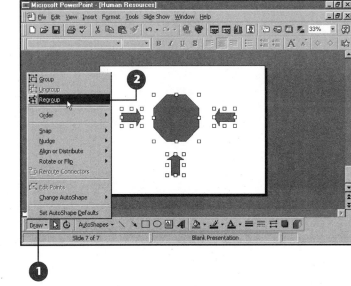

Adding
Multimedia
Clips

IN THIS SECTION

Inserting Multimedia Objects

Inserting Clips

Locating Clips

Adding and Removing Clips

Organizing Clips into Categories

Accessing Clip Gallery Live on the Web

Editing Clip Art

Recoloring an Object

Cropping an Image

Inserting Sounds

Playing and Recording Sounds

Using the Custom SoundTrack

Inserting and Playing Videos

Although well-illustrated slides can't make up for a lack of content, you have a much better chance of capturing your audience's attention if your slides are vibrant and visually interesting. You can easily enhance a slide by adding a picture—one of your own or one of the hundreds that come with Office 97. If you have the appropriate hardware, such as a sound card and speakers, you also might want to include sound files and video clips in your presentation.

You can insert a variety of non-PowerPoint objects into your presentation, such as clip art, pictures, sounds, and videos. If you have used other Microsoft Office 97 software products, you might already be familiar with the tools you use to insert these types of objects, because they are the same for all Office programs. You'll need to ensure that you have the necessary accessories installed before you perform all the tasks in this section.

Inserting Multimedia Objects

A vast collection of multimedia objects, called *clips*, comes with Microsoft PowerPoint 97 software. Clips include clip art, pictures, videos, and sounds. All Office 97 products provide a feature called the *Microsoft Clip Gallery*, which organizes these objects into categories and gives you tools to help locate the clips you need quickly. You can extend the usefulness of the Clip Gallery by importing your own objects into the Clip Gallery database.

Clip Art

Clip art objects are graphics developed by graphics software packages that can create vector images. *Vector images* are mathematically defined (made up of geometric shapes such as lines, curves, circles, squares, and so on) and therefore lend themselves extremely well to resizing and manipulating.

Pictures

Pictures, on the other hand, are not mathematically defined. They are *bitmaps*, images that are made up of dots. Bitmaps do not lend themselves as easily to resizing because the dots can't expand and contract. Instead, the software you are using must fill in the dots as best it can when you enlarge your picture, or must remove dots if you shrink your picture. You can create a bitmap using a bitmap graphics programs such as Windows *Paint*, by scanning an image, or by taking a digital photograph.

Sounds

A *sound* is a file that makes a sound. Some sounds can be played on your computer's internal speakers (such as the blip you hear when your operating system tries to alert you to an error), but others require a sound card and speakers. You can use the Windows accessory called *Media Player* to listen to sound clips.

Videos

A *video* is an animated movie file. Videos also use the Windows Media Player to play. Although you can play a video clip on most monitors, if it has sound, you probably need a sound card and speakers to hear the clip.

Inserting Clips

PowerPoint offers several easy methods for inserting clips. If you're including a clip on a new slide, you can choose an AutoLayout that includes a placeholder for that clip. To insert a clip on an existing slide, you can use the Insert menu. In either case, the Clip Gallery opens. The only clips that appear in the Clip Gallery are the ones provided by Microsoft Office 97. To include your own clips in the Clip Gallery, you need to first import them.

SEE ALSO

See "Adding and Removing Clips" on page 102 for information on importing clips.

Insert a Clip on a New Slide

1. Click the New Slide button on the Standard toolbar.

2. Click the AutoLayout that includes the clip type you want to insert.

3. Click OK.

4. Double-click the placeholder for the object type you want to insert.

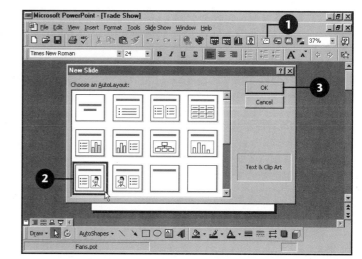

Insert a Clip from the Clip Gallery

1. Click the Insert menu.

2. Point to Picture or Movies And Sounds, and then click Clip Art, Sound From Gallery, or Movie From Gallery corresponding to the clip you want to add.

3. Click the category containing the clip you want.

4. Click the clip you want.

5. Click Insert.

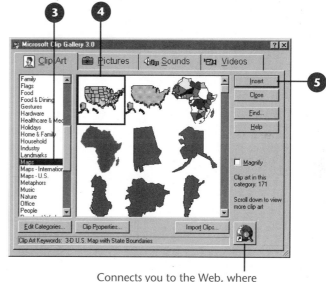

Connects you to the Web, where you can find additional clips.

6

Locating Clips

You can use the Clip Gallery's Find feature to locate a particular clip. Find gives you three different criteria for locating clips: keyword, file name, or clip type. A *keyword* is a word that describes the clip. Imagine, for example, that you need a piece of clip art to show how a recent bull market affected your company's returns. If you enter the keyword "bull," the Clip Gallery will display all images associated with bulls—from the animal to a bulldozer. You can also locate clips based on your presentation's content using AutoClipArt, which searches your presentation for words it can use as keywords.

Locate a Clip by Keyword

1 In the Clip Gallery, click Find.

2 Type a keyword that might be associated with the clip you are looking for.

3 Click Find Now.

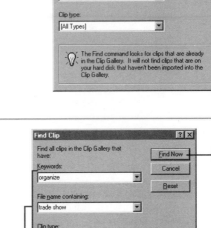

Locate a Clip by Clip Type

1 In the Clip Gallery, click Find.

2 Click the Clip Type drop-down arrow, and then click the clip type you want.

3 Click Find Now.

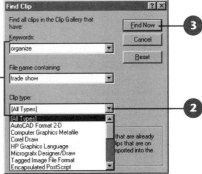

To narrow your search, enter criteria in all three boxes. Make sure you clear any previous search criteria before attempting a new search.

Use AutoClip Art to locate clip art. *To use AutoClipArt, you need to display the slide containing the text for which you'd like to locate accompanying clip art.*

"How can I find a clip that fits my ideas?"

Locate a Clip by Presentation Content

1 Display the slide for which you'd like to locate clip art, and then click the Tools menu. The Clip Gallery does not need to be open.

2 Click AutoClipArt.

3 Click the Select A Word drop-down arrow.

4 Click the word.

5 If necessary, click the On Slide drop-down arrow if the word occurs on more than one slide.

6 Click the View Clip Art button to view the list of clips that match the word.

7 In the Clip Gallery, click the clip you want.

8 Click the Insert button.

9 In the AutoClip Art dialog box, click the Close button.

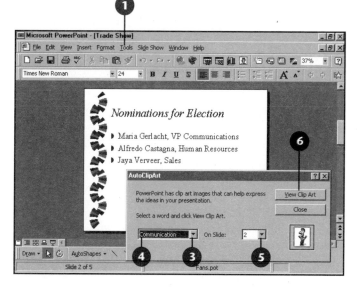

PowerPoint creates a temporary category with the results of the search.

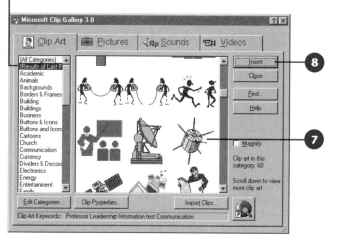

6

Adding and Removing Clips

You can import your own clips into the Clip Gallery one at a time, in groups, or in packages, so that their previews appear in the Clip Gallery window. If you regularly add, move, and remove clips to your hard drive, as active Web users often do, you will find the Update feature of the Clip Gallery especially useful. It automatically updates the locations of your clips if you try to insert a clip that needs updating, or you can update your clips manually.

SEE ALSO

See "Organizing Clips into Categories" on page 104 for information on setting clip properties.

Import a Clip

1 In the Clip Gallery, click Import Clips.

2 Click the Look In drop-down arrow, and then select the drive and folder that contain the clip you want to import.

3 Click the clip you want to import.

4 Click Open.

5 Set the clip properties.

6 Click OK.

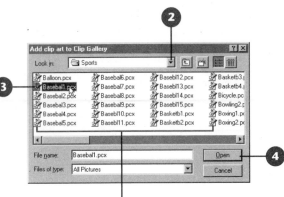

To import more than one file, press and hold the Ctrl key as you click the files you want.

Import a Clip Package

1 In the Clip Gallery dialog box, click Import Clips.

2 Click the Files Of Type drop-down arrow.

3 Scroll to, and then click Clip Gallery Packages.

4 Click the package you want to import.

5 Click Open.

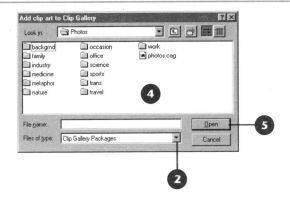

"I moved some clip art from one folder to another on my hard drive. How can I make sure the Clip Gallery will find it?"

Update the Clip Gallery

1 In the Clip Gallery, right-click a clip.

2 Click Update Clip Previews.

3 If you want to update clips on network drives, click the Network Drives check box.

4 If you want to update clips on removable disks, click the Removable Disks check box.

5 Click Update All.

6 If another Update dialog box appears, the Clip Gallery has found a preview for a clip that is no longer in its original location. You can do one of three things:

◆ Click Remove Previews to remove the previews for files that have been relocated.

◆ Click Skip This File to leave the preview in the Clip Gallery.

◆ Click Update Location, and then locate and select the folder that now contains the clip.

7 Click OK.

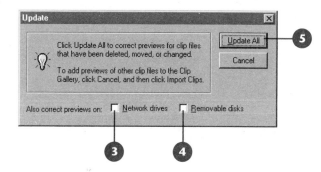

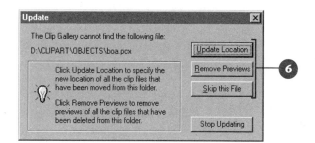

6

Organizing Clips into Categories

The clips that come with Office 97 are already organized, but if you've added clips without organizing them, you are probably underutilizing them because it's hard to find what you need in a hurry. To help you locate a clip quickly, you can place it in one or more categories, and you can assign one or more keywords to a clip. If the clip or picture you want is not in the Clip Gallery, you can insert it without opening the Clip Gallery.

TIP

What if the Clip Gallery is read-only? *You might not be able to edit the clip properties of the clips that are part of the shared read-only Clip Gallery database.*

Edit Clip Categories

1 In the Clip Gallery, click the Edit Categories button.

2 Choose the editing option you need:

- ◆ To add a new category to the category list, click New Category, type a new category name, and then click OK.

- ◆ To delete an existing category, click the category in the category list, and then click Delete Category.

- ◆ To rename an existing category, click the category in the category list, click Rename Category, type the new category name, and then click OK.

3 Click Close when you are finished editing the categories.

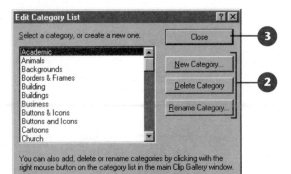

TRY THIS

Visit Web sites that offer clips other than the Microsoft clip site.

Download a few clips to your computer and categorize them into the Clip Gallery. Make sure, however, that the clips are not copyrighted. Some Web sites offer free clips, but others are copyrighted, and you must either pay to use the clips or you must acknowledge their source.

Categorize a Clip

1. In Clip Gallery, click the clip you want to categorize.

2. Click Clip Properties.

3. Check the check boxes corresponding to the categories in which you want the clips to appear.

4. Type keywords for the clip. For multiple keywords, type a space or comma between the words.

5. Click OK.

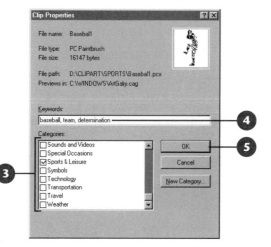

TIP

Use the Picture toolbar to insert an image. *To insert an image from a file, click Insert Picture From File on the Picture toolbar.*

Insert an Image from a File

1. Click the Insert menu, point to Picture, and then click From File.

2. Click the Look In drop-down arrow, and then select the drive and folder that contain the file you want to insert.

3. Click the file you want to insert.

4. Click Insert.

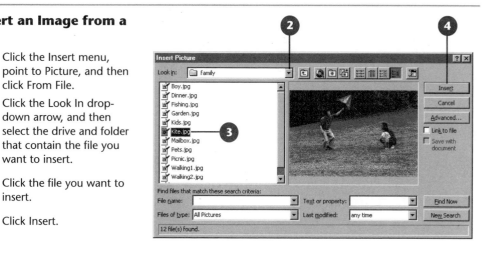

6

Accessing Clip Gallery Live on the Web

If the Clip Gallery contents are insufficient for your needs and you have a Web connection, you can go to a Web page from the Clip Gallery to browse through additional clips. You can then download those clips to your hard drive. Any clips you select there are automatically added to the Clip Gallery.

TIP

To use the Clip Gallery Live Web page, you must access it from the Office 97 Clip Gallery, not by entering its URL in your browser.

Open Clip Gallery Live

1. Open the Clip Gallery.

2. Click the Connect To Web For Additional Clips button.

3. If a message appears telling you about the Web feature, click OK. Your operating system software initiates your computer's Web connection.

4. Connect to the Web using whatever dialog box appears. Your browser automatically displays the Microsoft Clip Gallery Live page.

View Clips in a Category

1. If necessary, click the Accept button on the Clip Gallery Live Web page.

2. If necessary, click the Browse button.

3. Click the media type you want: ClipArt, Pictures, Sounds, or Videos.

4. Click the Select A Category drop-down list arrow, and then click the category you want.

5. Click the Go button.

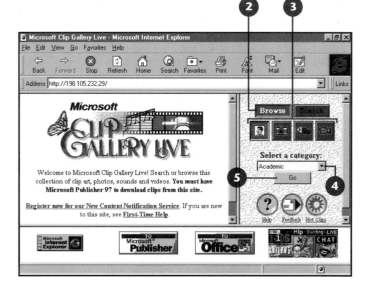

SEE ALSO

See "Adding and Removing Clips" on page 102 to import your own clips into the Clip Gallery.

TRY THIS

Locate Clips from PowerPoint Central. *You can also access clips from PowerPoint Central, a respository of information, tips and tricks, files such as sound and video clips, and tutorials, available via the Internet. Click Tools, click PowerPoint Central, and then click on the links that appear on your screen to access and use PowerPoint Central.*

Search for a Clip

1. On the Clip Gallery Live Web page, click the Search button, if necessary.

2. Type a keyword in the Enter Keywords box.

3. Click the Find button.

4. Click Yes if you are asked if you want to continue.

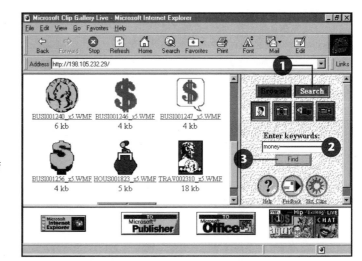

Download a Clip

1. Once you have displayed a list of clips on the Clip Gallery Live Web page, click the hypertext link underneath the clip you want.

2. If a virus warning dialog box appears, click the Save It To Disk option button.

3. Click OK.

4. In the Save As dialog box, enter a name and location for your clip.

5. Click the Save button. The clip is stored on your hard drive and added to the Clip Gallery.

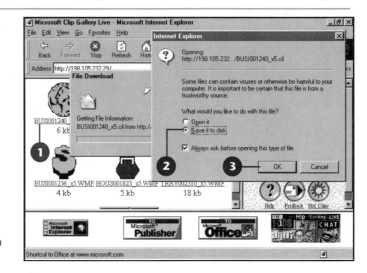

6

Editing Clip Art

Once you have inserted clip art into your presentation, you can adapt it to meet your needs. Perhaps the clip is too small to be effective, or you don't quite like the colors it uses. Like any object, you can resize or move the image. You can also control the image's colors, brightness, and contrast using the Picture toolbar. You can use these same methods with bitmapped pictures.

TIP

Open the Picture toolbar. *If the Picture Toolbar didn't open when you selected an image, right-click any toolbar, and then click Picture.*

Resize a Clip

1 Click the clip to select it.

2 Drag one of the sizing handles to increase or decrease the clip's size.

- Drag a middle handle to resize clip art up, down, left, or right.

- Drag a corner handle to resize clip art proportionally.

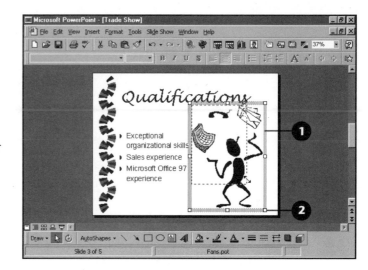

Change Image Contrast

1 Click the object whose contrast you want to increase or decrease.

2 To choose the contrast you want:

- Click the More Contrast button on the Picture toolbar to increase color intensity, resulting in less gray color.

- Click the Less Contrast button on the Picture toolbar to decrease color intensity, resulting in more gray color.

Change Image Brightness

1 Click the object whose brightness you want to increase or decrease.

2 To choose the image brightness you want:

♦ Click the More Brightness button on the Picture toolbar to lighten the object colors by adding more white.

♦ Click the Less Brightness button on the Picture toolbar to darken the object colors by adding more black.

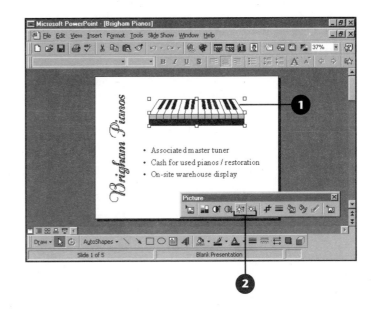

Restore Original Settings

"I made changes to my clip but I'd like to restore its original settings."

1 Click the object whose settings you want to restore.

2 Click the Reset Picture button on the Picture toolbar.

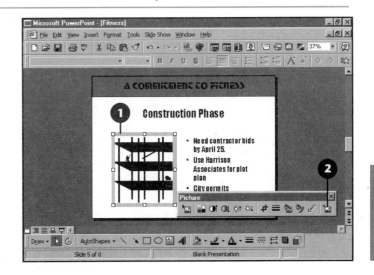

6

Recoloring an Object

An especially useful feature for working with clip art is the ability to recolor objects. For example, if you use a flower clip art as your business logo, you can change shades of pink in the spring to shades of orange in the autumn. You also might want to set a transparent background to your clip art to avoid conflict between a background color and your slide's background. With a transparent background, the clip art takes on the same background as your slide presentation.

Choose a Color Type

1 Click the object whose color you want to change.

2 Click the Image Control button on the Picture toolbar.

3 Click one of the Image Control options:

◆ Automatic gives the image the default coloring.

◆ Grayscale converts the default coloring into whites, blacks, and grays scaled between white and black.

◆ Black & White converts the default coloring into only white and black. Be careful when you choose this option because detail might be sacrificed.

◆ Watermark converts the default coloring into whites and very light colors. This option makes a nice slide background.

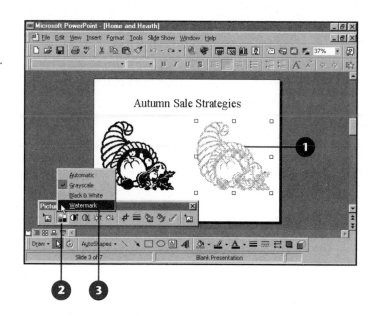

TIP

Setting a color as transparent only works with bitmaps.

SEE ALSO

See "Applying a Color to an Object" on page 64 for information on selecting a color.

Recolor a Picture

1 Click the picture you want to recolor.

2 Click the Recolor Picture button on the Picture toolbar.

3 Click the check box next to the original color you want to change.

4 Click the corresponding New drop-down arrow, and then select a new color.

5 Repeat steps 3 and 4 for as many colors as you want.

6 Click OK.

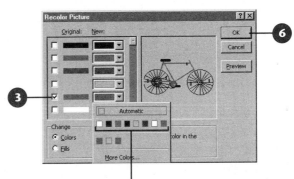

TRY THIS

Create a slide background. *To create an effective background to your presentation, place a clip art from the Clip Gallery on your Slide Master. Size it to fill the entire background. Right-click the object, point to Order, and then click Send To Back. Click the Image Control button on the Picture toolbar, and then click Watermark. The Watermark effect produces a picture light enough to serve as a background so that text in front is readable.*

Set a Transparent Background

1 Click the object.

2 Click the Set Transparent Color button on the Picture toolbar.

3 Move the pointer over the object until the pointer changes shape.

4 Click the color you want to set as transparent.

5 Click outside the image when you are finished.

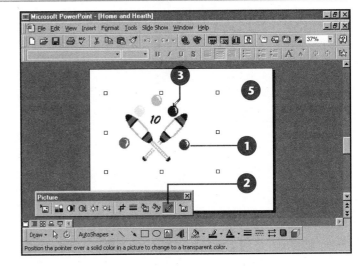

Cropping an Image

One of the things you will find especially useful with clip art is the ability to crop the clip art to isolate just one portion of it. Because clip art uses vector image technology, you can *crop*, or cut out, even the smallest part of it and enlarge it, and the clip art will still be recognizable. You can also crop bitmapped images, but if you try to crop a bitmapped image and then enlarge the area you cropped, you will lose picture detail. You can crop an image by hand using the Crop tool on the Picture toolbar. You can also crop using the Format Picture dialog box, which gives you precise control over the dimensions of the area you want to crop.

Crop an Image Quickly

1. Click the image to select the object.

2. Click the Crop button on the Picture toolbar.

3. Drag the sizing handles until the borders surround the area you want to crop.

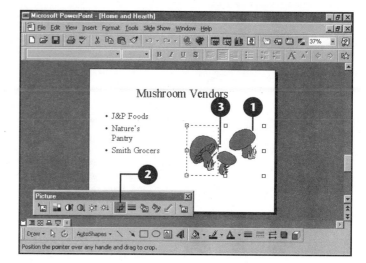

Redisplay a Cropped Image

1. Click the image, and then click the Crop button on the Picture toolbar.

2. Drag the sizing handles out to reveal the areas that were originally cropped.

3. Click outside the image when you are finished.

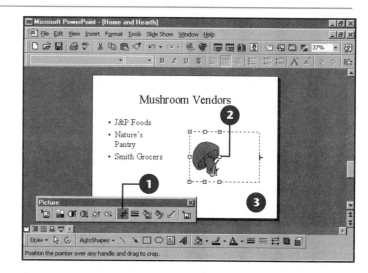

Crop an Image Precisely

1 Right-click the object you want to format.

2 Click Format Picture.

3 Click the Picture tab.

4 Adjust the values in the Left, Right, Top, and Bottom boxes to crop the image to the exact dimensions you want.

5 Click OK.

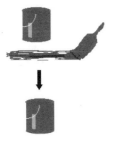

4 **3**

Format Picture

| Colors and Lines | Size | Position | Picture | Text Box |

Crop from

Left: `2"`   Top: `0"`

Right: `0"`   Bottom: `0"`

Image control

Color: `Automatic`

Brightness: `50 %`

Contrast: `50 %`

Recolor...   Reset

OK   Cancel   Preview

Values are distance from the border of the image. When you first insert an image the values are all 0. If you enter, for example, a value of 2" in the Left box, the leftmost two inches of the image will be cropped off.

6

Inserting Sounds

You can insert existing sounds into a presentation by either accessing them from a file or using the Clip Gallery. When you insert a sound in a slide, a small sound icon appears representing the sound file.

TIP

Scroll the AutoLayout dialog box to locate the Media clips, if necessary.

Insert a Sound Clip to a New Slide

1 Click the Insert New Slide button on the Standard toolbar.

2 Click the Media Clip & Text or Text & Media Clip AutoLayout.

3 Click OK.

4 Double-click the Media Clip placeholder.

5 Locate and select the file, and then click OK.

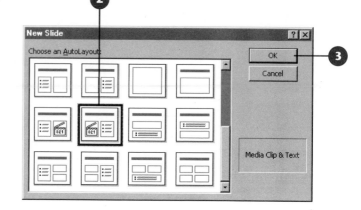

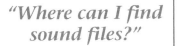

"Where can I find sound files?"

Insert a Clip Gallery Sound Clip

1 Click the Insert menu.

2 Point to Movies And Sounds.

3 Click Sound From Gallery.

4 Click the sound you want to insert.

5 Click Insert.

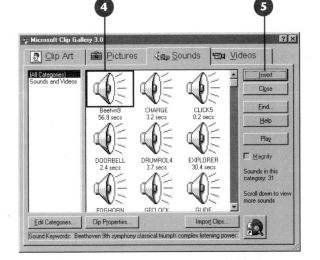

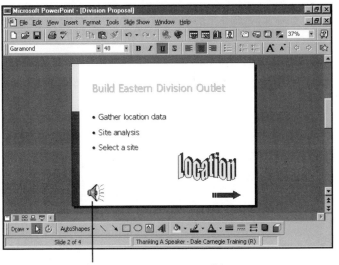

This icon appears on your slide when you insert a sound.

Playing and Recording Sounds

You can play sounds in Slide View and in Slide Show View. You can modify sound objects so they play continuously or one time through. To play sounds other than your computer's internal sounds, you need a sound card and speakers. You can record your own sounds if you have a microphone using the Windows Sound Recorder.

Play a Sound

1. Double-click the sound icon. In Slide Show view, click the sound icon.

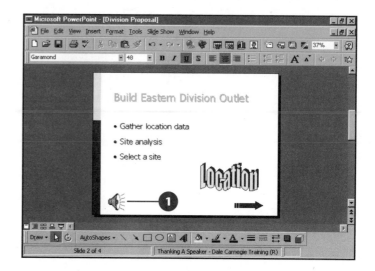

Edit a Sound

1. Right-click the sound icon.
2. Click Edit Sound Object.
3. Change the sound settings.
4. Click OK.

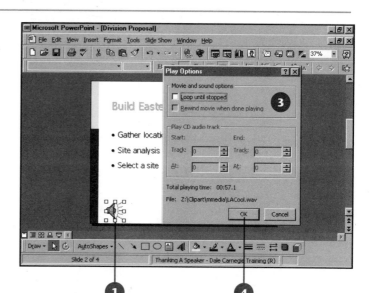

Record a Sound

1 Click the Start button on the taskbar.

2 Point to Programs, point to Accessories, point to Multimedia, and then click Sound Recorder.

3 Click the Record button. You will need a microphone to record your sounds.

4 Click the Stop button when you are finished.

5 Click the File menu, click Save As.

6 Click the Save In drop-down arrow and select a location to store the sound file.

7 In the File Name box, enter a name.

8 Click Save. You can now insert your sound file into a PowerPoint presentation.

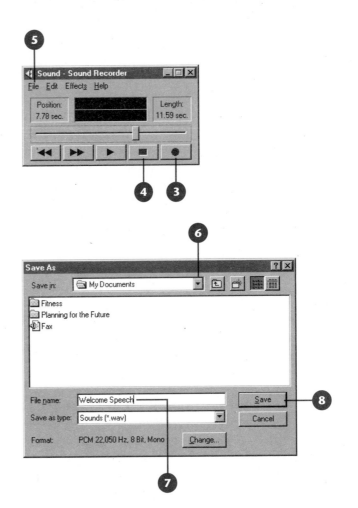

6

Using the Custom Soundtrack

One of the extra features available on your Office 97 CD-ROM is *Custom Soundtrack*, which automatically adds a soundtrack to your entire presentation or individual slides. You can choose music from 15 different music style groups, ranging from classical to funk. Each music style group has its own list of styles types. For example, you can choose ragtime jazz, big band jazz, or New Orleans jazz. You can specify personality, such as romantic, and define the band type—such as lounge or night club. Finally, you can specify a musical motif that matches your custom soundtrack to accompany any animations you've created.

Install Custom Soundtrack

1   Close PowerPoint if it is open, click the Start button on the taskbar, point to Settings, and then click Control Panel.

2   Double-click Add/Remove programs.

3   Click the Install button.

4   Insert your Office 97 CD-ROM, and then click the Next button.

5   Click the Browse button, and then click the Setup file in the Musictrk subfolder of the Valupack folder.

6   Click Open, and then click the Finish button.

Turn Off or Change a Soundtrack

1   Display the slide whose soundtrack you want to modify.

2   Click the Slide Show menu and then click Custom Soundtrack.

3   Choose one of the playing options for the slide.

4   Click the OK button to save your changes.

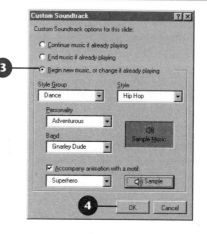

Load the SoundTracks Add-in to use the feature.
Custom Soundtrack is actually a separate program, called an add-in, which extends the functionality of PowerPoint 97. You can access other such programs by clicking the Tools menu, and then clicking Add-Ins.

Choose a Custom Soundtrack Sound Style

1 Click Slide Show menu, and then click Custom Soundtrack.

2 Click the Begin New Music option button.

3 Choose Style Group, Style, Personality and Band sound options.

4 Click the Sample Music button to preview the sound.

5 Click OK to close the dialog box and save your settings.

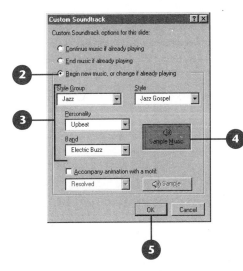

How do motifs work?
Musical motifs only work for animations that are activated by mouse clicks. They do not work for automatic animations.

Assign a Motif to an Animation

1 Display a slide containing an animation, click the Slide Show menu, and then click Custom Soundtrack.

2 Click the Begin New Music option button.

3 Select the Accompany Animation With Motif check box.

4 Choose a musical motif.

5 Click the Sample button.

6 Click OK.

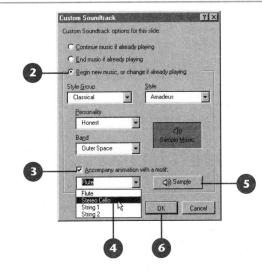

6

Inserting and Playing Videos

Video clips can be either *animations*, such as cartoons, or they can be real-life movies prepared with digitized video equipment. When you insert a video into PowerPoint, the Windows Media Player accessory automatically appears, which lets you play and work with your video. You can play videos on most monitors, but if you don't have a sound card and speakers, you won't be able to hear your videos if they include sound.

Insert a Video Clip to a New Slide

1. Click the Insert New Slide button on the Standard toolbar.

2. Click the Media Clip & Text or Text & Media Clip AutoLayout.

3. Click OK.

4. Double-click the Media Clip placeholder.

5. Locate and select the file you want to insert, and then click Open.

6. Click OK.

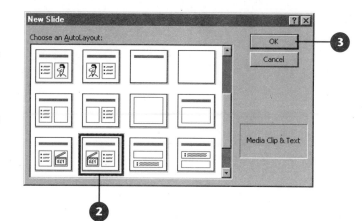

Insert a Clip Gallery Movie Clip

1. Click the Insert menu.

2. Point to Movies And Sounds.

3. Click Movie From Gallery.

4. Click the movie you want to insert.

5. Click Insert.

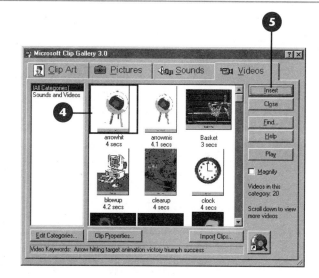

Play a Movie

1 Double-click the movie icon.

"How do I make a movie play continuously?"

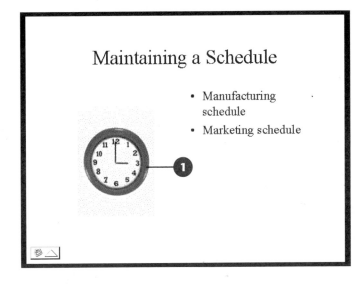

Edit a Movie

1 Right-click the movie icon.

2 Click Edit Movie Object.

3 Change the movie settings.

◆ Click the Loop Until Stopped check box to play the movie continuously or

◆ Click the Rewind Movie When Done Playing check box to complete the operation.

4 Click OK.

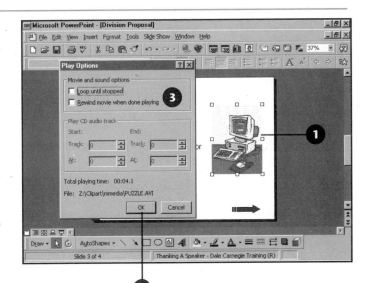

7

Inserting Linked and Embedded Objects

IN THIS SECTION

Sharing Information Among Documents

Copying and Pasting Objects

Embedding and Linking an Object

Modifying Links

Inserting an Excel Object

Inserting a Word Table

Creating WordArt Text

Editing WordArt Text

Applying WordArt Text Effects

Creating an Organization Chart

Structuring an Organization Chart

Formatting an Organization Chart

An effective presentation draws on information from many sources. Microsoft PowerPoint 97 helps you seamlessly integrate information such as Microsoft Word tables, Microsoft Excel worksheet and charts, Microsoft WordArt styled text, and Microsoft Organization Chart charts into your presentations. *Microsoft WordArt* lets you create interesting textual effects. *Microsoft Organization Chart* allows you to create an organization chart, usually used to display the personnel or reporting structure within an organization.

Object Linking and Embedding

In PowerPoint, you can insert an object created in another program into a presentation using a program-integration technology known as *Object Linking and Embedding* (OLE). OLE is a critical feature for many PowerPoint users because with it you can create a presentation that draws on information from any program that uses the technology—and these days, most Windows programs do. When you share objects using OLE, the menus and toolbars from the program that created the object are available to you from within your PowerPoint presentation. You can edit inserted information without having to leave PowerPoint.

Sharing Information Among Documents

One of the great technological steps forward recently in personal computing has been the ability to insert an object created in one program into a document created in another program. Terms that you'll find useful in understanding how you can share objects among documents include:

TERM	DEFINITION
source program	The program that created the original object.
source file	The file that contains the original object.
destination program	The program that created the document into which you are inserting the object.
destination file	The file into which you are inserting the object.

For example, if you place an Excel chart in your PowerPoint presentation, Excel is the source program and PowerPoint is the destination program. The chart is the source file; the presentation is the destination file.

There are three ways to share information in Windows programs: pasting, embedding, and linking.

Pasting

You can cut or copy an object from one document and then paste it into another using the Cut, Copy, and Paste buttons on the source and destination program toolbars.

Embedding

When you *embed* an object, you place a copy of the object in the destination file, and when you activate the object, the tools from the source program become available in your presentation. For example, if you insert an Excel chart into your PowerPoint presentation, the Excel menus and toolbars become available, replacing the PowerPoint menus and toolbars, so you can edit the chart if necessary. With embedding, any changes you make to the chart in the presentation do not affect the original file.

Linking

When you *link* an object, you insert a representation of the object itself into the destination file. The tools of the source program are available, and when you use them to edit the object you've inserted, you are actually editing the source file. Moreover, any changes you make to the source file are reflected in the destination file.

Copying and Pasting Objects

When you copy or cut an object, Windows temporarily stores the object in an area in your computer's active memory called the *Clipboard*. You can paste the object into the destination file using the Paste button or the Paste Special command, which gives you more control over how the object will appear in the destination file.

TIP

Be careful of file size when pasting objects. *When you click Paste, you are sometimes actually embedding. Because embedding can greatly increase file size you might want to use Paste Special if disk space is at a premium. You can select a format that requires minimal disk space, pasting the object as a simple picture or simple text instead of as an embedded object.*

Paste an Object into a Presentation

1   Select the object in the source program.

2   Click the Copy button on the source program's toolbar.

3   Switch to PowerPoint and display the slide on which you want to paste the object.

4   Click the Paste button on the PowerPoint Standard toolbar.

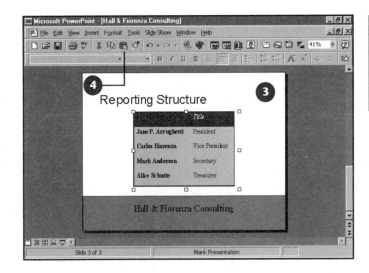

Paste Information in a Specified Format

1   Select the object in the source program.

2   Click the Copy button on the source program's toolbar.

3   Switch to PowerPoint and display the slide on which you want to paste the object.

4   Click the Edit menu, and then click Paste Special.

5   Click the object type you want in the As list box.

6   Click OK.

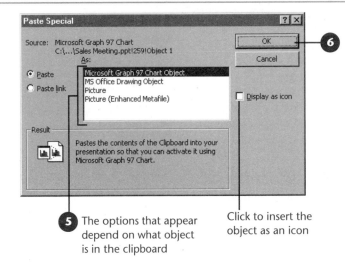

5   The options that appear depend on what object is in the clipboard

Click to insert the object as an icon

Embedding and Linking an Object

There are several ways to embed or link an object to a slide. If you are creating a new object from scratch, you can use the Insert Object command. If you want to insert an existing file, you can also use Insert Object and you can specify whether or not you want to link the object. If your object is already open in the program that created it, you can copy it, and in some cases, paste it onto a slide, automatically embedding it. Finally, you can use the Paste Special command to paste link a copied object—pasting and linking it at the same time.

Insert a New Object

1. Click the Insert menu.
2. Click Object.
3. Click the Create New option button.
4. In the Object Type list box, click the type of object you want to insert.
5. Click OK.
6. Use the source program tools to edit the object.
7. Click outside the object when you are finished.

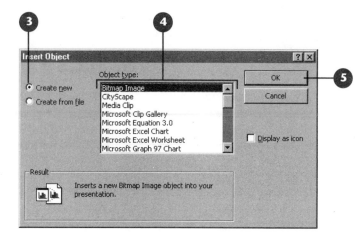

Insert a File

1. Click the Insert menu.
2. Click Object.
3. Click the Create From File option button.
4. Click the Browse button.
5. Click the Look In drop-down arrow, and then select the file you want to insert. Click OK.
6. To embed the object, make sure the Link check box is not checked. To link it, click the Link check box to select it.
7. Click OK twice.

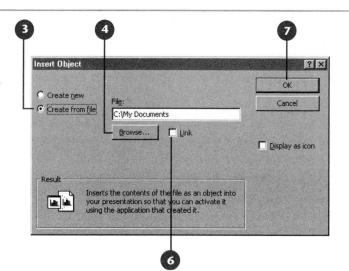

Inserting objects as icons.
If you insert an object as an icon, you can double-click the icon to view the object. This is especially handy for kiosk presentations.

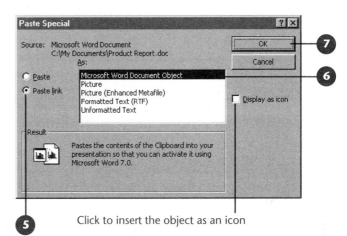

Paste Link an Object

1 In the source program, select the object you want to paste link.

2 Click the Cut or Copy button on the Standard toolbar in the source program.

3 Switch to your presentation.

4 Click the Edit menu, and then click Paste Special.

5 Click the Paste Link option button.

6 Click the format you want.

7 Click OK.

Click to insert the object as an icon

Modifying Links

When you modify a linked object, it will usually be automatically updated in the destination document. However, depending on your link settings, you might have to update it manually. All Office 97 programs give you control over the links you have established. You can change the source file and you can break a link at any time.

"I moved a linked object. How can I make sure the link will still work?"

Update Links

1. Open the presentation that contains the links you want to update.

2. Click the Edit menu, and then click Links.

3. Click the link you want to update.

4. Click the Update Now button.

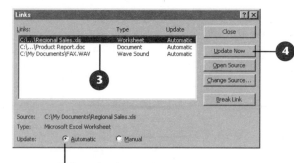

Click so that links will update automatically whenever the document is reopened

Change the Source of a Linked Object

1. Click the Edit menu, and then click Links.

2. Click the link whose source you want to change.

3. Click the Change Source button. The Change Source dialog box opens, displaying the contents of the folder that contains the linked object.

4. Locate and select the new source file.

5. Click the Open button.

6. Click the Close button.

7. Click outside the linked object to deselect it.

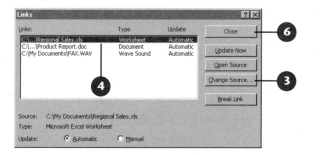

Open an object as a different type. *If more than one object type is available, you can specify that an object open as a different type.*

Break a Link

1. Click the Edit menu, and then click Links.

2. Click the link you want to break.

3. Click the Break Link button. The link no longer appears in the Links dialog box.

4. Click the Close button.

"How can I ensure that changes I make to the source file won't affect the object in my presentation?"

Convert a Linked Object

1. Click the linked object whose file type you want to convert.

2. Click the Edit menu.

3. Point to Linked Object. This command might appear as "Linked Chart Object," or some other file type, depending on the object type.

4. Click Convert.

5. Click the new object type you want.

6. Click OK.

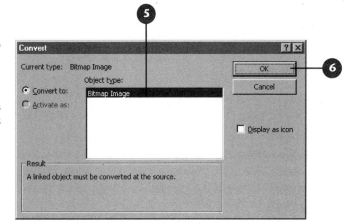

Inserting an Excel Object

There are several types of Excel objects that you can insert into your presentation. Two of the most common are worksheets and charts. You can insert a new Excel worksheet and then add data to it, or you can insert an existing Excel worksheet. You can also insert a chart from an Excel workbook.

TIP

To display only a certain portion of a worksheet.
Double-click the embedded Excel object, and then drag the sizing handles until only the rows and columns you want are displayed. You can also use the Crop tool on the Picture toolbar to crop unwanted portions.

Insert a New Excel Worksheet

1 Click the Insert Microsoft Excel Worksheet button on the Standard toolbar.

2 Click the cell representing the number of rows and columns you want.

3 In the worksheet, click the first cell into which you want to enter data.

4 Type the data. Press the Tab or Down arrow keys to move to the next cell, either to the right or down.

5 Edit and format the worksheet using the Excel tools.

6 Click outside the worksheet when you are finished.

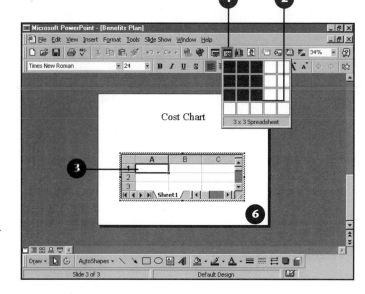

Insert Data Stored in an Excel Worksheet

1 Display the slide on which you want to insert the Excel worksheet.

2 Click the Insert menu, and then click Object.

3 Click the Create From File option button, click the Browse button, and then locate and select the worksheet you want. Click OK.

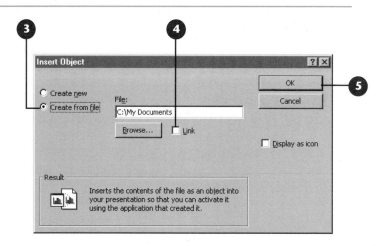

SEE ALSO

*See "Inserting a Graph Chart"
on page 146 for information on
inserting a chart using Microsoft
Graph—an alternative if you
need a chart in your presentation but don't have a program
like Excel.*

Month	Accidents
1	11
2	7
3	9
4	5
5	10
6	11
7	16
8	9
9	7

TIP

**You can also insert a chart
using drag-and-drop.** *Open
both Excel and PowerPoint,
select the chart in Excel, and
then drag it into PowerPoint.*

4 To link the worksheet,
click the Link check box.

5 Click OK.

6 If necessary, edit the
worksheet using the Excel
tools.

7 Click outside the worksheet when you are
finished.

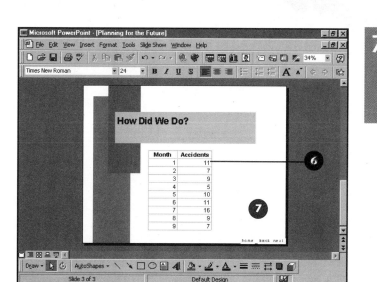

Insert an Existing Excel Chart

1 Open the worksheet
containing the chart in
Excel.

2 Click the chart, and then
click the Copy button on
Excel's Standard toolbar.

3 Switch to PowerPoint and
the slide on which you
want the chart.

4 Click the Paste button on
the Standard toolbar.

5 Click outside the chart to
deselect it.

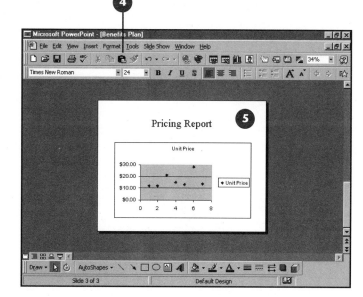

Inserting a Word Table

You use a Word table to organize non-numeric information into columns and rows. The intersection of a column and row is called a *cell*. When you insert a table into a PowerPoint presentation, the PowerPoint menus and toolbars change to the Word menus and toolbars.

TIP

Increase the size of a table after you have inserted it. *Click the Insert Rows button on the Word Standard toolbar, or right-click a cell, and then click Insert Rows.*

Insert a Word Table

1 In Slide view, click the Insert Microsoft Word Table button on the Standard toolbar.

2 Drag the pointer over the squares in the table grid to indicate the number of rows and columns you want to include.

3 Type the information you want into each cell, pressing Tab to move from one cell to the next.

4 Use the Microsoft Word menus and toolbars to edit and format the table.

5 Click outside the table to deselect it.

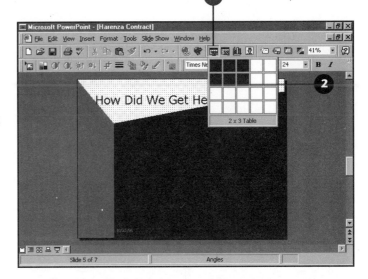

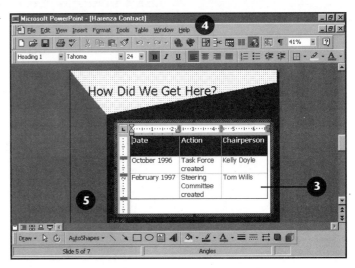

To create a new slide with a table. *Click the New Slide button, click the Table AutoLayout, and then click OK. Double-click the table placeholder on the new slide to enter the table information.*

"How can I format a table quickly?"

Edit a Word Table

1 Double-click the table to select it and display the Word menus and toolbar.

2 Use Word's Table tools to edit the table.

3 Click outside the table to deselect it.

Format a Word Table

1 Double-click the table in your presentation.

2 Right-click the table, and then click Table AutoFormat.

3 Scroll the list of formats, and then select the one you want to apply to the table.

4 Click OK.

5 Click outside the table to deselect it.

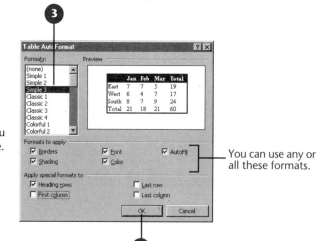

You can use any or all these formats.

Creating WordArt Text

The WordArt feature lets you create stylized text to draw attention to your most important words. Most users apply WordArt to short phrases or even just a word, such as "Our Customers Come First" or "Welcome." You should apply WordArt sparingly to a slide. Its visual appeal and unique look require uncluttered space. When you use WordArt, you can choose from a variety of text styles that come with the WordArt feature, or you can create your own using tools on the WordArt toolbar.

Insert WordArt

1. Click the Insert WordArt button on the Drawing toolbar to open the WordArt Gallery.

2. Click one of the WordArt styles. If you want to create your own WordArt, just click OK without selecting a WordArt style.

3. Click OK.

4. Type the text you want WordArt to use.

5. If applicable, use the Font, Size, Bold, and Italic options to modify the text you entered.

6. Click OK.

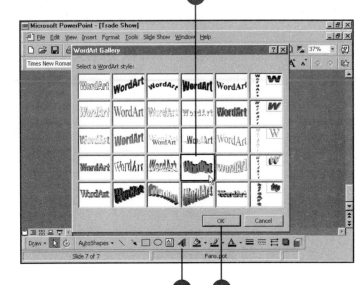

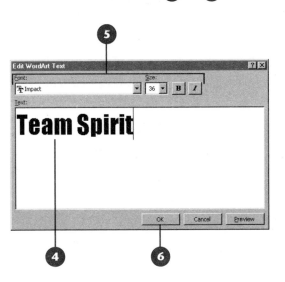

Different font

Different font

Different font

Edit WordArt Text

1 If necessary, right-click the WordArt object, and then click Show WordArt Toolbar.

2 Click the Edit Text button on the WordArt toolbar to open the Edit WordArt Text dialog box.

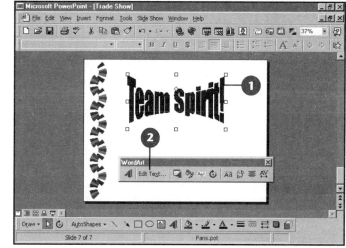

Apply a Different WordArt Gallery Style to Existing WordArt

1 Click the WordArt object whose style you want to change.

2 Make sure the WordArt toolbar is displayed.

3 Click the WordArt Gallery button on the WordArt toolbar.

4 Click the WordArt Gallery style you want to apply.

5 Click OK.

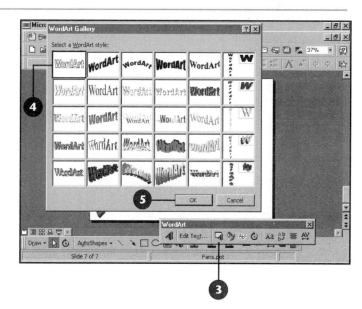

Editing WordArt Text

With WordArt, in addition to applying one of the preformatted styles, you can create your own style by shaping your text into a variety of shapes, curves, styles, and color patterns. The WordArt toolbar gives you tools for coloring, rotating, and shaping your text. You can also format your WordArt using the tools that are available through the Format dialog box that you have learned about in other sections, including positioning and sizing your WordArt.

Change the Shape of WordArt

1. Click the WordArt object.

2. Click the WordArt Shape button on the WordArt toolbar.

3. Click the shape you want to apply to the text.

Rotate WordArt

1. Click the WordArt object.

2. Click the Free Rotate button on the WordArt toolbar.

3. Drag one of the rotate handles that appear in the four corners to rotate the object in any direction you want.

4. When you are finished, click the Free Rotate button.

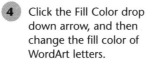

Color WordArt

1. Click the WordArt object.

2. Click the Format button on the WordArt toolbar.

3. Click the Colors And Lines tab.

4. Click the Fill Color drop down arrow, and then change the fill color of WordArt letters.

5. Click the Line Color drop down arrow to change the line color of WordArt letters.

6. Click OK.

Align WordArt

1. Click the WordArt object.

2. Click the WordArt Alignment button on the WordArt toolbar.

3. Click the alignment you want.

4. Click outside the object to deselect it.

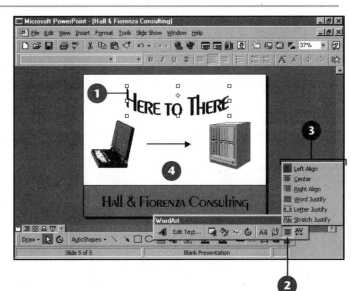

Applying WordArt Text Effects

You can apply a number of text effects to your WordArt objects that determine letter heights, justification, and spacing. The effect of some of the adjustments you make will be more pronounced for certain WordArt styles than others. Some of these effects will make the text unreadable for certain styles, so apply these effects carefully.

Make Letters the Same Height

1. Click the WordArt object.

2. Click the WordArt Same Letter Heights button on the WordArt toolbar.

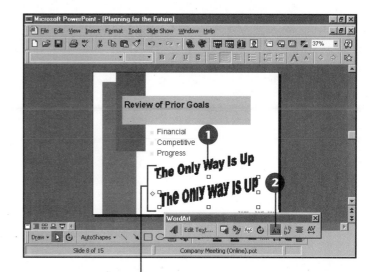

WordArt with and without same letter height.

Format Text Vertically

1. Click the WordArt object.

2. Click the WordArt Vertical Text button on the WordArt toolbar.

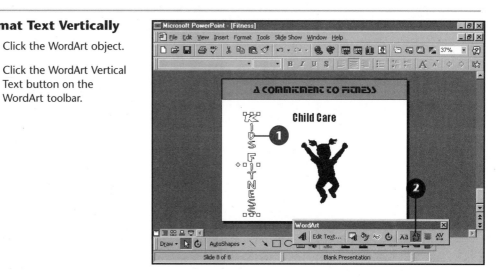

Reputation

Reputation

Reputation

Adjust Character Spacing

1 Click the WordArt object.

2 Click the WordArt Character Spacing button on the WordArt toolbar.

3 Click a spacing setting, including Very Tight, Tight, Normal, Loose, or Very Loose, to determine the amount of space between characters.

4 If necessary, select or deselect the Kern Character Pairs option to adjust the space between characters.

5 Click outside the object to deselect it.

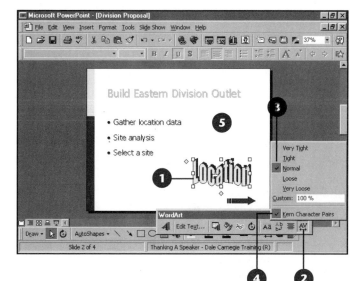

Creating an Organization Chart

An *organization chart*, also known as an *org chart*, shows the personnel structure in an organization. You can include an organization chart in a PowerPoint presentation using Microsoft Organization Chart, a program that comes with the Office 97 suite. When you start Organization Chart, chart boxes appear into which you enter company personnel. Each chart box is identified by its position in the chart. Managers, for example, are at the top, while Subordinates are below, Co-Workers to the sides, and so on.

SEE ALSO

See "Structuring on Organization Chart" on page142 for information on reorganizing your organization chart and see "Formatting an Organization Chart" on page 144 for information on formatting it.

Create an Organization Chart

1. Start Microsoft Organization Chart in one of the following ways:

    - On an existing slide, click the Insert menu, point to Picture, and then click Organization Chart, and then click OK.

    - On a new slide, click the Insert New Slide button on the Standard toolbar, click the Organization Chart AutoLayout, click OK, and then double-click the org chart placeholder to add an org chart.

2. Use the Organization Chart tools and menus to design your organization chart.

3. Click the File menu, and then click Exit And Return To [File Name] to return to your presentation.

4. Click Yes to update the presentation.

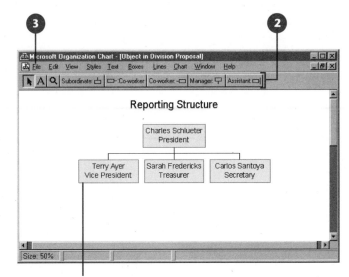

Each chart box represents one person or group in your company's structure. You can enter up to 4 lines of information.

SELECT AND DESELECT CHART BOXES	
Action	**Operation**
To select a single chart box	Select a chart box using the pointer
To select a set of chart boxes chart objects	Click the Edit menu, point to Select, and then click the set you want
To select one or more levels of chart boxes	Click the Edit menu, click Select Levels, enter the levels you want, and then click OK
To deselect a chart box	Click outside the chart box

7

TIP

Within a chart box, you can continue to press Enter to scroll through the lines and edit them, if necessary.

"How can I add a title to my organization chart?"

Enter Text into a Chart Box

1. If necessary, double-click a chart box in which you want to enter text.

2. Type a person's name, and then press Enter.

3. Type a person's title, and then press Enter.

4. Type up to two lines of comments. If you don't want to include comments, leave the comment line placeholders blank.

5. When you are finished, click outside the chart box.

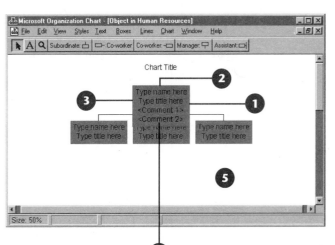

4. If you don't include comments, PowerPoint automatically removes the comment line placeholders from the chart box after you click outside it.

Add a Title

1. Highlight the sample title text "Chart Title" at the top of the organization chart.

2. Type a title you want for your org chart.

3. When you are finished, click outside the title area.

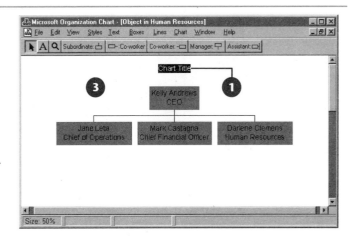

Structuring an Organization Chart

Chart boxes exist in relation to each other. For example, if you want to add a Subordinate chart box, you must select the chart box to which it will be attached. The buttons on the toolbar show the relationship between the different chart boxes you can add. When you add a Subordinate, it is automatically placed below the selected chart box. You can, however, display the chart box levels in a different structure, and you can customize the organization chart's appearance using the formatting options.

Add a Chart Box

1 Click the chart box button on the Organizational Chart toolbar you want to add, such as Subordinate or Co-Worker.

2 Click the chart box in the chart to which you want to attach the new chart box.

3 Enter the information in the box you just added.

4 Click outside the box.

Clicking the Subordinate button allows you to add a box below an existing box.

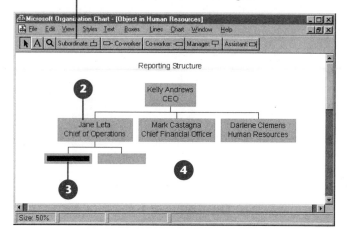

Change the Structure Style

1 Select the chart box or chart boxes whose style you want to change.

2 Click the Styles menu.

3 Click the button that provides the structure you want to use.

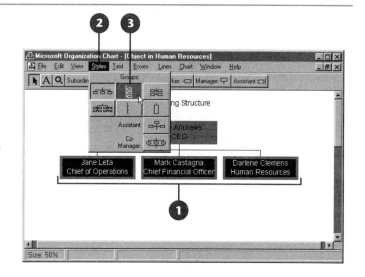

Rearrange a Chart Box

1. Make sure the chart box you want to move is deselected.

2. Drag the chart box over an existing chart box. The pointer changes to a four-headed arrow.

3. Continue to drag the chart box in the direction you want, and notice that the pointer changes to:

   ◆ A left arrow when you drag over the left side of a box

   ◆ A right arrow appears when you drag over the right side of a box

   ◆ A double-headed arrow and a small chart box appears when you drag over the bottom of a box

4. Release the mouse button when the chart box is in the correct position.

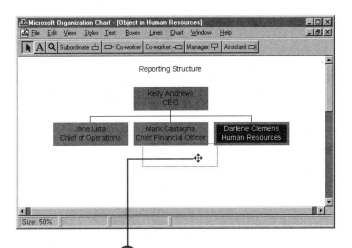

2 This pointer appears when you move the chart box below the highlighted chart box.

Formatting an Organization Chart

You can format the text and appearance of an organization chart with the same tools you use for other PowrePoint objects. You can modify text, colors, and lines.

Format Options

◆ Use the Text menu to format the text in a chart box by choosing a new font and font size, color, and alignment.

◆ Use the Boxes menu to change the color, shadow effect, border style, border color, and border line style of a selected chart box.

◆ Use the Lines menu to format the lines that connect the chart boxes, including their thickness, style, and color.

◆ Use the Chart menu to change the background of the entire chart.

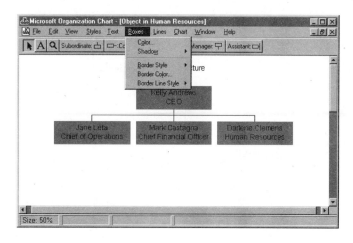

Format an Organization Chart

1. Click the Edit menu, point to Select, and then click the chart object or objects you want to format.

2. Click the format menu you want to use: Text, Boxes, Lines, or Chart.

3. Click the option you want to format.

4. Make the formatting changes.

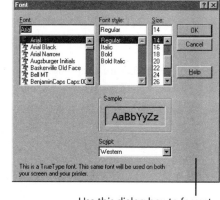

Use this dialog box to format an org chart's text.

8

Inserting Charts with Microsoft Graph

IN THIS SECTION

Inserting a Graph Chart

Opening an Existing Chart

Entering Graph Data

Selecting Graph Data

Importing Data

Editing Graph Data

Moving Graph Data

Hiding and Unhiding Graph Data

Formatting Graph Data

Selecting a Chart Type

Formatting Chart Objects

Choosing Advanced Features

Even if you don't have separate graphing software, you can include a graph in a PowerPoint presentation using a utility that comes with all the Office 97 programs: *Microsoft Graph*. With Graph, you can insert the data that make up the graph, and then generate the graph automatically.

Microsoft Graph Features

Microsoft Graph is a surprizingly versatile accessory. With it, you can enter new data or import or paste existing data from almost any source. Graph offers a variety of spreadsheet tools that make it easy to move, format, and manipulate the data that forms the basis of your chart.

You can also apply a variety of looks to your chart using pre-set chart types or by creating your own. Finally, Graph offers advanced graphing techniques that help your chart provide statistical information to your audience.

Inserting a Graph Chart

You can create a chart from scratch using the graph program that comes with the Office 97 suite, *Microsoft Graph*. Graph uses two views to display the information that makes up a graph: the *datasheet*, a spreadsheet-like grid of rows and columns that contains your data, and the *chart*, the graphical representation of the data.

A datasheet contains cells to hold your data. A *cell* is the intersection of a row and column. A group of data values from a row or column of data makes up a *data series*. Each data series has a unique color or pattern on the chart.

SEE ALSO

See "Selecting a Chart Type" on page 158 for information on selecting a different chart type.

Create a Graph Chart

1 Start Microsoft Graph in one of the following ways:

◆ To create a graph on an existing slide, display the slide on which you want the graph to appear, and then click the Insert Chart button on the Standard toolbar.

◆ To create a graph on a new slide, click the Insert New Slide button on the Standard toolbar, click the Chart AutoLayout, click OK, and then double-click the chart placeholder to add the chart and datasheet.

2 Replace the sample data in the datasheet with your own data.

3 Edit and format the data in the datasheet as appropriate.

4 Click the Close button on the datasheet to close it and view the chart.

5 If necessary, change the chart type, and format the chart.

6 Click outside the chart to exit Microsoft Graph.

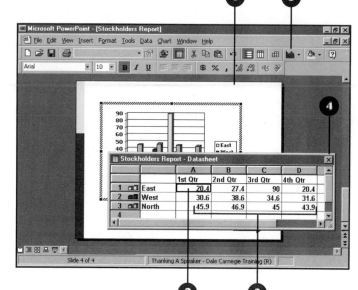

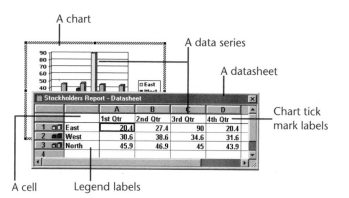

A chart

A data series

A datasheet

Chart tick mark labels

A cell

Legend labels

Opening an Existing Chart

Like any inserted object, you can open an existing chart in PowerPoint by double-clicking it. You can close the datasheet to view the chart.

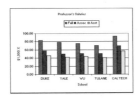

SEE ALSO

See "Selecting a Chart Type" on page 158 for information on selecting a different chart type, and see "Formatting Chart Objects" on page 160 for information on formatting a chart.

Open and View a Chart in Microsoft Graph

1 In PowerPoint, display the slide that contains the chart you want to open.

2 Double-click the chart to start Microsoft Graph. The Graph toolbars and menus appear.

3 Click the View Datasheet button on the Standard toolbar.

A chart consists of the following elements:

◆ Data markers: A graphical representation of a data point in a single cell in the datasheet. Typical data markers include bars, dots, or slices. Related data markers constitute a data series.

◆ Legend: A pattern or color that identifies each data series.

◆ x-axis: A reference line for the horizontal data values.

◆ y-axis: A reference line for the vertical data values.

◆ Tick marks: Marks that identify data increments.

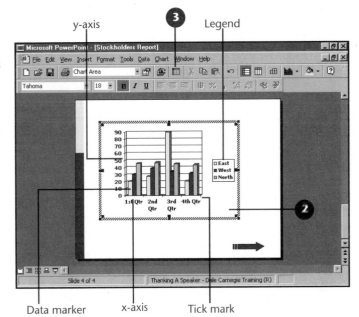

Entering Graph Data

You enter graph data in the datasheet either by typing it or by inserting it from a different source. The datasheet is designed to make data entry easy, but if your data resides elsewhere, it's better not to retype it—you might make mistakes, and you would have to update your data twice. When the data that form the bases of your graph are located elsewhere, it's usually best to link your data to the graph object.

If you type data into a cell already containing data, your entry replaces the cell contents. The cell you click is called the *active cell;* it has a thick border.

SEE ALSO

See "Inserting a Graph Chart" on page 146 for information on viewing a graph.

Enter Data in the Datasheet

1. In Microsoft Graph, click the View Datasheet button on the Standard toolbar.

2. Delete the sample data by clicking the upper-left heading button to select all the cells, and then pressing Delete.

3. Click a cell to make it active.

4. Type the data you want entered in the cell.

5. Press Enter to move the insertion point down one row to the next cell, or press Tab to move the insertion point right to the next cell.

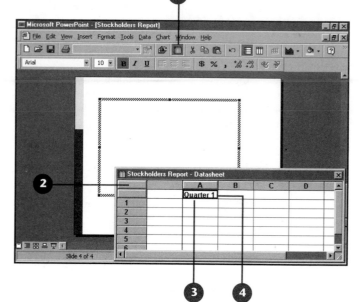

Selecting Graph Data

The extent to which you'll need to work with the datasheet depends on whether your data require editing. To edit data, you select it first in the datasheet. If you click a cell to select it, anything you type will replace the contents of the cell. If you double-click the cell, however, anything you type will be inserted at the location of the cursor.

Select Data in the Datasheet

◆ To select a cell, click it.

◆ To select an entire row or column, click the row heading or column heading.

◆ To select a range of cells, drag the pointer over the cells you want to select, or click the upper left cell of the range, press Shift, and then click the lower right cell. When you select a range of cells, the active cell has a thick border, and all other selected cells are highlighted in black.

Click here to select the entire datasheet

A column heading

		Year	A Month	B Dow Jones	C	D
1		1981	Jan	947.27		
2		1981	Feb	974.58		
3		1981	Mar	1003.87		
4		1981	Apr	997.75		
5		1981	May	991.75		
6		1981	Jun	976.88		

Stockholders Report - Datasheet

A row heading

A range of cells

Importing Data

Microsoft Graph makes it easy to insert data from other sources. You have control over how much of the data in a file you want to insert and, in the case of an imported text file, you can indicate how Graph should arrange your data once it is imported.

TIP

How much data can a datasheet accept? *Microsoft Graph can accept 4000 rows and 4000 columns of data and can display up to 255 data series.*

Import Data into the Datasheet

1. Switch to the datasheet.

2. If you want the data to begin at a cell other than the upper-left cell, click the cell.

3. Click the Edit menu, and then click Import File.

4. Select the file that contains the data you want to import.

5. If you are importing a text file, follow the Text Import Wizard steps. If you are importing Excel worksheet data, select the sheet that contains the data you want to import in the Import Data Options dialog box. You can only select one sheet.

   ◆ To import all the worksheet data, click the Entire Sheet option button.

   ◆ To import only a range, click the Range option button, and type the range of data. For example, to import cells A1 though C10, type A1:C10 in the Range box.

   ◆ If you selected a cell in step 2, clear the Overwrite Existing Cells check box.

6. Click OK.

This dialog box helps you import text files.

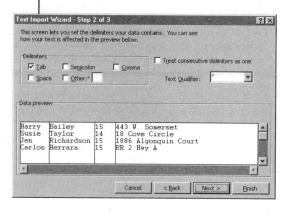

This dialog box helps you import spreadsheet data.

Paste Data into the Datasheet

1 Open the file that contains the data you want to paste in the source program.

2 Select the data you want to paste.

3 Click the Edit menu, and then click Copy.

4 Switch to PowerPoint, display the slide that contains the Microsoft Graph object, and then double-click the graph object.

5 If necessary, switch to the datasheet and, if necessary, clear its contents.

6 Paste the data into the datasheet using one of the following methods:

◆ To paste the data without linking it, click the Edit menu, and then click Paste.

◆ To link the data, click the Edit menu, click Paste Special, click the Paste Link option button, and then click OK.

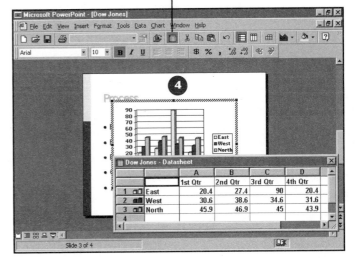

Formatting Graph Data

You also might need to reformat the datasheet itself—its size and how it displays the data—to make it easier to read. For example, you can format numbers in currency, accounting, percentage, and scientific formats, to name just a few.

"I want to format my numbers with percentages."

Change the Datasheet Font

1. In the datasheet, right-click any cell, and then click Font.

2. Make any changes to the font settings.

3. Click OK. Changes you make to the font affect all the data in the datasheet.

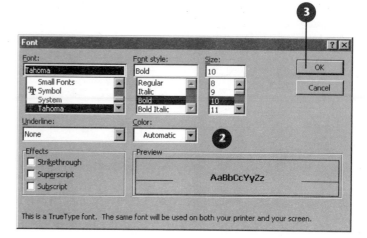

Format Datasheet Numbers

1. Select the data you want to format.

2. Right-click the selected data, and then click Number.

3. Click the style you want to apply.

4. Select the options you want to enable.

5. Click OK.

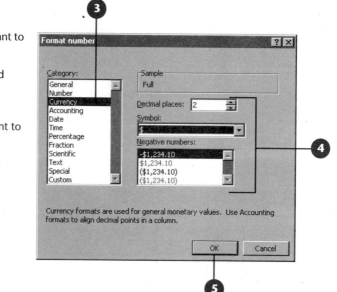

Change the Width of a Column

- ◆ To increase or decrease the width of a column, position the pointer on the vertical line to the right of the column heading, and then click and drag the pointer until the column is the correct width.

- ◆ To automatically adjust a datasheet column to display the widest data entry, position the pointer on the line to the right of the column heading, and then double-click to adjust the column width.

"How can I adjust the width of a column?"

Double-click here to resize column to its widest entry.

Drag to resize a column.

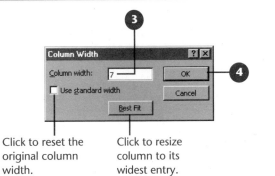

Enter a Precise Column Width

1 Click a cell in the column you want to format.

2 Click the Format menu, and then click Column Width.

3 Enter a new column width.

4 Click OK.

Click to reset the original column width.

Click to resize column to its widest entry.

Editing Graph Data

Although most of the time you edit Microsoft Graph data in the datasheet, you can change it in the chart by dragging a data marker. This method is easy, but it's hard to be accurate, and only works for 2-D charts, 3-D charts. You can edit data one cell at a time, or you can manipulate blocks of adjacent data called *ranges*. If you are familiar with electronic spreadsheets, you will find Microsoft Graph uses many of the same data editing techniques.

Edit Cell Contents

1 Click the cell you want to edit.

◆ To replace the cell contents, type the new data into the cell. It replaces the previous entry.

◆ To edit the cell contents, double-click the selected cell where you want to edit.

◆ Press the Delete and Backspace keys to delete one character at a time, and then type in the new data.

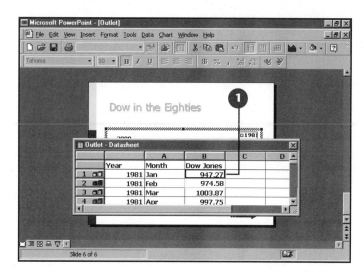

Edit Data by Dragging Data Markers

1 In the chart, click the data series that contains the data marker you want to change.

2 Click the data marker. When you select a data marker, a box appears that identifies the series and the value.

3 Drag the data marker for line or scatterplots, the top center selection handle for bar or column charts, and the largest selection handle on the edge of a pie chart.

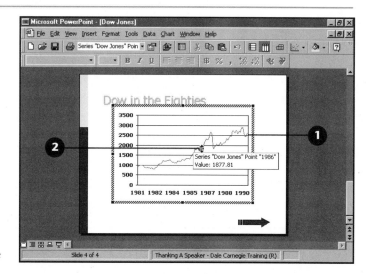

TIP

How does Graph create a legend? *Microsoft Graph has derived the legend and data labels from the first row and column in the datasheet, so if you type new ones in, the datasheet values are no longer used.*

TIP

Use Chart Options to display a table with a chart. *To show a table of the data with the chart, click the Chart menu, click Chart Options, click the Data Table tab, and then click the Show Data Table check box.*

Insert Cells

1 Click where you want to insert cells.

◆ To insert a column, click the column heading to the right of where you want the new column.

◆ To insert a row, click the row heading below where you want the new row.

◆ To insert a single cell, click an adjacent cell.

2 Click the Insert menu, and then click Cells.

3 Select how you want to insert the cells.

4 Click OK.

Delete Data from a Datasheet or a Graph

◆ Select the cell or range that contains the data you want to delete, and then press Delete.

◆ Click the data series in the graph, and then press Delete.

Select an entire row by clicking its row heading

Moving Graph Data

You can move data using the Cut, Copy, and Paste buttons on the Standard toolbar. If you try to move the data over existing data, the new data replaces the older data. Unlike Microsoft Excel, you can't drag data to move it in Microsoft Graph.

Move Data in the Datasheet

1. Select the cell or range that contains the data you want to move.

2. Click the Cut button on the Standard toolbar. You could also click Copy if you wanted to copy the data instead of cut it.

3. Click the first cell where you want to paste the data. Make sure there are enough adjacent cells to the right to accommodate the pasted data.

4. Click the Paste button on the Standard toolbar.

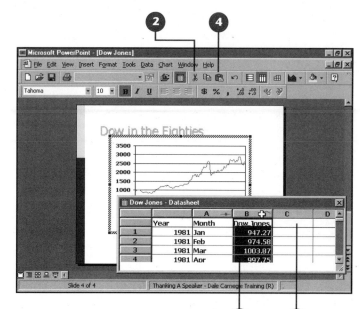

Hiding and Unhiding Graph Data

Sometimes you might want your chart to display only certain portions of the data in a datasheet. You can hide data so that it doesn't appear in the chart. This is not the same thing as deleting data, because you can always unhide the data if you want to redisplay it.

TIP

Click the By Column button on the Standard toolbar to represent the data series with columns. Click the By Row button on the Standard toolbar to represent the data series with rows.

Hide and Unhide Data

◆ In the datasheet, double-click the column or row heading for the column or row you want to hide. The data is grayed out and will not appear in the graph (the data is not deleted from the datasheet).

◆ To redisplay hidden data, double-click the column or row heading again.

Column heading

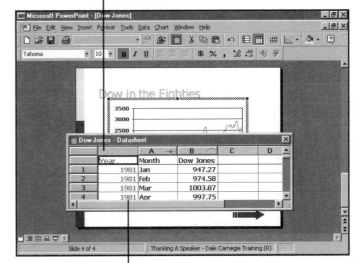

Gray data is hidden

Selecting a Chart Type

Your chart is what your audience will see, so make sure to take advantage of PowerPoint's chart formatting options. You start by choosing the chart type you want. There are 18 chart types, available in 2-D and 3-D formats, and for each chart type you can choose from a variety of formats. If you want to format your chart beyond the provided formats, you can customize any chart object to your own specifications and can then save those settings so that you can apply that chart formatting to any chart you create.

Select a Chart Type

1 In Graph, close the datasheet to view the chart, If necessary.

2 Click the Chart Type drop-down arrow on the Standard toolbar.

3 Click the button corresponding to the chart type you want.

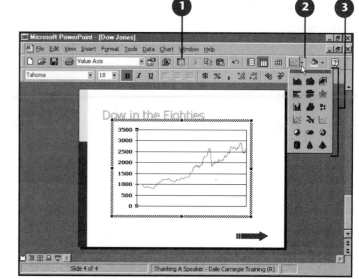

Apply a Standard Chart Type

1 Click the Chart menu, and then click Chart Type.

2 Click the Standard Types tab.

3 Click the chart type you want.

4 Click the chart sub-type you want. *Sub-types* are variations on the chart type.

5 Click OK.

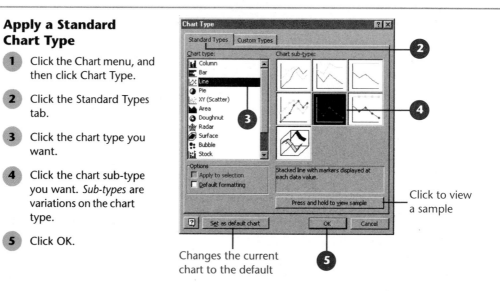

Click to view a sample

Changes the current chart to the default

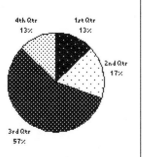

Apply a Custom Chart Type

1 Click the Chart menu, and then click Chart Type.

2 Click the Custom Types tab.

3 Click the Built-in option button.

4 Click the chart type you want.

5 Click OK.

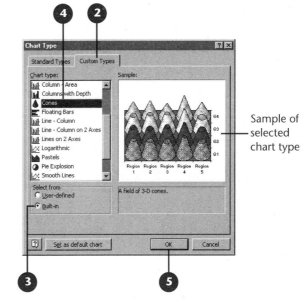

Sample of selected chart type

"I put a lot of work into creating this chart—how can I save the formatting to apply to other charts?"

Create a Custom Chart Type

1 Click the Chart menu, and then click Chart Type.

2 Click the Custom Types tab.

3 Click the User-defined option button.

4 Click Add.

5 Type a name and description for the chart.

6 Click OK twice.

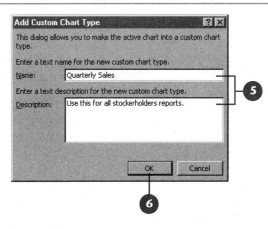

Formatting Chart Objects

Chart objects are the individual elements that make up a chart, such as an axis, the legend, or a data series. The *plot area* is the bordered area where the data are plotted. The *chart area* is the area between the plot area and the Microsoft Graph object selection box. As with any Microsoft utility, Graph treats all these elements as objects, which you can format and modify.

TIP

Use the mouse pointer to select a chart. *You can simply click a chart object to select it, but this can by tricky if you aren't using a zoomed view because the chart objects are often quite small.*

TIP

Use the Selected command on the Format menu to format an object you selected. *For an axis, for example, the command is Selected Axis.*

Select a Chart Object

1 Click the Chart Objects drop-down arrow on the Standard toolbar.

2 Click the chart object you want to select.

When a chart object is selected, selection handles appear.

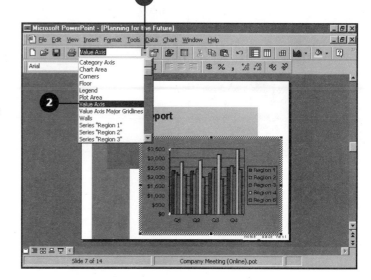

Format a Chart Object

1 Right-click the chart object you want to format, such as an axis or legend or data series.

2 Click the Format command that appears. For an axis, for example, the command is Format Axis.

3 Click the appropriate tab(s), and select the options you want to apply.

4 Click OK.

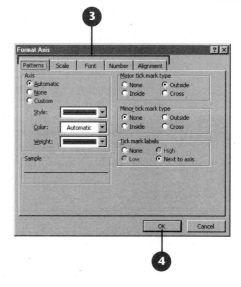

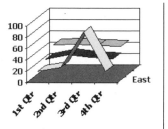

TIP

Use the Format Axis command to rotate the chart axis. *To change the angle of an axis, right-click the axis, click Format Axis, click the Alignment tab, then select a rotation.*

SEE ALSO

See "Selecting a Chart Type" on page 158 for information on applying a cutom chart.

Customize a Chart

1 Click the Chart menu, and then click Chart Options.

2 Click the tab corresponding to the chart object you want to customize.

3 Make the necessary changes.

4 Click OK.

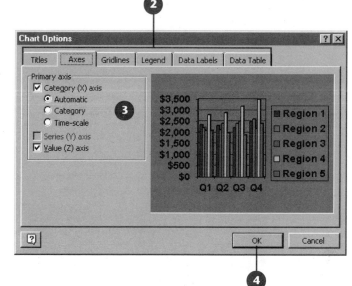

Choosing Advanced Features

Microsoft Graph offers a number of advanced graphing techniques that you can explore using the abundant information in online Microsoft Graph Help. You can:

- ◆ Add *trendlines* derived from regression analysis to show a trend in existing data and make predictions

- ◆ Create a *moving average*, a sequence of averages from grouped data points, that smoothes the fluctuations in data so you can more easily identify trends

- ◆ Add *error bars* that express the degree of uncertainty attached to a given data series

- ◆ Add drawing objects, including arrows, text boxes, and pictures to your charts

- ◆ Change chart object colors, fills, and patterns

- ◆ And much more!

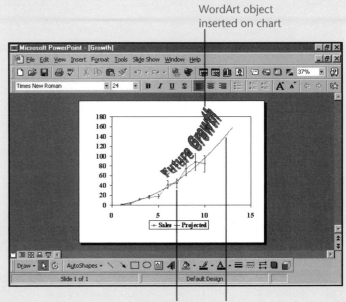

WordArt object inserted on chart

Error bar   Trendline

Finalizing a Presentation and Its Supplements

IN THIS SECTION

Finalizing a Presentation in Slide Sorter View

Inserting Slides from Other Presentations

Inserting Comments

Fine-Tuning Text and its Appearance

Setting Page Setup Options

Printing a Presentation

Preparing Handouts

Preparing Speaker Notes

Customizing Notes Pages

Documenting and E-Mailing a Presentation

Exporting Notes and Slides to Word

Creating 35-mm Slides

Saving Slides in Different Formats

As you wrap up the development of your presentation, you can use Microsoft PowerPoint 97 to add some last-minute enhancements such as creating a summary slide or presentation supplements, including speaker notes and handouts. You can send your presentation to others in your company, and when the slides are finished, you can convert them to 35-mm slides or save them in different formats.

Creating Supplements

Handouts are printed materials that you supply to your audience. Typically handouts include an outline for the audience to follow along as you speak, a copy of the slides in your presentation, printed one or more slides to a page, or a set of pages with blank lines next to reduced images of the slides for note-taking. PowerPoint gives you many options for printing handouts, including editing and formatting them in Microsoft Word.

Most speakers feel more comfortable giving a presentation with a "script" in front of them, and you can easily create one in Notes Page view. You can also work with your notes in Word.

Finalizing a Presentation in Slide Sorter View

Slide Sorter view helps you assess the final order of your slides because you can see them all at once. Slide Sorter view allows you to display the slides with or without color and formatting so that you can identify individual slides more easily. Slide Sorter view is also the easiest place to copy and paste slides between presentations. To finalize the presentation, you can create a summary slide. A *summary slide* compiles the titles of selected slides into one slide. It is an easy way to create a presentation agenda.

> **TIP**
>
> **Switch to Slide view quickly from Slide Sorter view.** *If you are in Slide Sorter view and you want to open a slide in Slide view, double-click the slide you want to open.*

View Slides in Slide Sorter View

◆ To view only a slide's title in Slide Sorter view, press Alt and click a slide.

◆ To view slides in black and white, click the View menu, and then click Black And White.

The selected slide appears with a black border

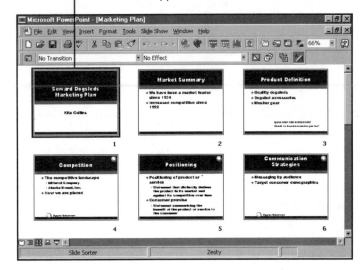

Create a Summary Slide

1. In Slide Sorter or Outline view, select the slides you want to include on your summary slide.

2. Click the Summary Slide button on the Slide Sorter or Outlining toolbar.

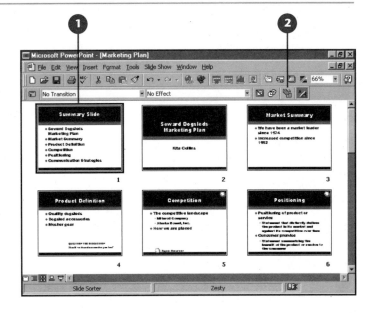

"How can I insert slides from a different presentation?"

Copy Slides from Other Presentations

1 Open the presentation that contains the slides you want to use.

2 In Slide Sorter view, select the slide or slides you want to copy. To select multiple slides, press and hold Shift, and then click each slide you want to include.

3 Click the Copy button on the Standard toolbar.

4 Switch to the presentation you are working on.

5 In Slide Sorter view, click before or after the slide to place the insertion point.

6 Click the Paste button on the Standard toolbar.

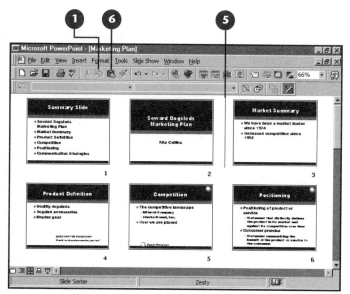

9

Inserting Slides from Other Presentations

To insert slides from other presentations in a slide show, you can open the presentation and copy and paste the slides you want, or you can use the *Slide Finder* feature. With Slide Finder, you don't have to open the presentation first; instead, you view "snapshots" of each slide in a presentation, and then insert only the ones you select. With Slide Finder, you can also create a list of favorite presentations that you often use as source material.

Insert Slides from Slide Finder

1 Click the Insert menu.

2 Click Slides From Files, and then click the Find Presentation tab, if necessary.

3 Click the Browse button, locate and select the file you want, and then click Open.

4 Click the Display button to display a miniature of each slide.

5 Select the slides you want to insert.

◆ To insert just one slide, click the slide and then click Insert.

◆ To insert multiple slides, click each slide, you want to insert, and then click Insert.

◆ To insert all the slides in the presentation, click Insert All.

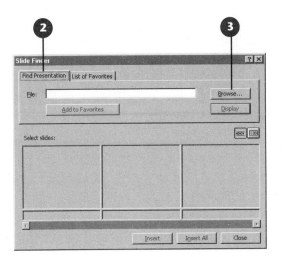

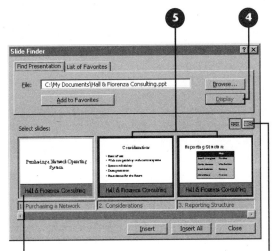

When you display miniatures, you see a miniature of each slide with its title underneath.

Click to display only the slide titles.

Display Slide Titles in Slide Finder

1 In Slide Finder, click the Titles button.

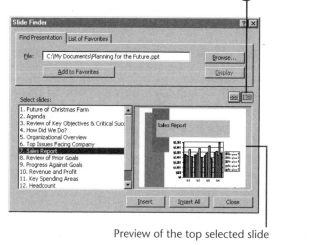

Preview of the top selected slide

Add a Presentation to List of Favorites

1 In Slide Finder, locate the file you want to add to the list of favorites.

2 Click Add To Favorites.

3 Click the List Of Favorites tab.

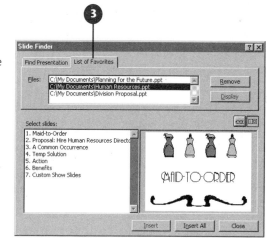

Inserting Comments

If you have been asked to review a presentation for a colleague, you can enter your comments right into the presentation file. When you return the presentation to your colleague, he or she can view the comments to process your feedback, deleting them as they are processed.

TIP

Use the Reviewing toolbar for easy access to commenting commands. *Reviewers might find it handy to display the Reviewing toolbar, which provides buttons for adding and viewing comments.*

Insert Comments

1 Click the Insert menu.

2 Click Comments.

3 Type your comment.

PowerPoint automatically inserts the name of the evaluator so the presentation developer knows who inserted the comment.

4 Click outside the comment selection box when you are finished.

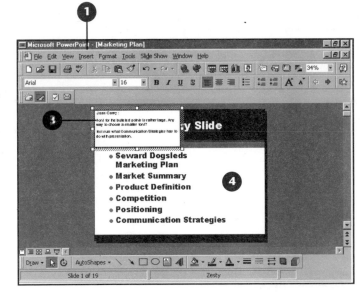

View or Hide Comments

1 Click the Show/Hide Comments button on the Reviewing toolbar.

Reviewing toolbar

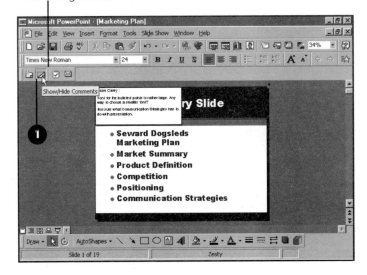

Delete Comments

1. Make sure comments are viewed.

2. Click the comment you want to delete, and then press Delete.

"I've read a comment and now I want to delete it."

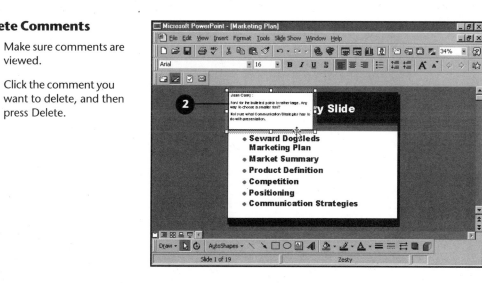

SEE ALSO

See "Creating Shadows" on page 86 or see "Creating a 3-D Object" on page 88 for information on formatting objects.

Format a Comment

1. Right-click the comment you want to format.

2. Click Format Comment.

3. Make the formatting changes you want.

4. Click OK.

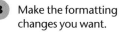

Click to make your new settings the default for all comment boxes.

Fine-Tuning Text and Its Appearance

PowerPoint offers an assortment of textual tools. When you are working with your text's fonts, you might want to embed the fonts you use so they "travel" with your presentation. If you decide you want to replace one font with another, you can easily do so with a single command. If your text is in more than one language, you can designate the language of selected text so the spelling checker uses the right dictionary. Finally, if you are searching for just the right word or for background information on a word or a concept, you can look it up right from PowerPoint using Microsoft Bookshelf, available on your Office 97 CD.

Embed TrueType Fonts in a Presentation

1. Click the File menu, and then click Save As.

2. Click the Embed TrueType Fonts check box.

3. If necessary, enter a file name and select a location for your presentation.

4. Click the Save button.

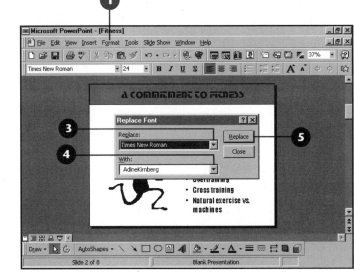

Replace Fonts

1. Click the Format menu.

2. Click Replace Fonts.

3. Click the Replace drop-down arrow, and then click the font you want.

4. Click the With drop-down arrow, and then click the font you want to subsitute.

5. Click the Replace button.

Mark Text as a Language

1. Select the text you want to mark.

2. Click the Tools menu and then click Language.

3. Click the language you want to assign to the selected text.

4. Click OK.

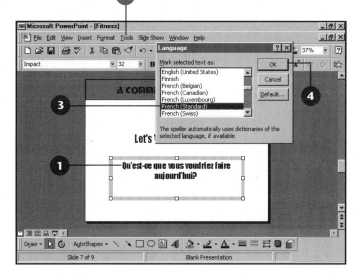

Look Up a Reference

1. Select the word or phrase you want to look up.

2. Click the Tools menu, and then click Look Up Reference.

3. Click Microsoft Bookshelf Basics (on the Office 97 CD-ROM) to use the reference tools.

4. View the information that appears.

5. Click a topic to explore further.

6. Click the Close button when you are finished.

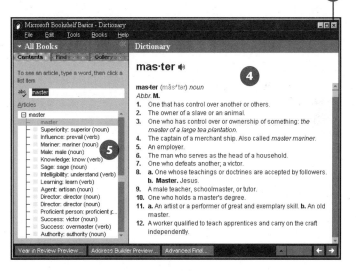

Setting Page Setup Options

Before you print a presentation you might want to work with the Page Setup dialog box to set the proportions of your presentation slides and their orientation on the printer. You can also control slide numbering from the Page Setup dialog box.

SEE ALSO

See "Creating a Web Page" on page 229 for information on creating Web pages with PowerPoint.

Control Slide Size

1 Click the File menu.

2 Click Page Setup.

3 Click the Slides Sized For drop-down arrow.

4 Click the size you want.

♦ Click On-Screen Show for 10-x-7 1/2" slides that fit a computer monitor.

♦ Click Letter Paper for slides that will fit on an 8 1/2-x-11" sheet of paper.

♦ Click A4 Paper for slides that will fit on a 210 mm x 297 mm sheet of paper.

♦ Click 35mm Slides for 11 1/4-x-7 1/2" slides that will fit the proportions of 35-mm slide cases.

♦ Click Overhead for 10-x 7 1/2" slides that will fit transparencies.

♦ Click Banner for 8-x 1" slides that are typically used as advertisements on a Web page.

♦ Click Custom to have PowerPoint set the width and height to fill the printing area for the active printer.

5 Click OK.

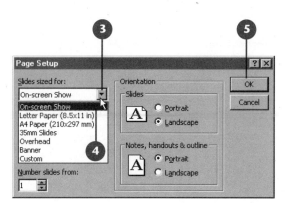

Scale Your Slides for Printing. *Although changing the page setup allows you to scale your slides, you can have PowerPoint scale your slides automatically to fit your printer's paper without changing the proportions of your slides. Click the File menu, click Print, and then click the Scale To Fit Paper check box.*

Customize Slide Proportions

1 Click the File menu.

2 Click Page Setup.

3 Enter a specific width in inches in the Width box.

4 Enter a specific height in inches in the Height box.

5 Click OK.

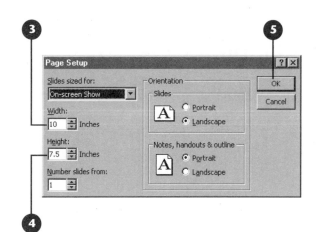

Change slide orientation. *All slides in a presentation use the orientation you select, but you can print your notes, handouts, and outlines in portrait orientation even if your slides are in landscape orientation. If you change orientation, check the masters to ensure that object placement is okay for the orientation you selected.*

Change Slide Orientation

1 Click the File menu, and then click Page Setup.

2 To orient your slides, click the Portrait or Landscape option buttons.

3 To orient your notes, handouts, and outline, click Portrait or Landscape under Notes, Handouts & Outline.

4 Click OK.

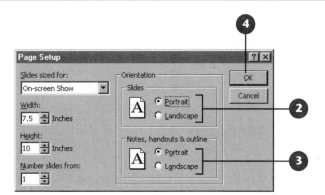

9

Printing a Presentation

You can print all elements of your presentation—the slides, an outline, the notes, and handouts—in either color or black and white. The Print dialog box offers standard Windows features, giving you the option to print multiple copies, to specify ranges, to access printer properties, and to print to a file.

When you print an outline, PowerPoint print the presentation outline as it is shown in Outline view. What you see is what you get.

SEE ALSO

See "Creating a Custom Slide Show" on page 210 for information on creating a custom slide show.

Print a Presentation

1. Click the File menu, and then click Print.

2. Click the Print What drop-down arrow.

3. Click what you want to print.

4. Change settings in the Print dialog box as necessary.

5. Click OK.

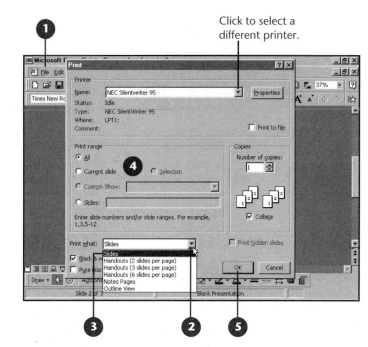

Click to select a different printer.

Print a Custom Show

1. Click the File menu, and then click Print.

2. Click the Custom Show drop-down arrow.

3. Click the custom show you want to print.

4. If applicable, set other print settings.

5. Click OK.

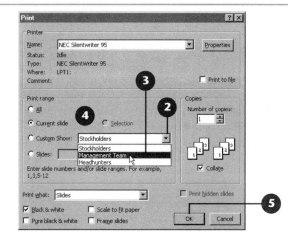

Print a Single Slide or a Range of Slides

1 Click the File menu, and then click Print.

2 If necessary, click the Print What drop-down arrow, and then click Slides.

3 In the Print Range area, select the slides you want to print.

4 Click OK.

"I'd like to print out my custom slide show."

Print an Outline

1 In Outline view, prepare your slide show for printing.

◆ To print only slide titles, click the Collapse All button on the Outlining toolbar.

◆ To print all text levels, click the Expand All button on the Outlining toolbar.

◆ To print with or without formatting, click the Show Formatting button on the Outlining toolbar.

2 Click the Print button on the Standard toolbar.

"How can I print out an outline of my presentation?"

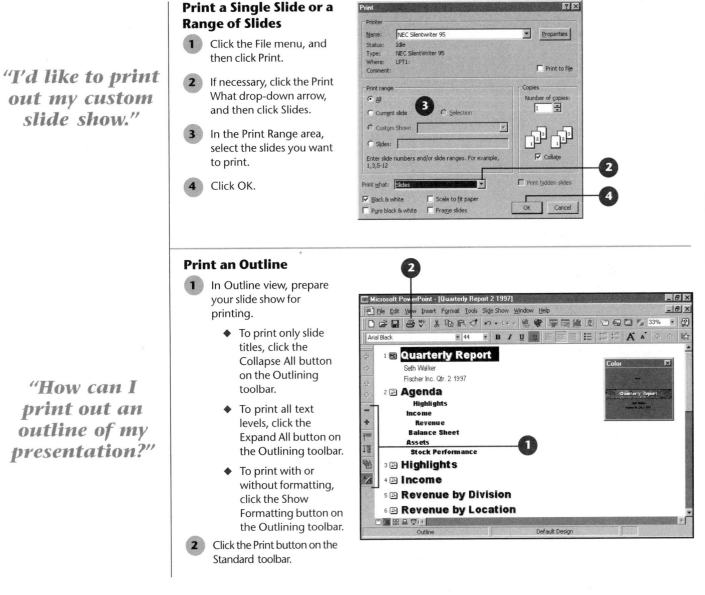

9

Preparing Handouts

Handouts are primarily created in the Print dialog box, where you specify what to print. You can, however, customize your handouts by formatting them in the Handout master first. You can also add a header and footer to your handouts.

TIP

Use Page Setup to change slide numbering. *To start numbering at a number other than one, click the File menu, click Page Setup, and enter the number you want to start with in the Number Slides From box.*

TIP

Add headers and footer to create consistent handouts. *Headers and footers you add to the Handout master are also added to notes pages and the printed outline.*

Format the Handout Master

1. Click the View menu, point to Master, and then click Handout Master.

2. Click one of the buttons on the Handout Master toolbar to specify how many slides you want per page.

3. If desired, add a header, footer, the date, and page numbering using the Header and Footer dialog box.

4. Click the Close button on the Master toolbar.

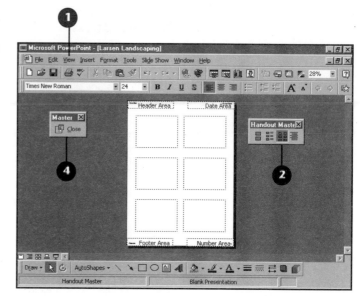

Add Headers and Footers to Handouts

1. Click the View menu.

2. Click Header and Footer.

3. If necessary, click the Notes And Handouts tab.

4. Enter the information you want to appear on your handouts.

5. Click Apply To All.

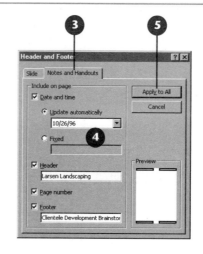

"I want to print my slides for my audience—2 slides per page."

Print Handouts

1 Click the File menu, and then click Print.

2 Click the Print What drop-down arrow.

3 Click Slides to print one slide per page or one of the three Handouts options.

4 Click OK.

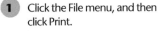

9

Preparing Speaker Notes

Every slide has a corresponding *notes page* that displays a reduced image of the slide and a text placeholder into which you can enter speaker's notes. You can also open up a Speaker Notes dialog box for each slide that shows the notes for just that slide. Once you have created speaker's notes, you can reference the notes pages as you give your presentation, either from a printed copy or from your computer. You can enhance your notes pages by including objects on the Notes master.

Enter Notes in Notes Page view

1. Switch to the slide for which you want to enter notes.

2. Click the Notes Page View button.

3. If necessary, click the Zoom drop-down arrow and increase the zoom percentage to more easily see the text you will type.

4. Click the text placeholder.

5. Type your notes.

Reduced image of a slide

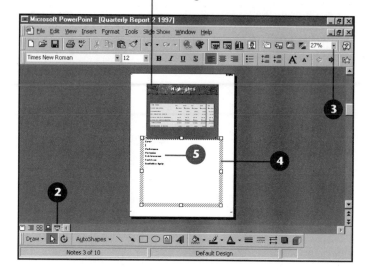

Enter Notes in Slide View

1. In Slide View, display the slide whose notes you want to work with.

2. Click the View menu.

3. Click Speaker Notes.

4. Type, edit, or view notes for the slide in the Speaker Notes dialog box.

5. Click Close.

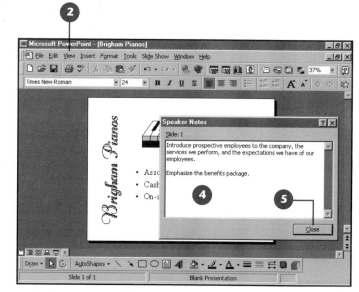

Different ways to edit notes. *You can edit notes in either Notes Page view or in the Speaker Notes dialog box using PowerPoint's text editing tools.*

"I want my notes pages to include the time and date."

Format the Notes Master

1 Click the View menu, point to Master, and then click Notes Master.

2 Make the format changes you want.

◆ You can add objects to the Notes Master that you want to appear on every page, such as a picture or a text object.

◆ You can add a header and footer by clicking the View menu, and then clicking Header And Footer.

◆ You can add the date, time, or page number to your notes pages.

3 Click the Close button on the Master toolbar.

Placeholder for slide miniature

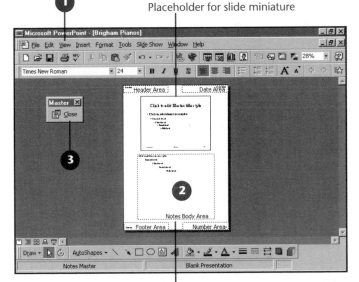

Placeholder for notes

Customizing Notes Pages

You can add dates, numbering, and header and footer text to your notes pages just as you do for your slides. If you have removed objects from the master and you decide you want to restore them, you can reapply any of the master placeholders (the slide image, the date, header, and so on) without affecting objects and text outside the placeholders. Moreover, if you have deleted, for example, the slide placeholder or text placeholder from a given notes page and you decide you want to reinsert it, you can do so.

SEE ALSO

See "Adding a Header and Footer" on page 58 for information on adding header and footer information to your presentation or see "Preparing Speaker Notes" on page 178 for information on viewing speaker notes on your computer as you give the presentation while your audience sees only the slides and not the notes.

Add a Header and Footer to Notes Pages

1. Click the View menu, and then click Header And Footer.

2. If necessary, click the Notes And Handouts tab.

3. Add the header and footer information you want.

4. Click Apply To All.

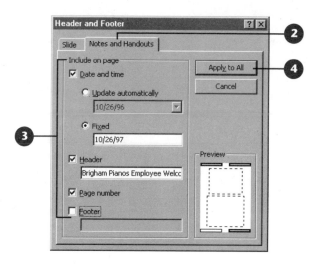

Reinsert Notes Placeholders to the Notes Master

1. Click the View menu, point to Master, and then click Notes Master.

2. Click the Format menu.

3. Click Notes Master Layout.

4. Click the check boxes corresponding to the placeholders you want to reinsert.

5. Click OK.

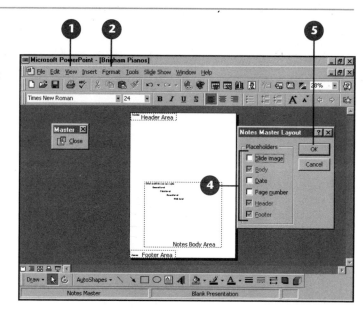

Reinsert Placeholders on an Individual Slide

1 In Notes Page view, switch to the slide whose placeholders you want to restore.

2 Click the Format menu.

3 Click Notes Layout.

4 Click the check boxes corresponding to the placeholders you want to reapply.

5 Click OK.

"I deleted a placeholder. How can I get it back?"

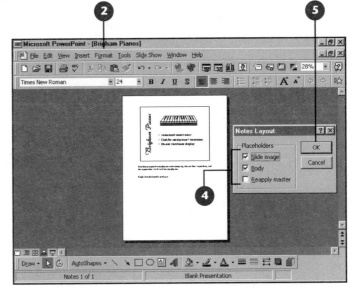

Customize Notes Pages

1 In Notes Page view, right-click a blank area of the notes area.

2 Click the item you want to format.

◆ Click Notes Color Scheme to open the Notes Color Scheme dialog box.

◆ Click Notes Background to open the Notes Background dialog box.

"How can I format my notes pages so they are more attractive?"

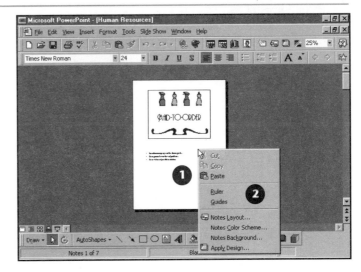

9

Documenting and E-Mailing a Presentation

When it's important to get feedback on your presentation before you present it, you can make use of PowerPoint's file properties to make the evaluation process as smooth as possible. PowerPoint allows you to document your presentation so your feedback team has all the information they need to evaluate it. You can send the presentation to your colleagues directly from PowerPoint if you have Microsoft Exchange installed.

Enter Information About a Presentation

1. Click the File menu, and then click Properties.

2. Click the Summary tab.

3. Enter information about the presentation that will help others identify it.

4. Click OK.

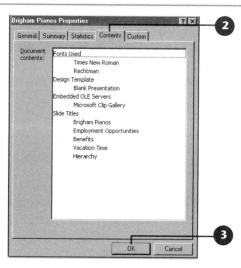

Check Presentation Contents

1. Click the File menu, and then click Properties.

2. Click the Contents tab to review the contents of the presentation.

3. Click OK.

Send a Presentation to a Colleague

1 Open the presentation you want to send.

2 Click the File menu, point to Send To, and then click the Send To option you want.

3 Fill in the dialog box that opens.

4 Click OK to send your file.

Outlook

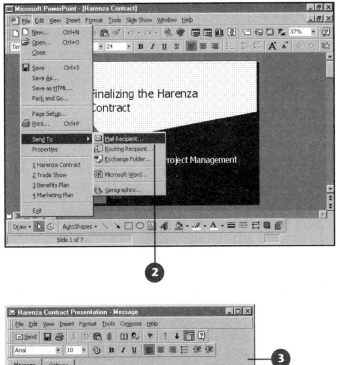

Exporting Notes and Slides to Word

You can send both your notes and slides to Word so that you can work with them with a full array of word processing tools. This is especially handy when you are developing more detailed materials, such as a training presentation and manual.

Winword

Create Handouts in Word

1. Click the File menu.

2. Point to Send To.

3. Click Microsoft Word.

4. Click the page layout option you want for handouts in the Write-Up dialog box.

5. Click OK. Word starts, creates a new document, and inserts your presentation with the layout you requested.

6. Print the document in Word, editing and saving it as necessary.

TIP

Settings to send notes to Word. *By default PowerPoint pastes your presentation into a Word document, so any changes you make to the presentation are not reflected in the Word document. If you click the Paste Link option button in the Write-Up dialog box, however, you create a link between the Word document and the presentation, and changes you make in one are reflected in the other.*

SEE ALSO

See "Sharing Information Among Document" on page 124 for information on linking documents.

Send Notes to Word

1. Click the File menu, point to Send To, and then click Microsoft Word.

2. Click the page layout option you want for notes pages.

3. Click OK. Word starts, creates a new document, and inserts your presentation with the layout you requested.

4. Print the document in Word, editing and saving it as necessary.

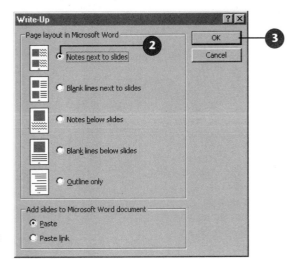

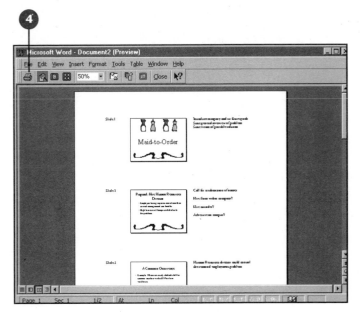

Creating 35-mm Slides

Although a PowerPoint presentation is most effective when it is shown electronically because you can make use of animations, transitions, and multimedia special effects, there are times when you need to convert an electronic presentation to physical 35-mm slides—perhaps your auditorium doesn't have the hardware necessary to display a computer presentation. PowerPoint offers an online service that downloads your presentation and prepares the physical medium you need, and ships it back to you in as little as a day.

Start the Genigraphics Wizard

1 Open the presentation you want to send.

2 Click the File menu, and then point to Send To.

3 Click Genigraphics.

4 Read the opening dialog box, and the click Next.

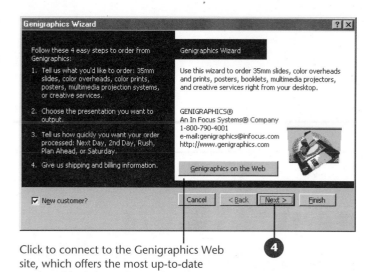

Click to connect to the Genigraphics Web site, which offers the most up-to-date genigraphics information and services.

Order Genigraphics Services

1 Click the services you want, from 35mm slides to prints or posters.

2 Click Next, and then follow the Wizard dialog box steps.

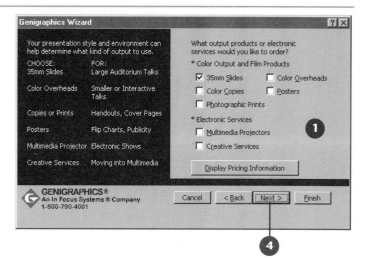

Saving Slides in Different Formats

You can save PowerPoint presentations in a number of different formats so that they can be accessed by many different programs. You can also save an individual slide as a graphic image that you can open in a graphics editor.

Save a Presentation in a Different File Type

1 Click the File menu.

2 Click Save As.

3 Click the Save As Type drop-down arrow.

4 Click the format you want, such as a previous version of PowerPoint or an RTF (Rich Text Format) outline, which allows your presentation to be read by many different software packages.

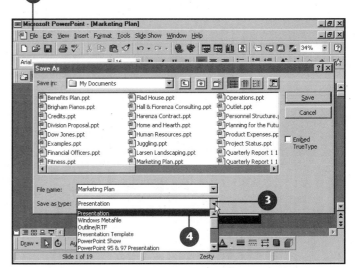

9

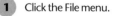

*"How can I
save a slide as
a graphic to my
hard drive?"*

Save a Slide as a Graphic Image

1 Click the File menu.

2 Click Save As.

3 Click the Save As Type drop-down arrow.

4 Click the graphics format you want to use, such as JPEG, or GIF.

5 Enter a filename.

6 Click OK.

7 When a message box opens asking if you want to export all slides in the presentation or just the current slide, click Yes to save all slides as separate graphic image files, or click No to save just the current slide as a graphic image file.

When you save a slide as a graphics file, you can work with it in a graphics editor.

IN THIS SECTION

Setting Up a Slide Show

Creating Slide Transitions

Adding Animation

Using Specialized Animations

Coordinating Multiple Animations

Adding Action Buttons

Adding Links to Objects

Creating Hyperlinks to External Objects

Timing a Presentation

Inserting a Presentation SoundTrack

Creating a Voice Narration

Creating a Custom Slide Show

10

Preparing a Slide Show

icrosoft PowerPoint 97 provides many tools to help you control how your slide show comes across to your audience.

A computer-generated slide show can feature special visual, sound, and animation effects. For example, you can program special *transitions* or actions between slides. You can also control how each element of the slide is introduced to the audience using *animations*. You can add *action buttons* to your presentation that the presenter can click to activate a hyperlink and jump instantly to another slide in the presentation.

PowerPoint also includes tools that you can use to time your presentation to make sure that it is neither too long nor too short. A PowerPoint presentation can really come alive with the proper use of narration and music. With PowerPoint, you can record a narration and insert it directly into your slide show. Some presentations include slides that are appropriate for one audience but not for another. PowerPoint lets you create custom slide shows that include only a selection of slides, in whatever order you want, intended for a given audience.

Setting Up a Slide Show

PowerPoint offers three different types of slide shows that accommodate a variety of presentation situations, from a traditional big-screen slide show to a show that runs automatically on a computer screen at a conference kiosk. In those situations when you don't want to show all of the slides in a PowerPoint presentation to a particular audience, you can specify only a range of slides to show, or you can hide individual slides.

SEE ALSO

See "Timing a Presentation" on page 206 for information on using rehearsed timings and "Adding Animation" on page 194 for information on adding animation to a slide.

Set Up a Show

1 Click the Slide Show menu.

2 Click Set Up Show.

3 Choose the show type you want:

◆ Click the Presented By A Speaker option button to run a traditional full screen slide show, where you can advance the slides manually or automatically.

◆ Click the Browsed By An Individual option button to run a slide show in a window and allow access to some PowerPoint commands.

◆ Click the Browsed At A Kiosk option button to create a self-running, unattended slide show for a booth or kiosk. The slides will advance automatically, or a user can advance the slides or activate hyperlinks.

4 Change additional show settings as appropriate.

5 Click OK.

Open a presentation in Slide Show view. *If you want a presentation file to open directly to a slide show rather than opening in a document window, click the File menu, click Save As, click the Save As Type drop-down arrow, and click PowerPoint Show.*

Show a Range of Slides

1 Click the Slide Show menu, and then click Set Up Show.

2 Click the From option button.

3 Enter the first and last slide numbers of the range you want to show in the From and To spin boxes.

4 Click OK.

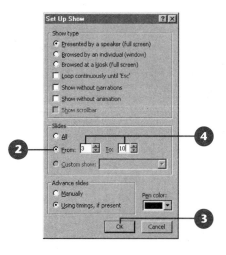

Hide slides in Slide view. *Display the slide you want to hide in Slide view, click the Slide Show menu, and then click Hide Slide. To unhide a slide, click it, and then click the Hide Slide option on the Slide Show menu again.*

Hide Slides

1 In Slide Sorter view, click the slide you want to hide.

2 Click the Hide Slide button on the Slide Sorter toolbar.

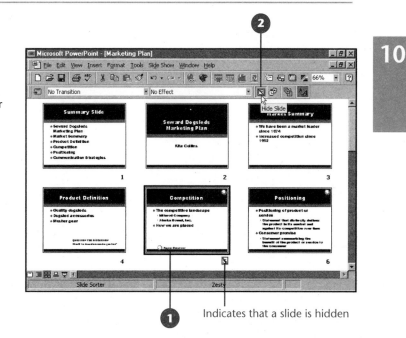

Indicates that a slide is hidden

Creating Slide Transitions

In order to give your presentation more visual interest, you can add transitions between slides. For example, you can create a "fading out" effect so that the old slide fades out and is replaced by the new slide, or you can have one slide appear to "push" another slide out of the way. You can also add sound effects to your transitions, though you need a sound card and speakers to play these sounds.

TIP

When you add a transition effect to a slide, the effect takes place between the previous slide and the selected slide.

Specify a Transition

1. Click the Slide Sorter View button.

2. Click the slide to which you want to add a transition effect.

3. Click the Slide Transition Effects drop-down arrow.

4. Click the transition effect you want.

Apply a Transition to All Slides in a Presentation

1. Click the Slide Show menu, and then click Slide Transition.

2. Click the Effect drop-down arrow.

3. Click the transition you want.

4. Click Apply To All.

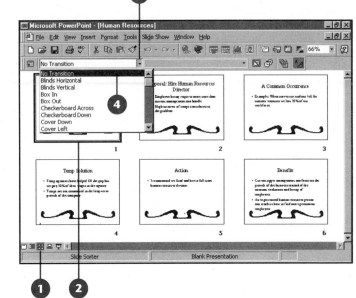

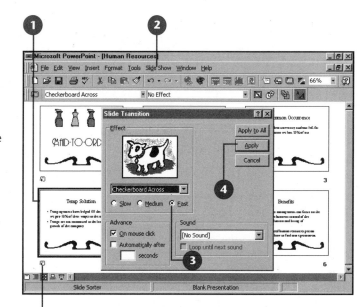

TIP

View a slide's transition quickly in Slide Sorter view. *In Slide Sorter view, click a slide's transition icon to view the transition's appearance.*

Set Transition Effect Speeds

1. In Slide or Slide Sorter view, click or display the slide whose transition effect you want to edit.

2. Click the Slide Show menu, and then click Slide Transition.

3. Click the Slow, Medium, or Fast option button in the Slide Transition dialog box.

4. Click Apply.

Icon indicates slide has a transition.

TRY THIS

Record your own sounds and use them as slide transitions. *If you have a microphone, use the Sound Recorder accessory that comes with Windows to record and save a sound. In the Slide Transition dialog box, click the Sound drop-down arrow, click Other Sound, locate and select the sound you created in the Add Sound dialog box, and then click OK.*

Add Sound to a Transition

1. In Slide or Slide Sorter view, click or display the slide for which you want to add a transition sound.

2. Click the Slide Show menu, and then click Slide Transition.

3. Click the Sound drop-down arrow, and then click the sound you want.

4. Click Apply.

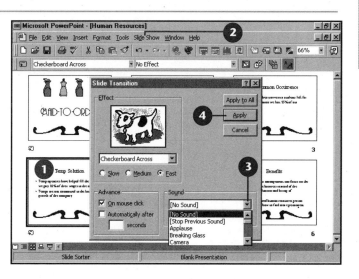

10

Adding Animation

You can use animation to introduce objects onto a slide one at a time or with special animation effects. For example, a bulleted list can appear one bulleted item at a time, or a picture or chart can fade gradually into the slide's foreground. PowerPoint supports many different kinds of animations. Some of these are called *preset animations* and are effects that PowerPoint has designed for you. Many of the preset animations contain sounds. You can also design your own *customized animations*, including your own special effects and sound elements.

Use Preset Animation

1 Select the slide or object you want to animate.

2 Click the Slide Show menu, and then point to Preset Animation.

3 Click the animation you want.

◆ Click the slide or object to see the animation.

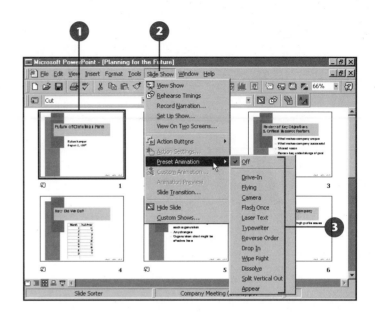

Preview an Animation

1 Click the Slide View button, and then display the slide containing the animation you want to preview.

2 Click the Slide Show menu, and then click Animation Preview.

Click the window to play the animation.

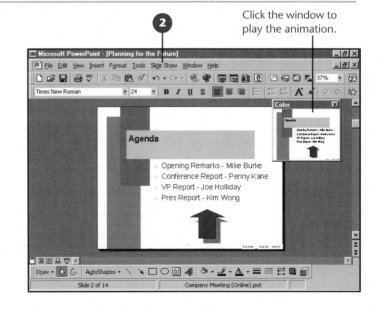

Apply a Customized Animation

1. In Slide view, right-click the object to which you want to apply a customized animation.

2. Click Custom Animation.

3. On the Effects tab, click the Entry Animation drop-down arrow.

4. Click the effect you want.

5. Click Preview.

6. Click OK.

List of custom animations

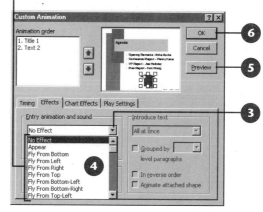

"How can I animate an object on my slide?"

Add Sound to an Animation

1. Right-click the object in Slide view, and then click Custom Animation.

2. Choose an effect from the list of animation effects.

3. Click the Sound drop-down arrow.

4. Click the sound effect you want.

5. Click Preview to preview the animation and sound effect.

6. Click OK.

10

TIP

PowerPoint sound effects.
You can insert one of PowerPoint's customized sound effects, or you can use one of your own sound files by clicking Other Sound at the bottom of the sound list and then selecting the sound you want.

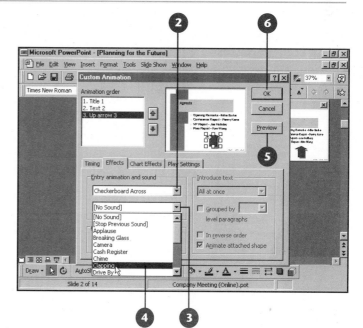

Using Specialized Animations

You can apply animations to your objects in different ways. For example, for a text object, you can introduce the text on your slide all at once or by word or letter. Similarly, you can introduce bulleted lists one bullet item at a time and apply different effects to older items, such as graying the items out as they are replaced by new ones. You can animate charts by introducing chart series or chart categories one at a time.

Animate Text

1. Right-click the selected text object, and then click Custom Animation.

2. Choose an effect from the list of animation effects.

3. Click the Introduce Text drop-down arrow, and click All At Once, By Word, or By Letter.

4. Click Preview.

5. Click OK.

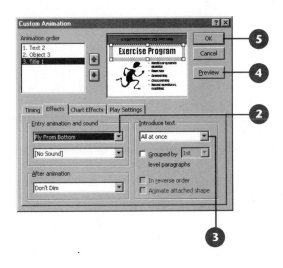

Animate Bulleted Lists

1. Right-click the bulleted text and then click Custom Animation.

2. Choose an effect from the list of animation effects.

3. If necessary, check the Grouped By check box.

4. Select at what level (1st, 2nd, 3rd and so forth) bulleted text will be animated.

5. Click Preview.

6. Click OK.

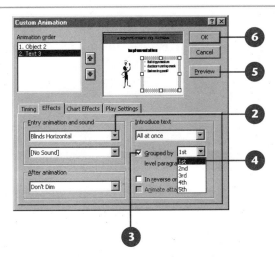

Dim Text After It Is Animated

1 Right-click the text, and then click Custom Animation.

2 Choose an effect from the list of animation effects.

3 Click the After Animation drop-down arrow.

4 Click the option you want.

5 Click Preview to see the animation.

6 Click OK.

Click to hide text as new objects enter the slide.

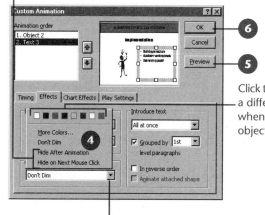

Click to give the text a different color when the next object is animated.

Chart Animation Options

1 In Slide view, right-click the chart, and then click Custom Animation.

2 On the Chart Effects tab, click the Introduce Chart Elements drop-down arrow.

3 Click the order in which chart elements should be introduced.

4 Click Preview.

5 Click OK.

"How can I make the bars on my bar chart appear one at a time with a neat animation effect?"

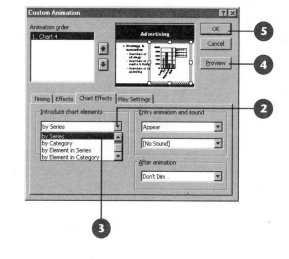

10

Coordinating Multiple Animations

The Custom Animation dialog box helps you keep track of your presentation's animations by listing all animated and unanimated objects in a single location. These lists are helpful if your slides contains more than one animation, because they help you determine how the animations will work together. For example, you can control the animation of each object, the order in which it appears, and what kind of time lag exists between animation effects. As you build up your animations, you can preview them to make sure that the combined effect is what you want.

Add Animation to Unanimated Slide Objects

1. Open the slide in Slide view, click the Slide Show menu, and then click Custom Animation.

2. Click the Timing tab.

3. Choose the slide object that you want to animate from the list of slide objects without animations.

4. Click the Animate option button.

5. Click the Effects tab.

6. Choose an animation effect and any additional animation options.

7. Click OK.

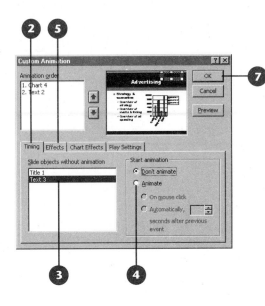

Modify the Animation Order

1. In the Custom Animation dialog box, click the slide object from the Animation Order list whose position you want to change.

2. Click the Up or Down arrow to move the object up or down in the animation order.

3. Click OK.

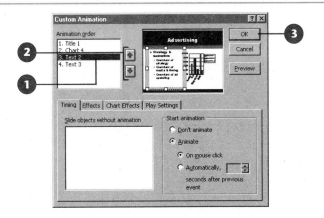

Set Time Between Animations

"How can I set a 2-minute lag between animations?"

1. In the Custom Animation dialog box, choose one of the animations from the Animation Order list.

2. Click the Timing tab.

3. Click the Animate Automatically option button.

4. Enter the number of seconds between this animation and the previous event.

5. Click OK.

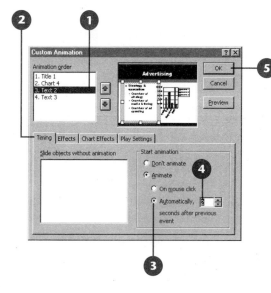

Remove an Animation

1. In the Custom Animation dialog box, click the animation you want to remove from the Animation Order list.

2. Click the Timing tab.

3. Click the Don't Animate option button.

4. Click OK.

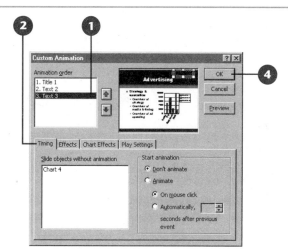

10

Adding Action Buttons

When you create a self-running presentation to be used at a kiosk, you might want a user to be able to move easily to specific slides or to a different presentation altogether. To give an audience this capability, you insert *action buttons*, which a user can click to jump to a different slide or different presentation. Clicking an action button activates a *hyperlink*, a connection between two locations in a the same document or a different document.

TIP

Insert the Return action button to help navigation in slide show. *If you want your audience to be able to return to the slide they were previously viewing, regardless of its location in the presentation, insert the Return action button.*

Insert a Foreward or Backward Action Button

1 Click the Slide Show menu.

2 Point to Action Buttons, and then choose the action button you want.

3 Drag on the slide, and then release the mouse button when the action button is the size you want.

4 If necessary, fill out the Action Settings dialog box, and then click OK

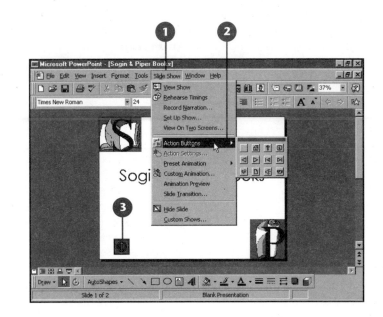

Test an Action Button

1 Click the Slide Show View button.

2 Display the slide containing your action button.

3 Click the action button.

Press Shift as you drag to create a square action button.

Create an Action Button to Go to a Specific Slide

1 Click the Slide Show menu, and then point to Action Buttons.

2 Click the Custom action button.

3 Drag to insert the action button on the slide.

4 Click the Hyperlink To option button, click the drop-down arrow, and then click Slide from the list of hyperlink destinations.

5 Select the slide you want the action button to jump to.

6 Click OK twice.

7 Right-click the action button, and click Add Text.

8 Type the name of the slide the action button points to.

9 Click outside the action button to deselect it.

10 Run the slide show and test the action button.

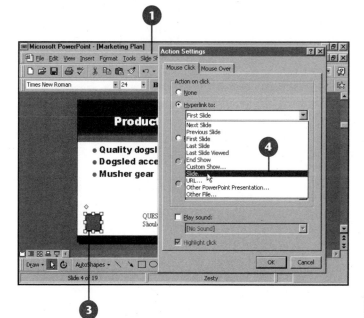

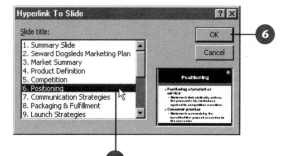

Adding Links to Objects

You can turn one of the objects on your slide into an "action button" so that when you click it you activate a hyperlink. You can point hyperlinks to almost any destination, including pages on the World Wide Web.

Add a Link to a Slide Object

1. Right-click an object on the slide.

2. Click Action Settings.

3. Click the Hyperlink To option button.

4. Choose a destination for the hyperlink.

5. Click OK.

6. Run the slide show and test the hyperlink by clicking the object in the slide show.

When you point at the action button, the pointer changes shape, and a ScreenTip appears indicating what the action button will do if you click it.

Add a Default Sound to a Hyperlink

1 In Slide view, right-click the object with the hyperlink.

2 Click Action Settings.

3 Click the Play Sound check box.

4 Click the Play Sound drop-down arrow.

5 Click the sound you want to play when the object is clicked during the show.

6 Click OK.

"I'd like a sound to play when I click a hyperlink."

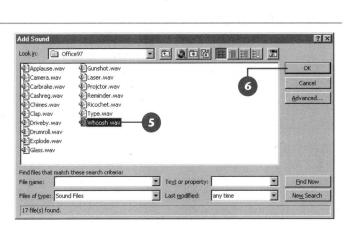

Add a Custom Sound to a Hyperlink

1 Right-click the hyperlinked object.

2 Click Action Settings.

3 Click the Play Sound check box and then click the Play Sound drop-down arrow.

4 Scroll to the bottom of the Play Sound list and then click Other Sound.

5 Locate and select the sound you want to use.

6 Click OK twice.

Creating Hyperlinks to External Objects

When objects on your PowerPoint slides are derived from other sources, you might want to make those sources available to your audience so that you can retrieve the source file during the presentation. You can create hyperlinks in your presentation that access those other sources: in other PowerPoint presentations, other files, a Web page, or even a program. This feature is especially useful for presentations intended to be used at a kiosk, where users might want more information on a topic, but you aren't there to provide it.

Create a Hyperlink to a Presentation

1. Right-click an object on your slide, and then click Action Settings.

2. Click the Hyperlink To option button, and then click Other PowerPoint Presentation from the list of hyperlinks.

3. Locate the presentation on your computer, and then click OK.

4. Display the slide in the presentation that you want to link to, and then click OK.

5. Click OK to save the hyperlink.

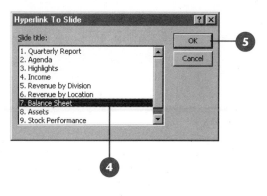

Create a Hyperlink to an External File

1. Right-click an object on your slide, click Action Settings, and then click the Hyperlink To option button.

2. Click Other File in the list of hyperlinks.

3. Locate the file on your computer, and then click OK.

4. Click OK to save the hyperlink.

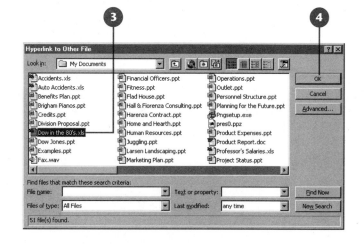

Create a Hyperlink to a Web Page

1 Right-click an object on your slide, click Action Settings, and then click the Hyperlink To option button.

2 Click URL in the list of hyperlinks.

3 Enter the URL of the Web page, and then click OK.

4 Click OK to save the hyperlink.

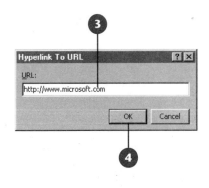

Create a Hyperlink to a Program

1 Right-click an object on your slide, and click Action Settings.

2 Click the Run Program option button.

3 Click the Browse button and locate the program on your computer or network.

4 Click OK.

5 Click OK to save the hyperlink that runs the program.

Enter the program's name and location here.

10

Timing a Presentation

If you will be presenting your slide show under a time limit, you can use PowerPoint's timing features to make sure that your presentation is not taking too long or going too fast. You can exactly specify the amount time given to each slide, and you can test yourself during rehearsal using the *slide meter*, which ensures that your timings are legitimate and workable. If you want the timings to take effect, make sure the show is set to use timings, if present, in the Set Up Show dialog box.

Set Timings Between Slides

1. Click the Slide Show menu, and then click Slide Transition.

2. Click the Automatically After check box.

3. Enter the time (in seconds) before the presentation automatically advances to the next slide after the entire slide is displayed.

4. Click Apply To All.

Create Timings Through Rehearsal

1. Click the Slide Show menu, and then click Rehearse Timings.

2. As the Slide Show runs, rehearse your presentation by clicking the Advance button to go the next slide as you finish with a slide.

3. Click Yes to accept the timings you just recorded.

4. Click Yes to review the timings in Slide Sorter view.

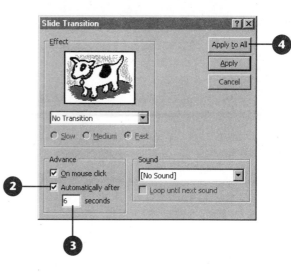

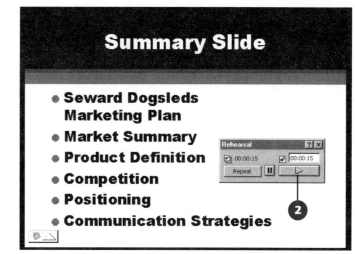

Controlling slide show timings. *To control whether your presentation uses timings you set or advances manually, click the Slide Show menu, click Set Up Show, click either the Manually option button or Using Timings option button in the Advance Slides section, and then click OK.*

See "Creating Slide Transitions" on page 192 for more information on creating transitions between slides.

"How can I set a particular slide so I have more time to talk?"

Test Timings

1. Start the slide show presentation.

2. Right-click the slide show, and then click Slide Meter.

3. Observe the slide meter as you rehearse your presentation and note when the meter goes into the red.

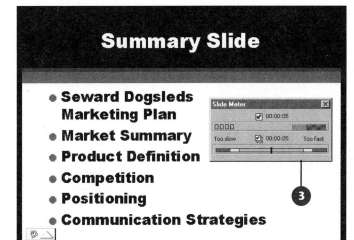

Edit Timings

1. In Slide Sorter view, click the slide whose timing you want to change.

2. Click the Slide Show menu, and then click Slide Transition.

3. Enter a new value in the Seconds box.

4. Click Apply to save the new timing.

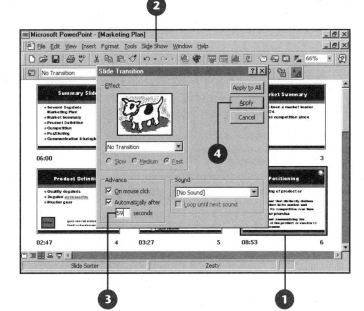

Recording a Narration

If you are creating a self-running presentation, you might want to add a narration to better emphasize the points you want to make. PowerPoint lets you to record your own narration as you are rehearsing your slide show. You can then insert that narration in the proper places on your slide. You can also augment your narration by including background music. Using these techniques you can create a self-running slide show that will be almost as good as the slide show you run yourself.

Record a Narration

1 Click the Slide Show menu, and then click Record Narration.

2 Click Settings.

3 Click the Name drop-down arrow, click the recording quality you want, and then click OK twice.

4 Speak clearly into the microphone attached to your computer, and go through the slide show, recording your narration for each slide.

5 Click Yes when prompted to save slide timings along with your narration.

6 Click Yes when asked to view the timings in Slide Sorter view.

7 Rerun the slide show and verify that your narration has been recorded along with the automatic timings.

Insert a Soundtrack from a File

1 Insert a sound clip anywhere on the slide.

2 Click the Slide Show menu, and then click Custom Animation.

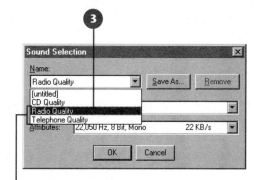

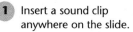

Higher quality sound files take up more disk space than lower quality sound files.

TIP

If the length of your presentation is longer than the length of the soundtrack, you can loop the soundtrack back to the beginning by clicking the More Options button on the Play Settings tab and choosing the Loop Until Stopped option button.

SEE ALSO

See "Inserting Sounds" on page 114 for more information on how PowerPoint handles sound files.

3 On the Timing tab, click the sound clip you just inserted, and then click Animate.

4 Click the Automatically option button, and then enter a delay time of 0.

5 Click the Up arrow button, and move the sound file to the top of the animation order.

6 Click the Effects tab and change the entry animation effect to No Effect.

7 Click the Play Settings tab, and click the Play Using Animation Order check box.

8 Make sure the Continue Slide Show option button is selected.

9 Enter the number of slides in your presentation in the Stop Playing After _____ Slides box so that the soundtrack will continue to play until you reach the end of the presentation.

10 Click the Hide While Not Playing check box.

11 Click OK.

12 Run the slide show and verify that your soundtrack plays correctly.

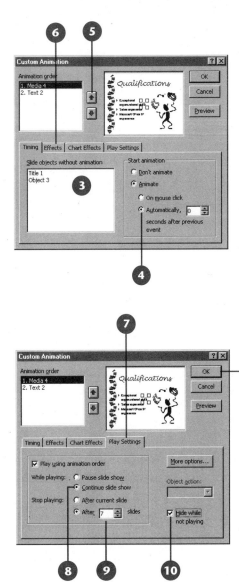

Creating a Custom Slide Show

If you plan to show a slide show to more than one audience, or you use a show regularly for different audiences, you don't have to create a separate slide show for each audience. Instead, you can create a *custom slide show* that allows you to specify which slides from the presentation you will use and the order in which they will appear.

TIP

Use the Set Up Show command to display a custom slide show. *Click Set Up Show on the Slide Show menu, click the Custom option button, and then choose the slide show from the custom slide show list.*

Create a Custom Slide Show

1. Click the Slide Show menu, and then click Custom Shows.

2. Click the New button.

3. Type a name for the show in the Slide Show Name box.

4. Double-click the slides you want to include in the show in the order you want to present them.

5. Click OK.

6. Click Close to close the Custom Shows dialog box.

List of custom slide shows for this presentation.

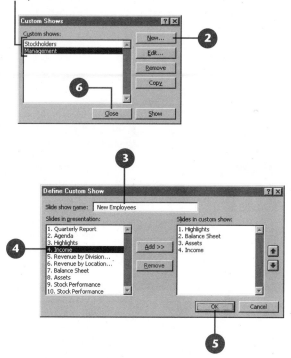

Show a Custom Slide Show

1. Click the Slide Show menu, and then click Custom Shows.

2. Click the custom slide show you want to run.

3. Click Show.

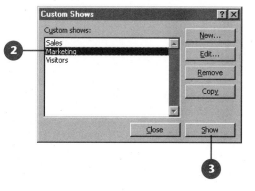

Edit a Custom Slide Show

1 Click the Slide Show menu, and then click Custom Shows.

2 Click the show you want to edit.

3 Click the Edit button.

4 In the Define Custom Show dialog box, edit the slides as necessary:

- ◆ To remove a slide from the show, click the slide in the Slides In Custom Show list, and then click Remove.

- ◆ To move a slide up or down in the show, click the slide in the Slides In Custom Show list, and then click the Up arrow or Down arrow.

- ◆ To add a slide, click the slide in the Slides In Presentation list and then click the Add button. The slide appears at the end of the Slides In Custom Show list.

5 Click OK.

6 Click Close.

Click to move the slide up in order

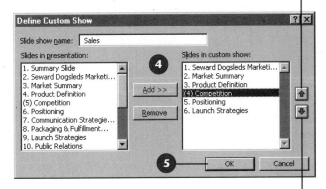

Click to move the slide down in order

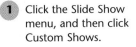

10

11

Presenting a Slide Show

IN THIS SECTION

Presenting a Show

Accessing Commands During a Show

Emphasizing Points

Navigating a Slide Show

Taking Notes

Running a Conference

Taking a Show on the Road

Using Web Templates

Creating a Web Page

Using the Web Toolbar

Viewing a Presentation in a Browser

Accessing Information on the Web

Accessing PowerPoint Central

Accessing the ValuPack

When you're ready to give a slide show, you'll find that Microsoft PowerPoint 97 provides many tools for presenting your show to audiences everywhere. PowerPoint accommodates the following situations:

◆ Presenting to a live audience in a conference room or auditorium

◆ Sharing a presentation with a remote audience over the Internet in "real-time"

◆ Running your presentation at a kiosk

◆ Showing your presentation on a computer that doesn't necessarily have PowerPoint installed

◆ Publishing your presentation on a World Wide Web page

In all these situations, PowerPoint not only gives you flexiblity in controlling how you run your show, but also helps you keep track of the ideas that arise over the course of your presentation. Finally, PowerPoint helps you use the World Wide Web to your advantage—an increasingly important consideration in today's information-oriented world.

Presenting a Show

Once your slide show is in its final state, it's time to consider how to show it to the world. PowerPoint lets you plan for a number of common presentation scenarios.

Presenting to a Live Audience

When you are giving the show in person, you can use PowerPoint's slide navigation tools to move around your presentation as you give it. You can move forward and backward or move to a specific slide. If you have set up custom slide shows, you can easily jump to one of those shows in the middle of your presentation. As you're presenting your slide show, you can highlight key ideas by using the mouse as a pointer or light pen. PowerPoint gives you the ability to control the color of your light pen so it complements your presentation's colors.

PowerPoint also provides tools for recording ideas that come up during the presentation, including using Meeting Minder, exporting ideas to a Word document file, or inserting them into your own personal calendar.

Presentation Conferencing

For presentations that take place over the Internet, PowerPoint provides a tool called the Presentation Conference Wizard. You, the presenter, see the conference on your computer, complete with all the tools you need to recall ideas or record notes. Participants in the conference can view your presentation on their own computer monitors, anywhere in the world. PowerPoint hides the tools you're using from them so they're not distracted. By supplementing the Internet conference with a telephone conference call, you can run a meeting over the phone almost as effectively as you can in a centrally located office building.

On the Road

If you are taking your presentation to another site, you might not need the entire PowerPoint package. Rather than installing PowerPoint on the site's computers, you can pack your presentation into one compressed file, storing it on a portable disk. Once you reach your destination, you can expand the compressed file onto your client's computer and play it, regardless of whether that computer has PowerPoint installed.

Internet Presentations

To reach the widest possible audience, consider placing your presentation on the World Wide Web. The Save As HTML Wizard formats your presentation in *HyperText Markup Language* (HTML), a simple coding system used to format documents for an intranet or the Internet. Using this language of the Web allows your presentation to be viewed by most Web browsers. To further assist you in creating Web pages, PowerPoint includes several Web templates that you can edit to fit your needs.

Accessing Commands During a Show

As you show your slide show, you can access certain PowerPoint commands without leaving Slide Show view using the Slide Show view popup menu. If your show is at a kiosk, you might want to disable this feature.

TIP

Use the Options dialog to customize slide show. *You can disable the popup menu using the View tab in the Options dialog box.*

Display the Popup Menu

1 In Slide Show view, right-click the slide you are showing.

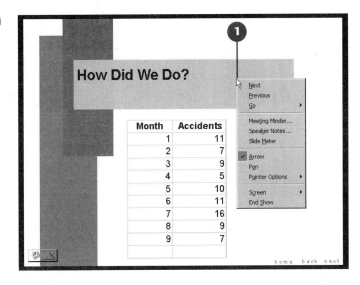

Set Popup Menu Options

1 Click the Tools menu.

2 Click Options.

3 Click the View tab.

4 Select the appropriate popup menu options.

5 Click OK.

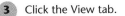

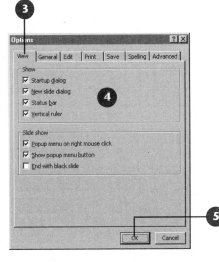

Emphasizing Points

When you are presenting your slide show, you can turn your mouse pointer into a light pen, capable of high-lighting and circling your key points. If you decide to use a light pen, you might want to set its colors to match the colors in your presentation. Marks you make on a slide with the light pen during a slide show are not permanent.

Pointer Options

1. In Slide Show view, right-click the slide.

2. Point to Pointer Options.

3. Click Hide Now to hide the pointer until you move the mouse, or click Hide Always to make the pointer invisible throughout the presentation.

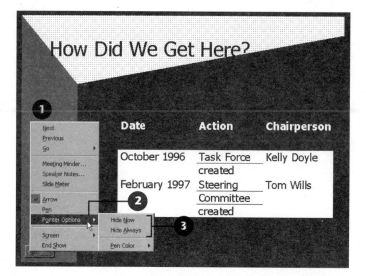

Use a Light Pen During a Slide Show

1. In Slide Show view, right-click an empty spot on the slide.

2. Click Pen. The pointer changes to the shape of a pen.

Return the pen back to the mouse pointer quickly. *To turn the light pen back to the normal mouse pointer, right-click a slide, and then click Arrow.*

3. Drag the mouse pointer to draw on your slide presentation with your pen. Use the pen to accentuate points on your slide.

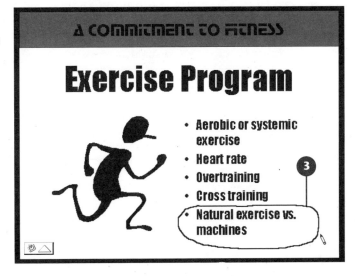

Set the Pen's Color

1. In Slide Show view, right-click a slide.

2. Point to Pointer Options.

3. Point to Pen Color.

4. Click the color you want to use for lines drawn by your pen.

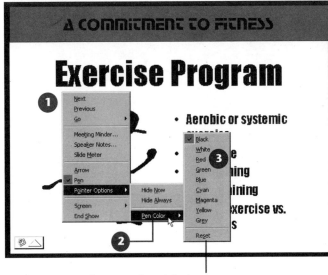

Click to return the pen to its original color

Navigating a Slide Show

In Slide Show view, you advance to the next slide by clicking the mouse button or pressing the Enter key on your keyboard. In addition to those basic navigational techniques, PowerPoint provides keyboard shortcuts that can take you to the beginning, end, or any particular slide in your presentation. You can also use the navigation commands on the popup menu to access slides in custom slide shows.

Slide Show View Navigation Shortcuts

Refer to the adjacent table for information on Slide Show view navigation shortcuts.

SLIDE SHOW VIEW SHORTCUTS	
Action	**Result**
Mouse click	Go to the next slide
Right-mouse click	Go to previous slide (popup menu on right-click option must be disabled first)
Press Enter	Go to the next slide
Press Home	Go to the first slide in the show
Press End	Go to the last slide in the show
Press PgUp	Go to the previous slide
Press PgDn	Go to the next slide
Press a slide number, and then press Enter	Go to the slide number you specified

Go to a Specific Slide

1. In Slide Show view, right-click a slide.

2. Point to Go, and then Point to By Title.

3. Click the title of the slide you want to go to.

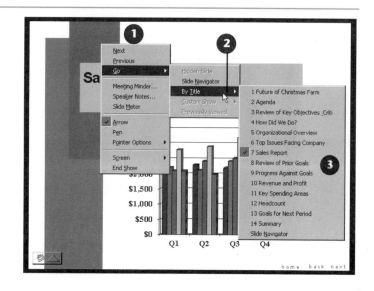

Use Slide Navigator

1. In Slide Show view, right-click a slide.

2. Point to Go, and then Click Slide Navigator.

3. If the slide you want to view is in a custom slide show, click the Show drop-down arrow, and then click the custom slide show you want.

4. Click the slide title for the slide you want to display.

5. Click Go To.

"How can I move easily through my slide show?"

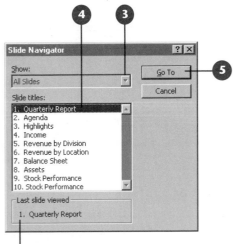

The slide you displayed most recently appears here.

Go to a Custom Slide Show

1. In Slide Show view, right-click a slide.

2. Point to Go, and then Point to Custom Show.

3. Click the custom slide show that you want to go to.

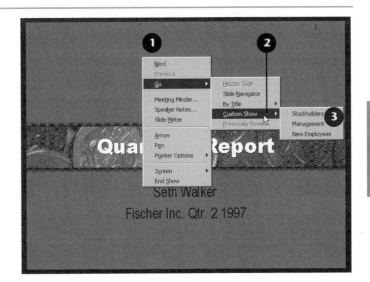

11

Taking Notes

When your presentation generates ideas or action items that need to be recorded, you can keep track of those items using PowerPoint's Meeting Minder. You can also use Meeting Minder to export your notes to a Word document or into Office 97's calendar and schedule program, Microsoft Outlook.

TIP

Edit information in Meeting Minder. *You can add or edit information from Meeting Minder even when you are not running your presentation. To access Meeting Minder outside of Slide Show view, click the Tools menu and then click Meeting Minder.*

Export Action Items and Minutes to Word

1. Click the Tools menu, and then click Meeting Minder.

2. Enter your minutes or action items.

3. Click Export.

4. Click the Send Meeting Minutes And Action Items To Microsoft Word check box.

5. Click Export Now.

6. Edit the items in Microsoft Word, and then save the document.

Create Meeting Minutes

1. In Slide Show view, right-click a slide.

2. Click Meeting Minder.

3. Type your minutes into the Meeting Minutes box.

4. Click OK.

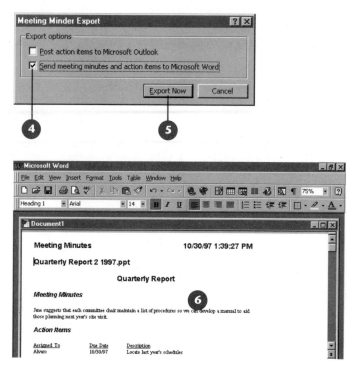

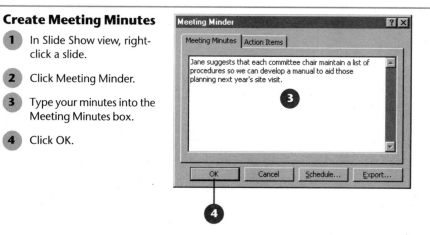

Create an Action Item

1 In Slide Show view, right-click a slide, and then click Meeting Minder.

2 Click the Action Items tab.

3 Type a description of the action you want to record.

4 Type the name of the person assigned to the action.

5 Type the due date of the action.

6 Click Add.

7 Click OK.

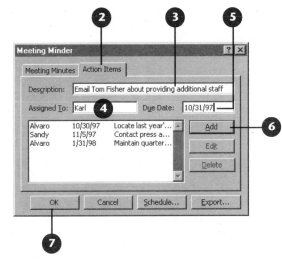

View and Edit Speaker Notes

1 In Slide Show view, right-click a slide, and then click Speaker Notes.

2 Enter new speaker notes or view the current notes in the Speaker Notes dialog box.

3 Click the Close button to close the Speaker Notes dialog box (you can leave it open if you want as you go from one slide to another.)

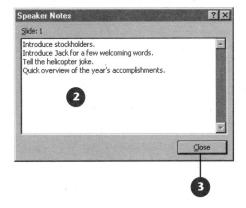

11

Running a Conference

If you're running a presentation for a group over your company's network or the Internet, you can use PowerPoint's Conference Wizard to set up your conference. If you are an audience member, you will also need to run this Wizard so that your computer is ready for the connection. If you are the presenter, you will probably want to hide the PowerPoint tools from your audience so that they see only your slide show.

Run the Presentation Conference Wizard as the Presenter

1 In Slide view, click the Tools menu.

2 Click Presentation Conference.

3 Verify that your party is ready to receive the slide show, and then click Next to continue.

4 Click the Presenter option button, and then click Next twice to continue.

5 If necessary, connect to your network or the Internet, and then click Next to continue.

6 Enter the computer name or Internet address of each participant in the conference, and then click Add for each address. Click Next when you are finished entering names.

7 Click Finish to start the conference.

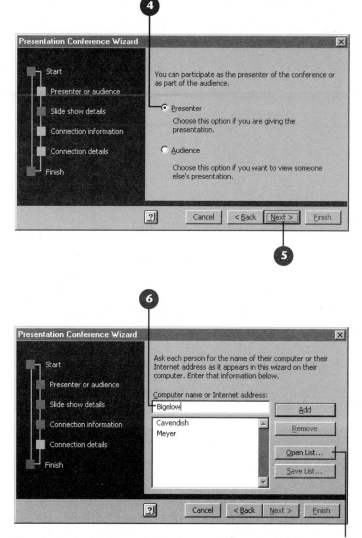

If you have previously saved a Conference Address List file that contains a list of addresses, click this button to locate and open that list.

Hide PowerPoint tools during a presentation. *You can hide your slide tools from any audience by running your show on two screens. You will need two computers connected by a serial or parallel cable. On the machine from which you are running the presentation, click the Slide Show menu, and then click View On Two Screens. Indicate the type of connection between the two computers and click the Presenter option button. On the audience's machine, issue the View On Two Screens command, enter the connection type, but this time click the Audience option button. Once the connection is made, the Presenter machine will have access to the PowerPoint tools, while the Audience screen will show only the slide show.*

Run the Presentation Conference Wizard as an Audience Member

1. In Slide view, click the Tools menu.

2. Click Presentation Conference.

3. Verify that the presenter is ready, and then click Next to continue.

4. Click the Audience option button, and then click Next to continue.

5. Specify whether you are connecting over a local area network or a dial-up Internet connection, and then click Next to continue.

6. If the presenter doesn't know your computer's name, read it off the dialog box, and then click Next to continue.

7. Click Finish and wait for the presenter to connect you.

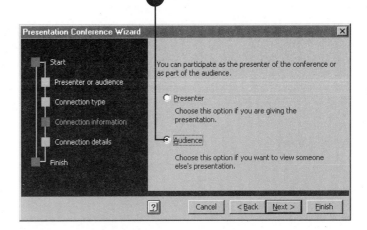

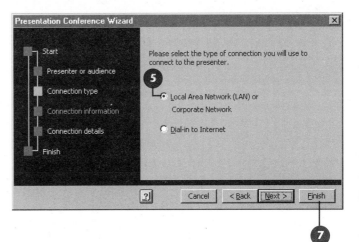

11

Taking a Show on the Road

If your audience can't come to you and you can't connect to them over the Internet, you might have to go to them, bringing your presentation with you. You don't need to bring the complete PowerPoint program. Instead, you can bring only those tools needed to show the slide show. PowerPoint provides the PowerPoint Viewer, a small program that runs PowerPoint slide shows. You can also use PowerPoint's Pack And Go Wizard to pack your presentation into a single compressed file that will fit on one or two floppy disks.

Run the Pack And Go Wizard

1. Click the File menu.

2. Click Pack And Go.

3. Click Next to start the Pack And Go Wizard.

4. Identify the presentation you want to pack, and then click Next to continue.

5. Identify where to send the packed file, and then click Next to continue.

6. Click the Include Linked Files check box to include any files you linked to your presentation and click the Embed TrueType Fonts check box to ensure that your fonts will appear correctly when you show the presentation. Click Next to continue.

7. If the computer on which you will show your presentation doesn't have PowerPoint installed, click the Viewer For Windows 95 or NT option button, and then click Next to continue.

8. Click Finish to pack your presentation.

9. When the Pack And Go Wizard has completed its task, click OK.

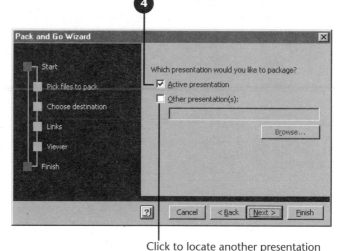

Click to locate another presentation

Click to locate the drive on which you want to pack the presentation

Unpack a Presentation

1 Open Windows Explorer.

2 Open the folder containing your packed presentation file.

3 Double-click PNGSETUP.

4 Enter a destination folder, and then click OK.

5 Click Yes if you want to view the slide show now, or click No tó view it later.

"I can take my presentation to anyone—even if they don't have PowerPoint on their system!"

④

Pack and Go Setup ⊠

Source Folder: A:

Destination Folder: **C:**

Extraction might take a few minutes and will ask you for additional disks if needed.

[OK] [Cancel]

View a Slide Show with the PowerPoint Viewer

1 Start Windows Explorer and open the folder containing your unpacked presentation.

2 Double-click PPVIEW32 to start the PowerPoint Viewer.

3 Click the name of your slide show in the Look In box.

4 Click Show to view your show.

③

Microsoft PowerPoint Viewer ?⊠

Look in: 📁 Present

📄 Electi~1

File name:

Files of type: Presentations(*.ppt;*.pps;*.pot)

[Show] ← **④**
[Exit]
[About] [Print...]

◉ SlideShow
  ☑ Popup Menu on Right Mouse Click
  ☑ Show Popup Menu Button
  ☑ End With Black Slide
  ☐ Run in a Window
◯ Password Locked SlideShow

☐ Show SlideShow Dialog

No Preview Available

11

Using Web Templates

If you intend to use PowerPoint to create your Web pages, you might want to take advantage of PowerPoint's specially-designed Internet templates. The AutoContent Wizard lets you add hyperlinks between the slides in your presentation or hyperlinks to your e-mail address. The Home Page template helps you create a customized home page for your Web site. Finally, if you want to create a logo for your page, you can use the Web Banner templates. You can save any page you design to an FTP server or HTML server using PowerPoint's Save As command.

SEE ALSO

See "Creating a Web Page" on page 228 for information on saving a presentation as an HTML file.

Create a Web Page with the AutoContent Wizard

1 Click the File menu, and then click New.

2 Click the Presentations tab, and then double-click the AutoContent Wizard icon.

3 Click Next to continue, and then choose the type of presentation you want to create. Click Next to continue.

4 Click the Internet, Kiosk option button to specify how the presentation will be used. Click Next to continue.

5 Enter your e-mail address in the E-mail Hyperlink text box and any other information requested.

6 Click Finish.

Click here to create a presentation suitable for the Web

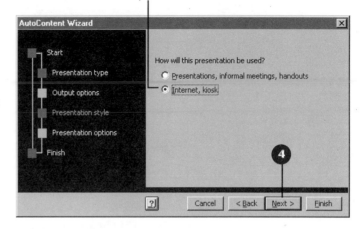

Instructions help you automate the presentation

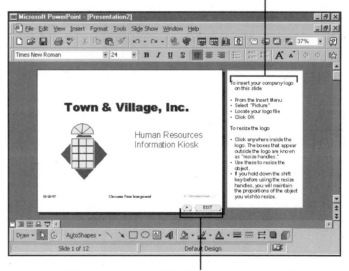

Slide contains hyperlinks to move forward and backward

Use the Animation Player to display slide show effects via the Internet. *If you use animation effects in your logo, be sure that your clients have the PowerPoint Animation Player added to their Web browser.*

Create a Home Page

1 Click the File menu, and then click New.

2 Click the Presentations tab, and then double-click the Personal Home Page (Online) icon.

3 Edit the presentation, and then save it as an HTML file.

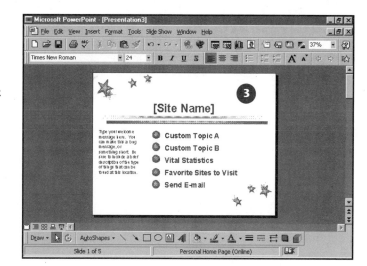

Save a Presentation to an FTP Server. *Click the File menu, and then click Save As. Click the Save In drop-down arrow, and then click Internet Locations (FTP). Double-click Add/Modify FTP locations. Type the address of the FTP server and any applicable user information, and then click Add. Click OK. Choose the FTP server from the list in the Save As dialog box, and click Open.*

Create a Web Page Banner

1 Click the File menu, and then click New.

2 Click the Web Pages tab, and then double-click one of the sample banners.

3 Edit the presentation, and then save it as a HTML file.

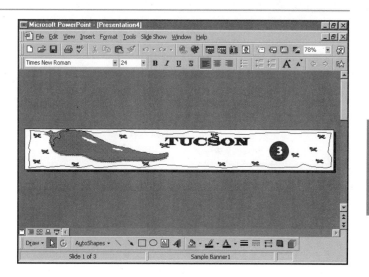

11

Creating a Web Page

PowerPoint allows you to save any presentation as a Web page, written in HTML, the language used by Internet browsers to interpret and display Web pages. PowerPoint provides the Save As HTML Wizard to facilitate the creation of your Web page. You can specify the appearance of the page, including button styles, colors, and layout. You can also include information such as your e-mail address and the URL of your home page. Finally, you can create a simple Web page presentation or you can create a page that uses frames.

What resolution should I use? *In choosing the monitor resolution for graphics in your Web page, note that higher values of resolution and width will create larger graphics that might be too large for smaller screens and will take longer to load into your page. If you're not sure what resolution to use, try a smaller value first.*

Start the Save As HTML Wizard

1 Click the File menu, and then click Save As HTML.

2 Click Next to continue.

3 Click the New Layout option button to create a new layout, or click the Load Existing Layout option button if you have already created and saved a layout and you want to use it again. Click Next to continue.

4 If you are creating a new layout, select the page style you want, and then click Next to continue.

5 Click the graphics type option you want: GIF files, JPG files, or files that use the PowerPoint Animation Player. Click Next to continue.

6 Choose a monitor resolution and width for the graphics in your Web page. Click Next to continue.

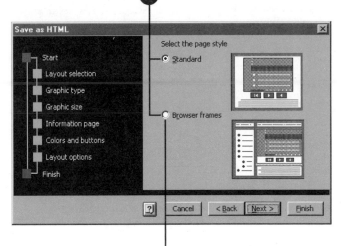

Click to create a web page that uses frames

Include animations in a Web Page. *If your presentation uses animation and special effects, you might want to save your slides as PowerPoint animations within your Web pages. You'll need to install the PowerPoint Animation player, a Web browser add-in that allows you to play animated PowerPoint presentations over the Internet and in real time. The PowerPoint Animation player works with Internet Explorer 2.0 or higher or Netscape version 1.22 or higher. You can get the latest version of the animation player from the PowerPoint Web page at http:// www.microsoft.com/ powerpoint/internet/player/ default.htm.*

7 After specifying graphic size and type, enter any relevant information about your page. Click Next to continue.

8 Choose whether to use the browser's colors for your Web page or your own defined colors for each Web page element. Click Next to continue.

9 Choose a button style for navigational buttons on your Web page. Click Next to continue.

10 Indicate whether or not to include speaker notes on each page. Click Next to continue.

11 Enter the folder in which PowerPoint will create a subfolder containing the files needed for your Web page presentation. Click Next to continue.

12 Click Finish to create a Web page with the settings you specified.

13 Enter a name for all of the settings you choose if you want to use them on other pages, and then click Save.

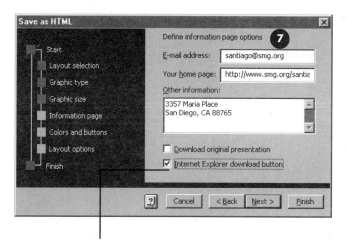

Click to include the PowerPoint presentation file along with the Web page so that others can download them

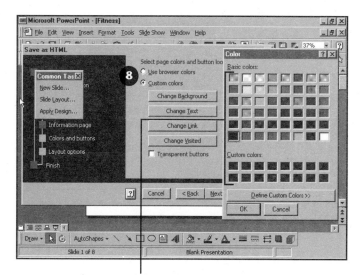

Click each button, and then select the color on the palette you want for that element.

11

Using the Web Toolbar

With the Web toolbar you are one click away from accessing the features of your Web browser. You can use the Web toolbar to go to your start page, access a Web search page, or open a specific URL.

Web Toolbar button

Display and Hide the Web Toolbar

1 Click the Web Toolbar button on the Standard toolbar.

2 Click the Show Only Web Toolbar button on the Web toolbar to hide the rest of the toolbars.

3 Click the Show Only Web Toolbar button on the Web toolbar again to restore the hidden toolbars.

4 Click the Web Toolbar button on the Standard toolbar again to hide the Web toolbar.

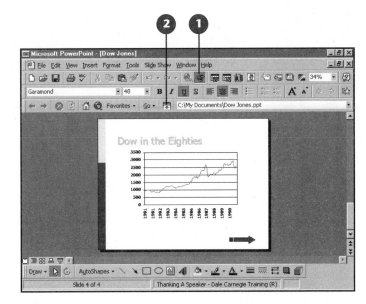

View your Start Page

1 Display the Web toolbar.

2 Click the Start Page button.

3 Connect to the Web if prompted.

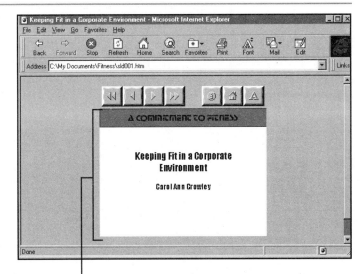

Your start page appears in your Web browser

Open a Specific URL or File

1 Display the Web toolbar.

2 Enter the URL of the Web page or location of the file that you want to access in the Address drop-down list box.

3 Press Enter.

4 Your browser opens, displaying your page or file.

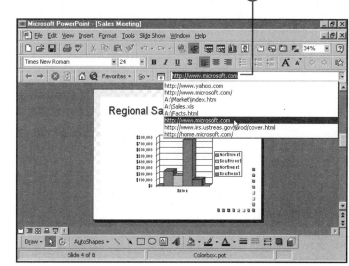

Search the Web

1 Display the Web toolbar.

2 Click the Search The Web button.

Viewing a Presentation in a Browser

Once you've created a Web page with the Save As HTML Wizard, you can test it by viewing it in your browser—Internet Explorer, Netscape Navigator, or another browser. To view your Web page presentation, you should start with the index page. The *index page* contains hyperlinks to all slide pages in your presentation—both in graphic and text-only form. You can open individual slides by opening the SLD00X.HTML file, where "x" is the number of the slide. Finally, opening the PPFRAME.HTML file opens the presentation using frames, if you specified that feature in the Save As HTML Wizard.

Open the Index Page

1. Start Internet Explorer or your browser.

2. Click the File menu, and then click Open.

3. Click Browse to locate and open the folder containing your Web presentation.

4. Locate and open Index.html.

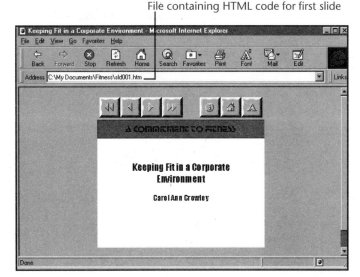

Click here to jump to a specific slide in your presentation

View a Slide in Graphics Mode

1. Start Internet Explorer or your browser.

2. Click the File menu, and then click Open.

3. Locate and open the folder containing your Web presentation.

4. Open the file SLD001.HTML (this will open the first slide).

File containing HTML code for first slide

View a Slide in Text Mode

1 Start Internet Explorer.

2 Click the File menu, and then click Open.

3 Locate the folder containing your Web presentation and open the file TSLD001.HTML.

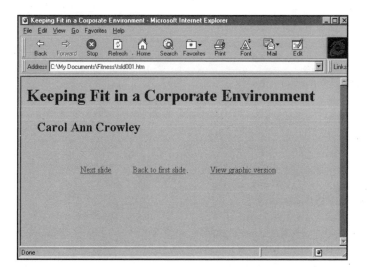

View a Presentation with Frames

1 Start Internet Explorer, click the File menu, and then click Open.

2 Locate the folder containing your Web presentation, and then open the file PPFRAME.HTML.

Click to show titles   Click to show titles and main points

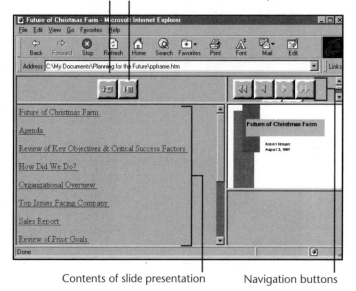

Contents of slide presentation   Navigation buttons

11

Accessing Information on the Web

Access to the World Wide Web gives you near-instant access to the latest information about PowerPoint. You can open Web pages about PowerPoint directly from the PowerPoint Help menu. With Web access you can get online support, view pages on frequently asked PowerPoint questions, or get the latest product news.

View an Online Support Web Page

1. Click the Help menu, and then point to Microsoft on the Web.

2. Click Online Support.

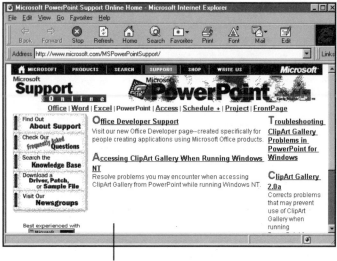

Online support page

View Product News

1. Click the Help menu and then point to Microsoft on the Web.

2. Click Product News.

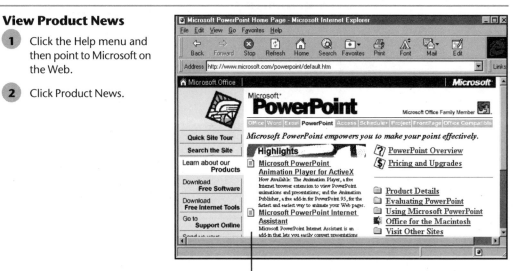

Product News Web page

Join a Newsgroup. *If you have a USENET newsreader, you might also consider accessing the newsgroup, microsoft.public.powerpoint to meet and share ideas with other PowerPoint users.*

View Frequently Asked Questions

1 Click the Help menu, and then point to Microsoft on the Web.

2 Click Frequently Asked Questions.

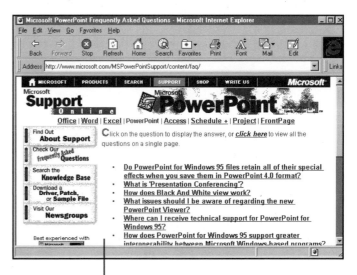

Frequently Asked Questions page

Accessing PowerPoint Central

You can explore the Web right from PowerPoint using the Web toolbar to access your favorite pages. You can also retrieve PowerPoint Central, a presentation showcasing the latest PowerPoint tips and tricks. Periodically accessing the Web and PowerPoint Central can help you grow and expand in your knowledge of PowerPoint.

View PowerPoint Central

1 Click the Tools menu, and then click PowerPoint Central.

2 Click Yes to check for an update when PowerPoint reports the time since you last updated PowerPoint Central.

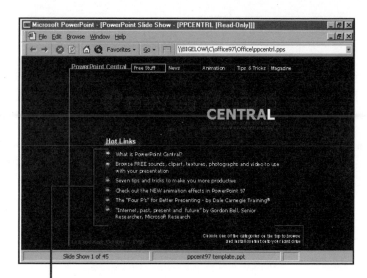

Run the PowerPoint Central presentation to get the latest tips and tricks on using PowerPoint.

Accessing the ValuPack

The Office 97 CD-ROM includes extra programs, files, and resource material that are not automatically installed when you install Office 97. These extra features can be found in the ValuPack on the installation CD-ROM. The features include a program to add a customized soundtrack to your presentations, new clip art images, sound files, extra templates for specialized tasks, and interactive presentations designed to help train new users on some of the finer points of PowerPoint.

"What other materials can I access with my Office 97 CD-ROM?"

Discovering the ValuPack

1. Click the Start button, point to Programs, and then click Windows Explorer.

2. Double-click the CD-ROM drive, and then double-click the ValuPack folder.

3. Double-click Overview.ppt, a presentation that gives you an overview of ValuPack features.

4. Run the presentation and close it when you are finished.

Click the links to view the ValuePack features you're interested in.

11

12

Customizing PowerPoint

IN THIS SECTION

Setting PowerPoint Options

Maximizing Efficiency with Macros

Controlling a Macro

Assigning a Macro to a Toolbar or Menu

Customizing PowerPoint Toolbars

Customizing Toolbar Buttons

Although Microsoft PowerPoint 97 is designed to be flexible and easy to use, you can customize the program to reflect your own preferences and the way you work. You can customize PowerPoint by automating frequent tasks and keystrokes with macros attached to buttons. Modifying PowerPoint's toolbars and menus to display the features you use most frequently increases your productivity. You can even create your own dialog boxes that appear when you first start PowerPoint. The purpose of each of these customization features is the same—to make PowerPoint even easier to use and permit you to accomplish more with less effort.

Setting PowerPoint Options

You can also customize the performance of many PowerPoint features including its editing, saving, spelling, viewing, and printing procedures. The initial settings for these procedures are called the *defaults*. If you change the default setting, PowerPoint will use the new setting for all subsequent PowerPoint sessions, until you change the setting again.

> **TIP**
>
> **Control viruses.** *If you open a file and receive a warning message about viruses, click Enable Macros to use the file with the macros or click Disable Macros to use the file without the macros.*

Change View Defaults

1. Click the Tools menu, and then click Options.

2. If necessary, click the View tab.

3. Change the View settings as necessary.

4. Click OK.

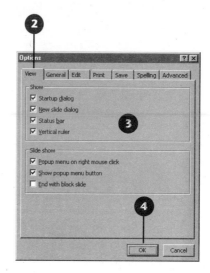

Change General Defaults

1. Click the Tools menu, and then click Options.

2. Click the General tab.

3. Change the General settings as necessary.

4. Click OK.

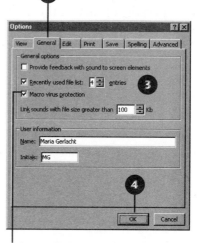

Select to turn on a warning message that appears whenever a file contains macros, which might contain viruses.

TIP

Use drag and drop to copy text. *To copy selected text, press and hold Shift while you drag the selection.*

SEE ALSO

See "Documenting and E-Mailing a Presentation" on page 182 for information on entering file properties.

Change Edit Defaults

 1 Click the Tools menu, and then click Options.

2 Click the Edit tab.

3 Change the Edit settings as necessary.

4 Click OK.

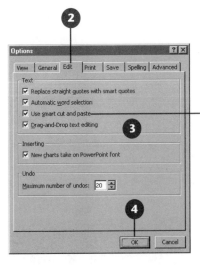

Select to add or remove spaces as needed when you edit text.

Change Advanced Defaults

1 Click the Tools menu, and then click Options.

2 Click the Advanced tab.

3 Change the Advanced settings as necessary.

4 Click OK.

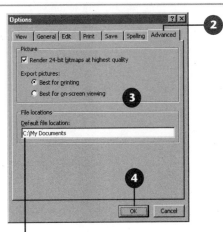

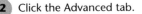

Enter the path of the folder you want PowerPoint to use as the default that appears when you open a new document or save an existing document.

12

Maximizing Efficiency with Macros

If you find yourself repeating the same set of steps over and over again or if you need to add new functionality to PowerPoint, you could create a macro. PowerPoint macros can run several tasks for you at the click of a button. You can easily create your own macros using PowerPoint's macro recorder utility, which records your actions, and then replays them. You can then add the macro to the PowerPoint toolbars or to the PowerPoint menu for easy access.

SEE ALSO

See "Customizing PowerPoint Toolbars" on page 248 for information on modifying toolbars.

Record a Macro

1 Click the Tools menu, point to Macro, and then click Record New Macro.

2 Type a name in the Macro Name box.

3 If necessary, click the Store Macro box and indicate the presentation where you want the macro to be placed.

4 If necessary, add to the description of the macro in the Description box.

5 Click the OK button.

6 Perform the actions you intend to place in the macro. Any action you perform in PowerPoint is recorded in the macro.

7 Click the Stop Recording button on the Macros toolbar.

"How can macros make my work easier?"

Run a Macro

1 Click the Tools menu, point to Macro, and then click Macros.

2 Click the name of the macro you want to run.

3 Click Run.

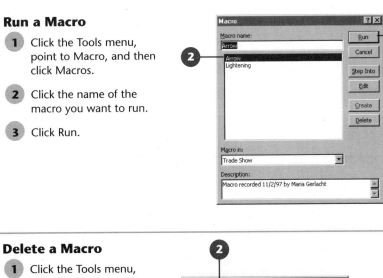

Delete a Macro

1 Click the Tools menu, point to Macro, and then click Macros.

2 Click the macro name.

3 Click the Delete button.

4 Click the Yes button to confirm the macro deletion.

12

Controlling a Macro

If your macro is not doing what you expect, you might want to run it one step at a time, rather than all at once, to find out where it is failing. This is a process known as "debugging." When you use the macro recorder, you are actually writing a program in a programming language called *Visual Basic*. All macros for a particular presentation are stored in a *macro module*, a collection of Visual Basic programming codes that you can copy to other presentation files. You can view and edit your Visual Basic modules using the Visual Basic editor. By learning Visual Basic you can greatly increase the scope and power of your programs.

Run a Macro One Step at a Time

1. Click the Tools menu, point to Macro, and then click Macros.

2. Click the name of the macro you want to run.

3. Click the Step Into button.

4. If necessary, display the Debug toolbar.

5. Click the Step Into button on the Debug toolbar.

6. Continuing clicking the button until you have worked through all the steps in the macro.

7. Click the File menu, and then click Close And Return To Microsoft PowerPoint.

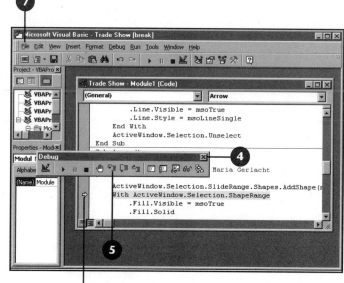

Arrow indicates current step

Edit a Macro

1. Click the Tools menu, point to Macro, and then click Macros.

2. Click the macro you want to edit, and then click the Edit button.

3. Click the Module window containing the Visual Basic code for your macro.

Module window contains your Visual Basic macros

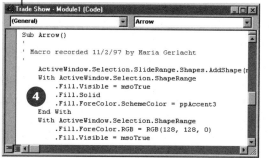

TIP

Use the Visual Basic Editor to help correct macro problems. *If a problem occurs while you step through your macro, you have probably discovered why your macro wasn't working. You can correct the problem using the Visual Basic Editor.*

TIP

Use the keyboard to access the Visual Basic Editor quickly. *To quickly access the Visual Basic Editor, press Alt+F11.*

TIP

Get help on Visual Basic. *To learn more about Visual Basic, place your macro in Edit mode, click the Help menu, and then click Microsoft Visual Basic Help.*

4 Type new Visual Basic commands or edit the commands already present.

5 Click the File menu, and then click Close And Return To Microsoft PowerPoint.

Copy a Macro Module to Another Presentation

1 Open the presentation files you want to copy the macro from and to.

2 Click the Tools menu, point to Macro, and then click Visual Basic Editor.

3 Click the View menu, and then click Project Explorer.

4 Drag the module you want to copy from the source presentation to the destination presentation.

5 Click the File menu, and then click Close And Return To Microsoft PowerPoint.

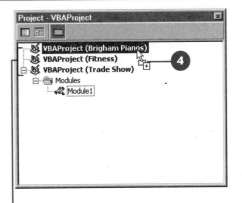

Presentation files currently open

12

Assigning a Macro to a Toolbar or Menu

Once you create a macro, you can then add the macro to the PowerPoint toolbars or to the PowerPoint menu for easy access.

"I'd like to be able to access my macro from the menu bar."

Assign a Macro to a Toolbar

1 Click the Tools menu, and then click Customize.

2 Click the Commands tab.

3 Click Macros from the Categories list box.

4 Click the Macro name in the Commands box, and drag it to the toolbar.

5 Click Modify Selection.

6 Choose a style and button image for your macro button.

7 Click the Close button to close the Customize dialog box and save your changes.

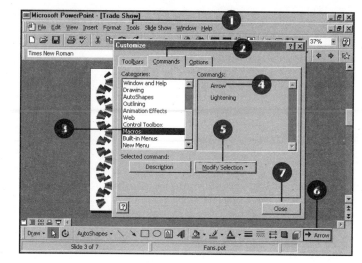

Delete a macro button from a toolbar. *Click Tools, click Customize, and then clickmacros. Select the macro button you want to delete on a toolbar, and drag it off the toolbar. Click Close to exit the Customize dialog box.*

Assign a Macro to a Menu

1. Click the Tools menu, click Customize, and then click the Commands tab.

2. Click Macros from the Categories list box.

3. Click the Macro name in the Commands box and drag it to a spot on the PowerPoint menu bar.

4. Click the Modify Selection button and choose a style and text for your menu entry.

5. Click the Close button to close the Customize dialog box and save your changes.

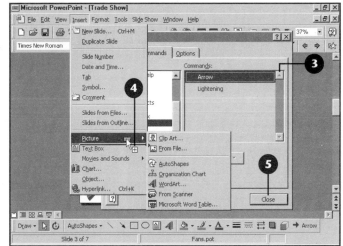

12

Customizing PowerPoint Toolbars

You can create new toolbars and customize the existing ones to maximize your efficiency. When you create a new toolbar and begin filling it with the buttons you use most for a given task, you can place icons on those buttons by either selecting an icon from the set that comes with PowerPoint or creating a new button using the Button Editor.

TIP

Enlarge a toolbar for easy readability. *If you have limited vision, you might want to create a toolbar with the buttons you use most frequently, and then enlarge those buttons by clicking the Options tab in the Cutomize dialog box, and then clicking the Large Icons check box.*

Add a Toolbar

1 Click the Tools menu and then click Customize.

2 Click the Toolbars tab.

3 Click the New button.

4 Type a name for your new toolbar.

5 Click OK.

6 Click Close.

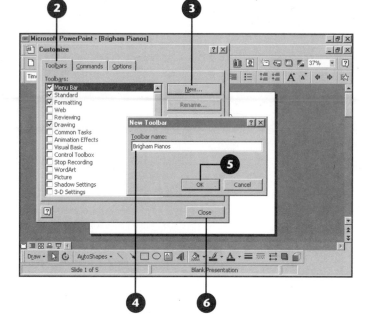

TIP

Delete a toolbar. *Click it on the Toolbars tab in the Customize dialog box, and then click the Delete button. You can also open the Customize dialog box, and then simply drag the button off the toolbar in the PowerPoint window.*

Add Buttons to a Toolbar

1 In the Customize dialog box, display the toolbar to which you want to add buttons. You can do this by double-clicking the toolbar on the Toolbars tab.

2 Click the Commands tab.

3 Click the category in the Categories list containing the button you want to add to your toolbar.

4 Scroll the Commands list to locate the command you want to add as a button on your toolbar.

5 Drag the command to your toolbar. If the command has a button icon associated with it, that icon appears. If it doesn't, the name of the command appears.

6 Click Close.

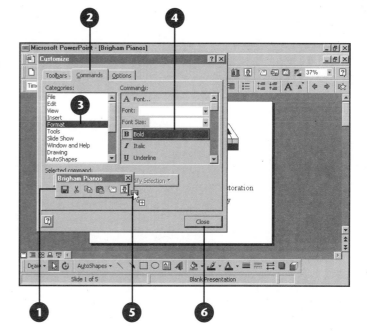

12

Customizing Toolbar Buttons

You can modify existing toolbars or create new ones using the Button Editor, which works like a "fill in thedots" drawing package. You fill each square with the color you want to create your button image.

TIP

Restore a toolbar to its original appearance. *If you have changed one of the default toolbars and you want to restore it to its original appearance, click it on the Toolbars tab in the Customize dialog box, and then click the Reset button.*

Modify a Toolbar Button

1. In the Customize dialog box, display the toolbar containing the button you want to modify, click the Commands tab.

2. Click the Modify Selection button.

3. Enter a name for your button in the Name box.

4. If applicable, select an icon for your button by pointing to Change Button Image, and then clicking the icon you want.

5. If applicable, edit the icon for your button using the Edit Button Image command.

   ◆ Click a color on the Colors palette.

   ◆ Click each square with the selected color to draw the object.

   ◆ Click the Move arrows to move the icon you create to a different location on the Picture grid.

6. Click OK.

7. Click Close.

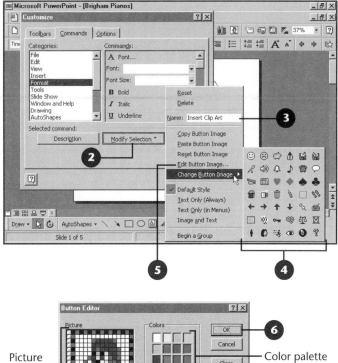

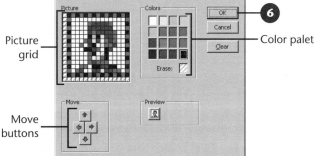

Picture grid

Color palette

Move buttons

Index

SPECIAL CHARACTERS

▶ (arrow symbol), menu
symbol, 14
… (ellipsis), menu/dialog box
symbol, 15

NUMBERS

3-D effects, 71, 88-89
3-D objects
adding surfaces to, 89
creating, 88
setting depth, 89
setting lighting, 89
spinning, 88
35-mm slides, converting
presentations to, 186

Accent & Followed Hyperlink
color, 59
Accent & Hyperlink color, 59
accent colors, 59
action buttons, 189
inserting, 200, 201
and the pointer, 202
testing, 200

turning objects into, 202
See also hyperlinks
action items (from slide shows)
creating, 221
exporting to Word, 220
Action Settings dialog box, 201,
202, 203, 205
actions
identifying undoable/
redoable actions, 33
undoing/redoing, 33
active cell (in worksheets/
datasheets), 148
Add clip art to Clip Gallery
dialog box, 102
Add Custom Chart Type dialog
box, 159
add-in programs, installing, 119
Add Sounds dialog box, 203
adjusting AutoShapes, 75
Advanced tab (Options dialog
box), 241
aligning
objects, 92-93
with the guides, 90
text, 43
in chart boxes, 144
WordArt text, 137
alignment guides. *See* guides
Alt key, dragging objects, 91
angles (of freeform vertices),
modifying, 79

animating
bulleted lists, 194, 196
Graph charts, 194, 196, 197
logos for Web pages, 227
objects, 198
text, 196, 197
then dimming, 197
See also animations
animations, 194-99
adding sound to, 195
adding to slides, 194
applying customized, 195
assigning musical motifs
to, 119
including in Web pages, 229
inserting video clips, 120
modifying the animation
order, 198
previewing, 194
removing, 199
setting the time between,
199
specialized, 196-97
See also animating
Apply button (in dialog
boxes), 15
Apply Design dialog box,
applying templates, 9
arrow keys, selecting text, 32
arrow symbol (▶), menu
symbol, 14
Arrow tool, 72

arrows
  coloring, 84
  drawing, 73
  editing, 73
  resizing, 73
AutoClipArt, locating clips with, 100, 101
AutoContent Wizard
  creating Web pages with, 226
  designing presentations with, 8
AutoCorrect, correcting errors while typing, 48
AutoLayouts
  applying to slides, 24
  placeholders, 25
AutoShapes, 46, 71
  adding text to, 47
  adjusting, 75
  drawing, 74-75
  replacing, 75
  reshaping, 74
  resizing, 74
axes (in Graph charts), 147
  labeling, 151
  rotating, 161

Background color, 59
  specifying, 65, 110
Background dialog box, 54, 65
background fill effects, applying, 66
background objects (on masters), hiding, 54
backgrounds
  applying fill effects, 66
  creating, 111
  setting transparent, 111
Backward action buttons, inserting, 200

banners, creating for Web pages, 227
bitmaps, 98
  cropping, 112
  displaying, 241
black and white
  converting default colors to, 110
  printing in, 64
bold typeface, applying, 42
Bookshelf (Microsoft), looking up references in, 170, 171
borders, formatting chart box borders, 144
breaking links, 128
Browse dialog box, 118
browsers, viewing presentations on the Web, 232-33
Bullet dialog box, 45
bulleted lists, 28, 29
  adding items to, 37
  animating, 194, 196
  creating slides from, 31
  customizing, 44-45
bulleted text
  adding/removing bullets, 44
  entering, 31
  See also bulleted lists
bullets
  adding/removing from text, 44
  formatting, 45
  spacing between text and, 44
Button Editor dialog box, 250
buttons
  option buttons (in dialog boxes), 15
  view buttons, 10

Cancel button (in dialog boxes), 15

category option buttons (PowerPoint window), 8
cell contents (datasheet cells), editing, 154
cells, 132, 146
  active cell, 148
  editing datasheet cell contents, 154
  inserting into datasheets, 155
centering objects, 92
Change Source dialog box, 128
characters
  adjusting WordArt text character spacing, 139
  See also bullets; special characters
chart area (in Graph), 160
chart box borders, formatting, 144
chart box lines, formatting, 144
chart boxes (in Organization Chart), 140
  adding, 142
  aligning text in, 144
  editing, 141
  entering text into, 141
  formatting, 144
  moving, 143
  restructuring, 142
  selecting/deselecting, 140
chart objects, selecting/formatting, 160-61
Chart Options dialog box (Excel/Graph), 161
Chart Type dialog box (Graph), 158, 159
charts. See Excel charts; Graph charts
check boxes, in dialog boxes, 15
checking
  grammar, 49
  presentation contents, 182

spelling, 48
clip art, 98
  changing image brightness, 108, 109
  changing image contrast, 108
  editing, 108
  resizing, 98, 108
  restoring original settings, 109
clip categories, editing, 104
Clip Gallery, 98
  adding/deleting clips to/from, 99, 102, 103
  inserting clips from, 99, 115, 120
  inserting movies from, 120
  inserting sounds from, 115
  locating clips in, 100
  updating, 102
Clip Gallery Live (on the Web)
  downloading clips from, 107
  opening, 106
  searching for clips in, 107
  viewing clips in, 106
clip packages, importing, 102
Clip Properties dialog box, 105
Clipboard, copying/cutting and pasting objects via, 124, 125
clips, 23, 97-119
  adding/deleting to/from the Clip Gallery, 99, 102, 103
  categorizing, 105
  downloading from the Web, 105, 107
  importing, 102
  inserting, 99, 114-15, 120
  locating, 100-101
    in Clip Gallery Live, 107
    in PowerPoint Central, 106

clips, *continued*
  organizing, 104-5
  types, 23, 98
  viewing in Clip Gallery
    Live, 106
Close button (PowerPoint
  window), 10
closing
  dialog boxes, 15
  presentations, 21
collapsing slides Outline view,
  40, 41
Color dialog boxes, 62, 63
color scheme colors, 59, 64
  adding, 65
  changing, 62-63
  choosing nonstandard
    colors, 62-63
  dialog boxes, 62, 63
  previewing, 62
  and printing in black and
    white, 64
  properties, 62
Color Scheme dialog box
  changing colors, 62
  choosing/deleting color
    schemes, 60
  saving color schemes, 63
color schemes, 51, 59
  applying to slides, 60, 61
  changing, 62-63
  choosing, 60, 64
  deleting, 60
  picking up and applying, 61
  saving, 63
coloring
  objects, 64, 84, 110
  shadows, 87
  slides, 60-63
  WordArt text, 137
colors
  properties, 62
  specifying object colors, 84

specifying the default
  type, 110
specifying the light pen
  color, 217
See also color scheme colors
column labels, entering, 151
columns (in datasheets)
  inserting, 155
  selecting, 149
  specifying widths, 153
command buttons, in dialog
  boxes, 15
commands
  accessing during slide
    shows, 215
  issuing, 14, 16
comments
  deleting, 169
  displaying/hiding, 168
  formatting, 169
  inserting, 168
constraining drawing, 72,
  74, 201
constraining rotation, 83
content templates, 51
  storing, 68
  See also templates
Contents tab (Help Topics
  dialog box), 18
Convert dialog box, 129
converting
  default colors to black and
    white/grayscale/
    watermark, 110
  linked objects, 129
  presentations to 35-mm
    slides, 186
copying
  macro modules between
    presentations, 245
  objects, 125
  slides between presentations,
    165

correcting errors while
  typing, 48
cropping images, 112-13
  with precision, 113
Ctrl key
  drawing lines, 72
  selecting slides in Outline
    view, 41
Ctrl+Enter keys, adding new
  slides in Outline view, 37
curves
  drawing irregular curves,
    76-77
  switching between open and
    closed, 77
Custom Animation dialog box,
  195-99
Custom Shows dialog box, 210
custom slide shows, 189, 210-11
  creating, 210, 211
  editing, 211
  going to, 219
Custom Soundtrack, 118, 119
  installing, 118
Customize dialog box, 246-50

D

Dash Style tool, 72
data
  entering into datasheets, 148
  importing into datasheets,
    150
  pasting into datasheets, 151,
    156
  See also datasheets; Graph
    data
data labels (in charts), 155
data markers (in charts), 147
  editing data with, 154
data series (in Graph), 146
datasheets (in Graph), 146

entering data into, 148
importing data into, 150
pasting data into, 151, 156
selecting, 149
showing with charts, 155
specifying column widths,
  153
See also Graph data
date formats, 56
dates
  adding to notes pages,
    179, 180
  inserting into slides, 56, 58
debugging macros, 244, 245
defaults, setting, 240-41
  arrow size, 73
  color type, 110
  document folder, 241
  Graph charts, 159
  line style, 85
  object color, 85
Define Custom Show dialog
  box, 210, 211
deleting
  animations, 199
  clips, 102, 103
  color schemes, 60
  comments, 169
  Graph data, 155
  guides, 91
  macros, 243
  objects, 27
  slides, 35
    from slide shows, 211
  text, 33
  toolbars, 249
  vertices (in freeforms), 79
Demote button, 36
demoting text, 31, 36, 37
depth, of 3-D objects, 89
deselecting
  chart boxes, 140
  objects, 26

design templates, 51
  applying, 70
  changing, 69
  storing, 68
  See also templates
destination file, defined, 124
destination program,
    defined, 124
dialog boxes, 15
  choosing options, 15
  closing, 15
  for color scheme colors, 62
dimming animated text, 197
distributing objects across
    slides, 92
document windows, 10
documenting presentation
    contents, 163, 182
documents
  default folder, 241
  sharing information among,
    123-44
  starting PowerPoint as a new
    document, 6
dotted selection boxes, 42
downloading clips from the
    Web, 105, 107
drag and drop, inserting Excel
    charts, 131
dragging data markers, editing
    data, 154
dragging objects, overriding the
    grid/guides, 91
drawing freehand, 77
drawing objects, 71-95
  arrows, 73
  coloring, 84
  in Graph charts, 162
  irregular curves, 76-77
  irregular polygons, 76
  lines, 73
  moving, 80-81
    with precision, 81

nudging, 80
ovals, 74
rectangles, 74
Drawing toolbar, 16, 47, 72, 73
drop-down arrows (in
    toolbars), 16
drop-down lists (in dialog
    boxes), 15
drop shadows. *See* shadows

E

Edit Category List dialog
    box, 104
Edit tab (Options dialog
    box), 241
editing
  arrows, 72
  cell contents, 154
  chart boxes, 141
  clip art, 108
  clip categories, 104
  custom slide shows, 211
  freeforms, 78-79
  Graph data, 154
  lines, 72
  macros, 244-45
  movies, 121
  slide timings, 206, 207
  sounds, 116, 117
  speaker's notes, 221
  text, 28, 32-33
    adding/removing spaces
      as needed, 241
    in text boxes, 46
  Word tables, 133
  WordArt text, 135, 136-37
ellipsis (...), menu/dialog box
    symbol, 15
embedded objects
  activating, 126
  selecting, 126

embedding
  fonts, 170, 171
  objects, 124, 126
  pasting as, 125
Enter key, adding new slides in
    Outline view, 37
entering
  bulleted text, 31
  data into Graph datasheets,
    148
  notes, 178
  text
    into chart boxes, 141
    in Outline view, 29, 34
    in Slide view, 25, 28,
      30-31
error bars, in Graph charts, 162
Excel charts, inserting, 130, 131
Excel worksheets
  importing data from, 150
  inserting data from, 130-31
  inserting new, 130
exiting PowerPoint, 21
expanding slides Outline view,
    40, 41
exporting
  meeting minutes to
    Microsoft Outlook,
    220
  notes pages/slides to Word,
    184, 185
  slide show action items/
    minutes to Word, 220

F

FAQ (frequently asked ques-
    tions) Web page, 235
favorite presentations,
    listing, 167

file formats, saving slides/
    presentations in different
    formats, 187-88
files
  closing, 21
  creating hyperlinks to, 204
  finding, 11
  inserting, 126
  inserting pictures from, 105
  opening, 11
  printing presentations
    to, 174
  protecting, 21
  temporary files, 20
fill effects, 66
  choosing, 66-67
Fill Effects dialog box, 66-67
filling
  objects, 66-67
  WordArt text, 137
fills, 66
Fills color, 59
  applying, 84
finalizing presentations, 163,
    164-65
Find Clip dialog box, 100
Find tab (Help Topics dialog
    box), 18
finding
  clips, 100-101
    in Clip Gallery Live, 107
  presentations, 11
  text, 33
finding and replacing text, 33
flipping objects, 82
folders, default document
    folder, 241
Font dialog box, 42, 152
fonts
  embedding, 170, 171
  formatting, 42-43
  replacing, 170
  resizing, 43

fonts, *continued*
specifying in datasheets, 152
footers
as added to printed notes/
outlines, 175
adding to handouts, 176
adding to notes pages, 179, 180
adding to slides, 58
changing, 58
foreign languages
marking text in, 170, 171
spell checking, 49
Format Comment dialog box, 169
Format dialog boxes
formatting org charts, 144
resizing objects, 81
rotating objects, 83
specifying colors/lines, 84
Format dialog boxes (Graph), 160
Format Number dialog box, 152
Format Painter
picking up and applying color schemes, 61
picking up and applying styles, 42, 43
Format Picture dialog box, cropping images, 113
Format Text Box dialog box, 47
Format WordArt dialog box, 137
formatting
bullets, 45
chart boxes, 144
chart objects, 160-61
comments, 169
fonts, 42-43
Graph data, 152-53
the Handout Master, 176
lines, 84-85
of chart boxes, 144
the Notes Master, 179

org charts, 144
presentations in HTML, 214
text, 28, 42-43, 170-71
in chart boxes, 144
in text boxes, 47
Word tables, 133
WordArt text, 136-39
formatting (of text), displaying/
hiding in Outline view, 43
Formatting toolbar, 16
changing fonts, 43
formatting text, 42
Forward action buttons, inserting, 200
frames, viewing presentations with, 233
freeforms, 71, 76
creating, 76-77
editing, 78-79
freehand drawing, 77
frequently asked questions Web page, 235
FTP servers, saving presentations to, 226, 227

G

General tab (Options dialog box), 240
Genigraphics services, ordering, 186
Genigraphics Wizard, starting, 186
gradient fill effects, applying, 67
grammar, checking, 49
Graph (Microsoft), 145, 150
advanced features, 162
starting, 214
Graph charts, 146
animating, 194, 196, 197
applying chart types, 158-59

axes, 147, 151
creating, 146
creating chart types, 159
custom types, 159
customizing, 161
drawing objects in, 162
elements, 146, 147, 162
error bars, 162
formatting chart objects, 160-61
hiding/unhiding data from, 157
moving averages in, 162
opening, 147
selecting chart objects, 160
selecting chart types, 158
setting the default type, 159
showing datasheets with, 155
trendlines, 162
Graph data
deleting, 155
editing, 154
formatting, 152-53
formatting numbers, 152
hiding/unhiding from charts, 157
moving, 156
selecting, 149
showing tables with charts, 155
specifying fonts, 152
See also datasheets (in Graph)
graphic images. *See* images
graphs. *See* Excel charts; Graph charts
grayscale, converting default colors to, 110
grid
overriding, 91
snapping objects to, 90
grouping objects, 94
guides

adding/moving/removing, 91
aligning objects with, 90
overriding, 91

handles, sizing handles, 27, 47
Handout Master
formatting, 176
viewing, 53
handouts, 163
adding headers/footers to, 175, 176
creating, 176
in Word, 184
printing, 173, 177
Header and Footer dialog box, 58, 176, 180
headers
as added to printed notes/
outlines, 175
adding to handouts, 176
adding to notes pages, 179, 180
adding to slides, 58
changing, 58
Help, 18
asking the Office Assistant for, 17
frequently asked questions Web page, 235
online support Web page, 17, 234
on particular objects, 18, 19
on particular topics, 18
PowerPoint user newsgroup, 234
Visual Basic Help, 245
Help Topics dialog box, 18
hiding
background objects, 54

hiding, *continued*
    comments, 168
    slides from slide shows,
        13, 191
    text formatting in Outline
        view, 43
    toolbars, 16
    tools during presentations,
        223
highlighting. *See* selecting
home pages (on the Web),
    creating, 226, 227
HTML (Hypertext Markup
    Language), formatting
    presentations in, 214
hue (of colors), 62
Hyperlink To Slide dialog box,
    201, 204
Hyperlink To URL dialog
    box, 205
hyperlinks
    activating, 205
    adding sounds to, 203
    adding to objects, 202
    to files, 204
    to other programs, 205
    to slides, 201, 204
    to web pages, 205
    See also action buttons

icons
    hidden slide icon, 191
    inserting objects as, 127
    toolbar button icons, 250
images
    bitmaps, 98, 112, 241
    cropping, 112-13
    redisplaying cropped
        images, 112

saving slides as graphic
    images, 187, 188
specifying color type, 110
vector images, 98
See also clip art; pictures
Import Data Options dialog
    box, 150
importing
    clips, 102
    data, 150
indenting text, 31, 36-37
index pages (on the Web),
    opening, 232
Index tab (Help Topics dialog
    box), 18
information
    accessing on the Web, 234
    entering into placeholders,
        25
    pasting in a specified
        format, 125
    sharing among documents,
        123-44
Insert dialog box, 155
Insert Object dialog box,
    126, 130
Insert Outline dialog box, 35
Insert Picture dialog box, 105
inserting
    action buttons, 200-201
    cells into datasheets, 155
    clips, 99, 114-15, 120
    comments, 168
    dates/times/slide numbering,
        56-57, 58
    Excel charts, 130, 131
    Excel worksheets, 130-31
    files, 126
    movies, 120
    objects, 126-27
    outlines from other applica-
        tions, 34, 35
    pictures, 105

placeholders, 180-81
slides
    new, 24
    from other presentations,
        166, 167
    sounds, 114-15, 118-19
    text between words, 30
    videos, 120
    Word tables, 132
    WordArt text, 134
    See also embedding; import-
        ing; linking; pasting
insertion point, on slides, 30
installing add-in programs,
    118, 119
Internet
    getting Help from
        PowerPoint Central,
        19
    presentations on, 214
intranets, inserting slides
    from, 167
irregular curves, drawing, 76-77
irregular polygons, drawing, 76
italics, applying, 42

K

keyboard
    selecting text, 32
    See also shortcut keys
keywords, locating clips by,
    100-101
kiosks, creating presentations
    for, 190, 204

L

languages
    marking text in other
        languages, 170, 171

spell checking other
    languages, 49
legend labels (in charts),
    146, 155
legends (in charts), 147
light pen
    setting the color, 217
    using in slide shows, 216-17
lighting, of 3-D objects, 89
line patterns, creating, 85
Line Style tool, 72
Line tool, 72
lines, 71
    coloring, 84
    creating line patterns, 85
    drawing, 72
    editing, 72
    formatting, 84-85
        chart box lines, 144
linked objects
    converting types, 129
    modifying, 128
    modifying sources of, 128
linking
    Excel worksheets, 130-31
    objects, 124, 126, 127
    See also hyperlinks; paste
        linking
links
    breaking, 128
    updating, 128
    See also action buttons;
        hyperlinks
Links dialog box, 128, 129
locating. *See* finding
logos
    adding to every slide in a
        presentation, 54
    creating for Web pages,
        226, 227
luminosity (of colors), 62, 63

macro modules, 244
  copying between presentations, 245
macros, 242
  assigning to toolbars/menus, 246-47
  debugging, 244, 245
  deleting, 243
  editing, 244-45
  recording, 242
  running, 243
    one step at a time, 244
  virus protection, 240
masters, 51
  designing slides with, 54-55
  hiding background objects on slides, 54
  overriding, 55
  reapplying, 55
  viewing, 52-53
Maximize button (PowerPoint window), 10
Media Player, 98
Meeting Minder, 220, 221
Meeting Minder Export dialog box, 220
meeting minutes
  creating, 220
  exporting, 220
menu bars (PowerPoint window), 10
menu commands, 14
menus
  assigning macros to, 247
  issuing commands with, 14
  popup menu, 215
Microsoft Bookshelf, looking up references in, 170, 171
Microsoft Clip Gallery. *See* Clip Gallery

Microsoft Organization Chart. *See* Organization Chart (Microsoft)
Microsoft Outlook, sending meeting minutes to, 220
Microsoft PowerPoint 97 At a Glance, 1-3
Microsoft Web pages
  frequently asked questions, 235
  online support, 17, 234
  Product News, 234
Microsoft Word. *See* Word (Microsoft)
Microsoft WordArt. *See* WordArt (Microsoft)
Minimize button (PowerPoint window), 10
monitor resolution for Web page graphics, 228
motifs (musical), assigning to animations, 119
mouse
  activating hyperlinks, 205
  drawing objects, 81
  selecting text, 32
  slide show navigation shortcuts, 218
mouse pointer. *See* pointer
Move Down button, 40
Move Up button, 40
movies
  editing, 121
  inserting, 120
  playing, 121
moving
  chart boxes, 143
  drawing objects, 80-81
    with precision, 81
  Graph data, 156
  guides, 91
  objects, 27
  vertices in freeforms, 78

See also navigating; rearranging
moving averages, in Graph charts, 162
multimedia objects. *See* clips
multiple animations, coordinating, 198-99
music
  adding background music to slide shows, 208-9
  assigning motifs to animations, 119
  See also soundtracks

narrations, recording, 208
navigating
  objects, 95
  slide shows, 214, 218-19
  slides in Slide view, 12
New Office Document dialog box, starting PowerPoint from, 6
New Presentation dialog box
  creating new presentations with templates, 9
  starting new presentations, 7
New Slide dialog box
  default display, 240
  inserting clips, 99, 114, 120
newsgroups, PowerPoint users', 234
notes, 163, 178
  adding to presentations, 13
  entering, 178
  meeting minutes, 220
  printing, 173
  taking notes during slide shows, 220-21
  See also comments; notes pages

Notes Master
  formatting, 179
  reinserting placeholders on, 180
  viewing, 53
Notes Page view, 13
  entering notes, 178
notes pages, 178
  adding dates/times/headers/footers/numbering to, 179, 180
  adding headers/footers to, 175
  customizing, 180-81
  sending to Word, 184, 185
nudging drawing objects, 80
numbering
  adding to notes pages, 179, 180
  See also slide numbering

Object Linking and Embedding (OLE), 123, 124, 126-29
objects, 64, 84
  adding hyperlinks to, 202
  adding to every slide in a presentation, 54
  aligning, 92-93
    with the guides, 90
  animating, 198
  chart objects, 160-61
  coloring, 64, 84, 110
  deleting, 27
  deselecting, 26
  distributing across slides, 92
  dragging, overriding the grid/guides, 91
  embedding, 124, 126
  filling, 66-67, 137
  flipping, 82

objects, *continued*
  getting Help on, 18, 19
  grouping/ungrouping/
    regrouping, 94-95
  inserting, 126-27
  linking, 124, 126, 127
  moving, 27
  moving through, 95
  pasting, 124, 125
  placing, 90-91
  recoloring, 110-11
  resizing, 26, 80, 81
    with precision, 81
    proportionally, 27, 80
  rotating, 82-83
  selecting, 26, 27, 32, 36
  snapping into place, 90-91
  stacking, 94
  title objects, 54
  turning into action
    buttons, 202
  types, 23
  See also images
Office 97 CD-ROM
  Custom Soundtrack, 118-19
  ValuPack, 171, 237
Office Art drawing tools, 73
Office Assistant
  asking for Help from, 17
  changing the display, 17
OLE (Object Linking and
    Embedding), 123, 124,
    126-29
online help. *See* Help
Open dialog box
  finding presentations, 11
  opening presentations, 11
opening
  Clip Gallery Live, 106
  Graph charts, 147
  index pages, 232
  presentations, 11
    in Slide Show view, 191

URLs (uniform resource
  locators), 231
option buttons (in dialog
  boxes), 15
options. *See* defaults, setting
Options dialog box
  Advanced tab, 241
  Edit tab, 241
  General tab, 240
  Spelling tab, 49
  View tab, 215, 240
org charts
  adding titles to, 141
  creating, 140
  formatting, 144
Organization Chart (Microsoft),
    123, 140
  starting, 140
Outline view, 12, 28, 29
  adding slides, 34, 37
  collapsing/expanding slides,
    40, 41
  displaying/hiding text
    formatting, 43
  entering text, 29, 34
  rearranging slides, 40, 41
  selecting slides, 41
outlines, 34
  adding headers/footers
    to, 175
  adding slides to, 34, 37
  entering text into, 29, 34
  inserting from other
    applications, 34, 35
  printing, 173, 175
  rearranging slides in, 40, 41
  selecting slides in, 41
  See also Outline view
Outlook (Microsoft), sending
    meeting minutes to, 220
ovals, drawing, 74

Pack And Go Wizard, 224
packing/unpacking presenta-
    tions, 224-25
Page Setup dialog box, 172, 173
page setup options, 172-73
  changing slide orientation,
    173
  specifying slide size, 172-73
paragraphs
  spacing, 31
  tabs and, 38
Paste command (Edit
    menu), 125
paste linking
  data, 151
  notes pages, 185
  objects, 126, 127
Paste Special command (Edit
    menu), 125, 126
Paste Special dialog box,
    125, 127
pasting
  data into datasheets,
    151, 156
  information in a specified
    format, 125
  objects, 124, 125
  See also paste linking
pattern fill effects, applying, 67
Patterned Lines dialog box, 85
patterns, creating line
    patterns, 85
picking up and applying
  color schemes, 61
  styles, 42, 43
picture fill effects, applying, 66
pictures
  animating, 194
  inserting, 105
  recoloring, 111
  resizing, 98

placeholders, 25
  entering text into, 25, 30-31
  reinserting, 180-81
  See also text boxes
Play Options dialog box,
    116, 121
playing
  movies, 121
  sounds, 116
plot area (in Graph), 160
pointer
  action buttons and, 202
  in chart boxes, 143
  slide show options, 216
points, modifying vertex
    points, 79
polygons, drawing irregular
    polygons, 76
popup menu, 215
PowerPoint (Microsoft), 5, 123
  customizing, 239-50
  exiting, 21
  program window
    elements, 10
  starting, 6
  user newsgroup, 234
  views, 12-13
  Web pages, 17, 234, 235
  See also masters
PowerPoint Animation
    Player, 229
PowerPoint Central, 234, 236
  accessing, 236
  getting Help from, 19
  locating clips in, 106
PowerPoint dialog box, starting
    new presentations, 7
PowerPoint Viewer, 224
  showing slide shows, 225
PowerPoint window
    elements, 10
precision
  cropping images, 113

precision, *continued*
  resizing objects, 81
  specifying datasheet column
    widths, 153
presentation agendas,
  creating, 164
Presentation Conference
  Wizard, 214
  as an audience member, 223
  as a presenter, 222
presentation conferencing, 214,
  222-23
presentation window
  (PowerPoint window), 10
presentations
  adding notes to, 13
  applying designs from, 70
  applying templates to, 9, 70
  checking contents, 182
  closing, 21
  conferencing, 214, 222-23
  copying macro modules
    between, 245
  copying slides between, 165
  creating, 7
    for kiosks, 190, 204
    with templates, 9
  creating hyperlinks to, 204
  designing, 8
  documenting contents,
    163, 182
  embedding fonts in,
    170, 171
  finalizing, 163, 164-65
  finding, 11
  formatting in HTML, 214
  with frames, viewing, 233
  hiding tools during, 223
  inserting outlines from other
    applications, 34, 35
  inserting slides from other
    presentations,
    166, 167

on the Internet, 214
listing favorites, 167
before live audiences, 214,
  215-21
locating clips in, 100, 101
navigating, 214, 218-19
opening, 11
  in Slide Show view, 191
packing into floppy
  disks, 224
pasting objects into, 125
placing on Web pages, 214
printing, 174-75
recording ideas during, 214
on the road, 214, 224-25
saving, 20
  in different formats, 187
  to FTP servers, 226, 227
  as templates, 68, 69
  as Web pages, 214, 226,
    228-29
scenarios, 214
sending, 183
specifying templates for, 9
starting, 7
supplements, 163-88
switching between open, 7
timing, 206-7
unpacking, 225
viewing, with Web browsers,
  232-33
See also slide shows
previewing
  animations, 194
  color scheme colors, 62
Print dialog box, 174, 175, 177
printing
  handouts, 173, 177
  headers/footers in notes/
    outlines, 175
  notes, 173
  outlines, 173, 175
  presentations, 174-75

setting up slides for, 172-73
slide shows, 174
slides, 175
Product News (Microsoft),
  viewing on the Web, 234
programs
  creating hyperlinks to other
    programs, 205
  installing add-in programs,
    119
Promote button, 36
promoting text, 31, 36, 37
properties
  entering, 182
  locating, 182
Properties dialog boxes,
  documenting/checking
  presentation contents,
  182
protecting files, 21

R

ranges (in datasheets)
  importing, 150
  selecting, 149
  See also Graph data
rearranging
  chart boxes, 143
  slides, 40, 41, 211
  See also moving
Recolor Picture dialog box, 111
recoloring objects, 110-11
Record dialog box, 242
Record Macro dialog box, 242
Record Narration dialog
  box, 208
recording
  macros, 242
  narrations, 208
  sounds, 116, 117
rectangles, drawing, 74

Redo button, identifying
  redoable actions, 33
redoing actions, 33
reference resources, accessing,
  170, 171
regrouping objects, 95
rehearsing slide timings, 206
reinserting placeholders, 180-81
replacing
  AutoShapes, 75
  fonts, 170
  text, 33
reshaping
  AutoShapes, 74
  WordArt text, 136
resizing
  arrows, 73
  AutoShapes, 74
  clip art, 98, 108
  fonts, 43
  objects, 26, 80, 81
    with precision, 81
    proportionally, 27, 80
  pictures, 98
  text boxes, 47
  Word tables, 132
Restore button (PowerPoint
  window), 10
Return action buttons, 200
rotating
  Graph chart axes, 161
  objects, 82-83
  WordArt text, 136
row labels, entering, 151
rows (in datasheets)
  inserting, 155
  selecting, 149
ruler
  changing indents, 37
  displaying, 36
  selected objects and, 36
running macros, 243
  one step at a time, 244

running slide shows, 13, 210
  on other computers, 171

S

saturation (of colors), 62
Save As dialog box
  recording sounds, 117
  saving presentations, 20
    in different formats, 187
    as templates, 69
Save As HTML Wizard, 214,
  228-29
saving
  color schemes, 63
  presentations, 20
    in different formats, 187
    to FTP servers, 226, 227
    as templates, 68, 69
    as Web pages, 214, 226,
     228-29
  slides, as graphic images,
    187, 188
scaling slides, 172-73
ScreenTips
  for action buttons, 202
  identifying undoable/
    redoable actions, 33
Scribble tool, 77
scroll boxes, 12
selecting
  chart boxes, 140
  chart objects, 160
  embedded objects, 126
  Graph data, 149
  objects, 26, 27, 32, 36
  slides, 32
    in Outline view, 41
  text, 32
  text objects, 36
  words, 32, 241

selection boxes, slanted versus
  dotted, 42
sending
  presentations, 183
  See also exporting
Set Up Show dialog box, 190,
  191, 210
shadows
  applying to text, 42, 87
  coloring, 87
  locating, 86
  preset, 86
Shadows color, 59
shapes
  snapping to other shapes, 90
  See also AutoShapes
sharing information among
  documents, 123-44
Shift key
  drawing circles/squares,
    74, 201
  drawing lines, 72
  resizing objects, 80
  selecting data ranges, 149
  selecting text, 32
Shift+Enter keys, adding new
  lines in Outline view, 37
Shift+Tab keys, promoting text,
  31, 36, 37
shortcut keys
  issuing commands with, 14
  slide show navigation
    shortcuts, 218
  See also Alt key; Ctrl key;
    Shift key
shortcut menus, 14
  displaying, 14
  selecting commands, 14
sizing handles, 27, 47
slanted selection boxes, 42
Slide Finder
  displaying slide titles in, 167

inserting slides from other
  presentations, 166,
  167
listing favorite presentations,
  167
slide icons, 12, 13
Slide Master
  opening the Title Master
    from, 52
  viewing, 52
slide meter, 206, 207
Slide Navigator, 219
slide numbering
  inserting into slides, 56, 58
  specifying, 57, 172
slide orientation, changing, 173
Slide Show view, 13
  displaying the popup
    menu, 215
  opening presentations
    in, 191
slide shows
  accessing commands
    during, 215
  action items, 220, 221
  adding background music to,
    208-9
  adding slides to, 211
  copying slides into, 165
  custom, 189, 210-11
    creating, 210, 211
    editing, 211
    going to, 219
  emphasizing points, 216
  enabling return to previous
    slide, 200
  going to custom shows, 219
  going to specific slides, 218
  hiding slides from, 13, 191
  hiding tools during, 223
  inserting slides from other
    presentations into,
    166, 167

light pen use, 216-17
before live audiences, 214,
  215-21
meeting minutes, 220
navigating, 214, 218-19
navigation shortcuts, 218
pointer options, 216
preparing, 189-211
presenting, 213-37
printing, 174
rearranging slides in, 211
recording narrations for, 208
removing slides from, 211
on the road, 214, 224-25
scenarios, 214
setting up, 190
showing, 13, 210
  on other computers, 171
  with the PowerPoint
    Viewer, 225
showing ranges of slides, 191
taking notes during, 220-21
types, 190
See also presentations
Slide Sorter view, 12-13
  finalizing presentations,
    164-65
  hiding slides from slide
    shows, 13, 191
  opening slides in Slide
    view, 164
  rearranging slides, 40,
    41, 211
  vertical bar, 40
  viewing slides, 164
slide timings
  activating, 206, 207
  editing, 206, 207
  setting, 206
  testing, 206, 207
slide titles, displaying, 167
Slide Transition dialog box, 192,
  193, 206, 207

slide transitions, 189
    adding, 12-13
    adding sound to, 192, 193
    applying to all slides, 192
    effects, 192
    setting transition effect
        speeds, 193
    specifying, 192
Slide view, 12, 28
    entering notes, 178
    entering text, 25, 28, 30-31
    hiding slides from slide
        shows, 191
    manipulating objects, 26-27
    moving through slides, 12
slides
    adding animation to, 194
    adding headers/footers to, 58
    adding to outlines, 34, 37
    adding to slide shows, 211
    applying individual slide
        changes globally, 55
    collapsing/expanding in
        Outline view, 40, 41
    coloring, 60-63
    copying between presenta-
        tions, 165
    creating, 24-25
        from bulleted lists, 31
        with Word tables, 133
    creating hyperlinks to,
        201, 204
    deleting, 35
        from slide shows, 211
    designing
        with AutoLayouts, 24
        with masters, 54-55
    displaying titles, 167
    distributing objects
        across, 92
    duplicating, 35
    hiding slides from slide
        shows, 13, 191

icons, 12, 13
inserting
    new slides, 24
    from other presentations,
        166, 167
inserting action buttons into,
    200-201
inserting clips into, 99,
    114-15, 120
inserting comments
    into, 168
inserting dates/times/slide
    numbering into,
    56-57, 58
inserting Excel charts/
    worksheets into,
    130-31
inserting pictures into, 105
inserting sounds into,
    114-15, 118-19
inserting Word tables
    into, 132
inserting WordArt text
    into, 134
making global changes to, 52
moving through, in Slide
    view, 12
in Outline view, 12
printing, 175
rearranging, 40, 41, 211
reinserting placeholders
    into, 181
saving as graphic images,
    187, 188
scaling for printing, 172-73
selecting, 32
    in Outline view, 41
sending to Word, 184, 185
setting up for printing,
    172-73
sizing, 172-73
summary slides, 164
title slides, 53

viewing
    in Slide Sorter view, 164
    on Web pages, 232-33
viewing miniatures, 12, 55
See also slide shows
snapping objects into place, 90
Sound Selection dialog box, 208
sounds, 98
    adding to animations, 195
    adding to hyperlinks, 203
    adding to slide transitions,
        192, 193
    editing, 116, 117
    inserting, 114-15, 118-19
    playing, 116
    recording, 116, 117, 193
soundtracks
    inserting, 208-9
    installing, 118
    looping, 209
    recording narrations, 208
    specifying, 118-19
source file, defined, 124
source program, defined, 124
spaces, adding/removing in
    editing text, 241
Speaker Notes dialog box, 178,
    221
speaker's notes
    editing, 221
    preparing, 178-79
    viewing, 221
special characters
    inserting, 30
    See also WordArt text; and
        Special Characters
        section of this index
special effects
    for drawing objects, 71
    fill effects, 66-67
    three-dimensional effects, 71
    WordArt text effects, 138-39
spelling

checking, 48
correcting while typing,
    48, 49
Spelling dialog box, 48
Spelling tab (Options dialog
    box), 49
spinning 3-D objects, 88
stacking objects, 94
Standard toolbar, 16
Start menu, starting PowerPoint
    from, 6
start pages (on the Web),
    viewing, 230
starting
    the Genigraphics Wizard,
        186
    Graph, 214
    Organization Chart, 140
    PowerPoint, 6
    presentations, 7
status bar (PowerPoint
    window), 10
style, checking grammar, 49
Style Checker, 49
styles, picking up and applying,
    42, 43
subordinate chart boxes,
    adding, 142
summary slides, creating, 164
supplements to presentations,
    163-88
surfaces, for 3-D objects, 89
switching between open
    presentations, 7
symbols. See special characters
system failures, temporary files
    and, 20

Tab key
    demoting text, 31, 36, 37

Tab key, *continued*
moving through objects, 95
selecting objects, 26
Shift+Tab keys, promoting
text, 31, 36, 37
Table AutoFormat dialog
box, 133
tabs (in dialog boxes), 15
tabs (in documents), 38
button alignments, 38
changing, 39
clearing, 39
setting, 38-39
templates, 9, 51
applying to presentations,
9, 70
changing, 69
creating, 68
creating presentations
with, 9
saving presentations as,
68, 69
storing, 68
types, 51
temporary files, and system
failures, 20
text
adding to AutoShapes, 47
aligning, 43
in chart boxes, 144
animating, 196, 197
then dimming, 197
applying shadows to, 42, 87
deleting, 33
editing, 28, 32-33
adding/removing spaces
as needed, 241
in text boxes, 46
entering
into chart boxes, 141
in Outline view, 29, 34
in Slide view, 25, 28,
30-31

finding and replacing, 33
formatting, 28, 42-43,
170-71
in chart boxes, 144
in text boxes, 47
indenting, 31, 36-37
inserting between words, 30
marking text in other
languages, 170, 171
replacing, 33
selecting, 32
spacing between bullets
and, 44
See also bulleted text
Text & Lines color, 59
text boxes (in dialog boxes), 15
text boxes (in Slide view), 28,
29, 46-47
creating, 46
editing, 46
formatting, 47
resizing, 47
text formatting, displaying/
hiding in Outline
view, 43
text objects, 23
selecting, 36
35-mm slides, converting
presentations to, 186
three-dimensional effects, 71
three-dimensional objects
adding surfaces to, 89
creating, 88
setting depth, 89
setting lighting, 89
spinning, 88
tick mark labels (in charts), 146
tick marks (in charts), 147
time formats, 56
times
adding to notes pages,
179, 180
inserting into slides, 56, 58

timing presentations, 206-7
title bar (PowerPoint
window), 10
Title Master, viewing, 52
title objects, placing, 54
title slides, 53
title text, 28, 29
Title Text color, 59
titles
adding to org charts, 141
placing title objects, 54
slide title text, 28, 29
toolbar buttons, 10
adding to toolbars, 248-49
customizing, 250
enlarging, 248
issuing commands with, 16
toolbars, 10, 16
adding, 248
adding buttons to, 248-49
assigning macros to, 246
deleting, 249
displaying, 16
Drawing toolbar, 16, 47,
72, 73
Formatting toolbar, 16, 42,
43
hiding, 16
restoring, 250
Standard toolbar, 16
Web toolbar, 230-31
tools
hiding during presentations,
223
Office Art drawing tools, 73
See also toolbar buttons;
toolbars; *and specific
toolbar buttons*
transitions. *See* slide transitions
trendlines, in Graph charts, 162
TrueType fonts, embedding, 170
typing errors, correcting while
typing, 48, 49

underlining, applying to
text, 42
Undo button, identifying
undoable actions, 33
undoing actions, 33
ungrouping objects, 95
Update dialog box, 103
updating
the Clip Gallery, 102
links, 128
URLs (uniform resource
locators)
creating hyperlinks to, 204
opening, 231

V

ValuPack (Office 97 CD-ROM),
171, 237
accessing, 237
vector images, 98
vertex/vertices (in freeforms)
deleting, 79
inserting, 78
modifying angles, 79
modifying point types, 79
moving, 78
vertical bar (in Slide Sorter
view), 40
videos, 98
inserting, 120
view buttons (PowerPoint
window), 10
View tab (Options dialog box),
215, 240
views, 12-13
changing, 12
Visual Basic, 244
Help, 245
visual objects, 23

watermark, converting default
colors to, 110
Web
    accessing information
      on, 234
    downloading clips from,
      105, 107
    getting Help from, 17
    searching, 231
    See also Microsoft Web pages;
      Web pages
Web browsers, viewing presenta-
    tions with, 232-33
Web pages
    creating, 214, 226-27, 228-29
    creating banners for, 227
    creating home pages,
      226, 227
    creating hyperlinks to, 204
    including animations in, 229

monitor resolution for
    graphics, 228
    opening index pages, 232
    saving presentations as, 214,
      226, 228-29
    viewing presentations with
      frames, 233
    viewing slides on, 232-33
    viewing start pages, 230
    See also Microsoft Web pages
Web toolbar, 230-31
    displaying/hiding, 230
Windows Media Player, 98
wizards, AutoContent Wizard, 8
Word (Microsoft)
    creating handouts in, 184
    exporting action items/
      meeting minutes
      to, 220
    exporting notes pages/slides
      to, 184, 185
Word tables

creating slides with, 133
    editing, 133
    formatting, 133
    inserting, 132
    resizing, 132
word wrap, in text boxes, 47
WordArt (Microsoft), 123, 134
WordArt text
    adjusting character
      spacing, 139
    aligning, 137
    coloring, 137
    editing, 135, 136-37
    filling, 137
    formatting, 136-39
    formatting vertically, 138
    inserting, 134
    making letters the same
      height, 138
    reshaping, 136
    restyling, 135
WordArt text effects, applying,
    138-39

WordArt toolbar, 136
words
    inserting text between, 30
    looking up, 170, 171
    red-underlined, 49
    selecting single words,
      32, 241
worksheets. *See* Excel worksheets
World Wide Web. *See* Web
Write-Up dialog box, 184, 185

x-axis (in Graph charts), 147
    labeling, 151

y-axis (in Graph charts), 147
    labeling, 151

The manuscript for this book was prepared and submitted to Microsoft Press in electronic form. Text files were prepared using Microsoft Word for Windows 95. Pages were composed by Steven Payne, Patricia Young, and Gary Bedard using PageMaker for Windows, with text in Stone Sans and display type in Stone Serif and Stone Serif Semibold. Composed pages were delivered to the printer as electronic prepress files.

Cover Designer
Tim Girvin Design

Interior Graphic Designer
designlab
Kim Eggleston

Graphic Layout
Steven Payne

Principal Compositor
Patrica Young

Compositor
Gary Bedard

Indexer
Michael Brackney

Joan and Patrick Carey, husband-and-wife team, have authored, developed, or managed over 40 books in the software industry, for both academic and trade audiences. The topics range from a ground-breaking, internationally acclaimed text that teaches statistically analysis with Microsoft Excel to texts on surfing the World Wide Web or understanding operating systems and networks. When they're not staying up late writing, they keep busy with their four young children. When they're not writing and rearing, they sleep. Joan, Patrick, and the kiddies live in Madison, Wisconsin, but can also be found peak-bagging in Estes Park, Colorado during the summer.

Acknowledgments

We would like to thank David Beskeen and Steve Johnson and all the staff at Perspection for their vision, hard work, and enthusiastic support for this project. Perspection is one of the most vibrant companies in today's fast-paced publishing industry, and we are honored to be associated with them. We are especially grateful for their team spirt and active desire to make book production a positive, affirming experience. Copyeditor Jane Pedicini deserves special mention for her high editorial standards. We dedicate this book to our four little sons, John Paul, Thomas, Peter, and Michael, who have so cheerfully accommodated the demands that go with such a project.

Take
productivity
in
stride.

Microsoft® Excel 97 Step by Step
U.S.A. $29.95   ($39.95 Canada)
ISBN 1-57231-314-5

Microsoft® Word 97 Step by Step
U.S.A. $29.95   ($39.95 Canada)
ISBN 1-57231-313-7

Microsoft® PowerPoint® 97
 Step by Step
U.S.A. $29.95   ($39.95 Canada)
ISBN 1-57231-315-3

Microsoft® Outlook™ 97 Step by Step
U.S.A. $29.99   ($39.99 Canada)
ISBN 1-57231-382-X

Microsoft® Access 97 Step by Step
U.S.A. $29.95   ($39.95 Canada)
ISBN 1-57231-316-1

Microsoft® Office 97 Integration
 Step by Step
U.S.A. $29.95   ($39.95 Canada)
ISBN 1-57231-317-X

Microsoft Press® *Step by Step* books provide quick and easy self-paced training that will help you learn to use the powerful word processor, spreadsheet, database, desktop information manager, and presentation applications of Microsoft Office 97, both individually and together. Prepared by the professional trainers at Catapult, Inc., and Perspection, Inc., these books present easy-to-follow lessons with clear objectives, real-world business examples, and numerous screen shots and illustrations. Each book contains approximately eight hours of instruction. Put Microsoft's Office 97 applications to work today, *Step by Step.*

Microsoft Press® products are available worldwide wherever quality computer books are sold. For more information, contact your book retailer, computer reseller, or local Microsoft Sales Office.

To locate your nearest source for Microsoft Press products, reach us at www.microsoft.com/mspress/, or call 1-800-MSPRESS in the U.S. (in Canada: 1-800-667-1115 or 416-293-8464).

To order Microsoft Press products, call 1-800-MSPRESS in the U.S. (in Canada: 1-800-667-1115 or 416-293-8464).

Prices and availability dates are subject to change.

Microsoft *Press*

Keep things **running** smoothly around the **Office.**

These are *the* answer books for business users of Microsoft® Office 97 applications. They are packed with everything from quick, clear instructions for new users to comprehensive answers for power users. The Microsoft Press® *Running* series features authoritative handbooks you'll keep by your computer and use every day.

Running Microsoft® Excel 97
Mark Dodge, Chris Kinata, and Craig Stinson
U.S.A.   **$39.95**   ($53.95 Canada)
ISBN 1-57231-321-8

Running Microsoft® Office 97
Michael Halvorson and Michael Young
U.S.A.   **$39.95**   ($53.95 Canada)
ISBN 1-57231-322-6

Running Microsoft® Word 97
Russell Borland
U.S.A.   **$39.95**   ($53.95 Canada)
ISBN 1-57231-320-X

Running Microsoft® PowerPoint® 97
Stephen W. Sagman
U.S.A.   **$29.95**   ($39.95 Canada)
ISBN 1-57231-324-2

Running Microsoft® Access 97
John Viescas
U.S.A.   **$39.95**   ($53.95 Canada)
ISBN 1-57231-323-4

Get quick, easy answers— anywhere!

Microsoft Press® Field Guides are a quick, accurate source of information about Microsoft® Office 97 applications. In no time, you'll have the lay of the land, identify toolbar buttons and commands, stay safely out of danger, and have all the tools you need for survival!

Microsoft® Excel 97 Field Guide
Stephen L. Nelson
U.S.A. $9.95 ($12.95 Canada)
ISBN 1-57231-326-9

Microsoft® Word 97 Field Guide
Stephen L. Nelson
U.S.A. $9.95 ($12.95 Canada)
ISBN 1-57231-325-0

Microsoft® PowerPoint® 97 Field Guide
Stephen L. Nelson
U.S.A. $9.95 ($12.95 Canada)
ISBN 1-57231-327-7

Microsoft® Outlook™ 97 Field Guide
Stephen L. Nelson
U.S.A. $9.99 ($12.99 Canada)
ISBN 1-57231-383-8

Microsoft® Access 97 Field Guide
Stephen L. Nelson
U.S.A. $9.95 ($12.95 Canada)
ISBN 1-57231-328-5

Microsoft Press® products are available worldwide wherever quality computer books are sold. For more information, contact your book retailer, computer reseller, or local Microsoft Sales Office.

To locate your nearest source for Microsoft Press products, reach us at www.microsoft.com/mspress/, or call 1-800-MSPRESS in the U.S. (in Canada: 1-800-667-1115 or 416-293-8464).

To order Microsoft Press products, call 1-800-MSPRESS in the U.S. (in Canada: 1-800-667-1115 or 416-293-8464).

Prices and availability dates are subject to change.

Things are looking up!

Here's the remarkable, *visual* way to quickly find answers about the powerfully integrated features of the Microsoft® Office 97 applications. Microsoft Press® *At a Glance* books let you focus on particular tasks and show you with clear, numbered steps the easiest way to get them done right now.

Microsoft® Excel 97 At a Glance
Perspection, Inc.
U.S.A. **$16.95** ($22.95 Canada)
ISBN 1-57231-367-6

Microsoft® Word 97 At a Glance
Jerry Joyce and Marianne Moon
U.S.A. **$16.95** ($22.95 Canada)
ISBN 1-57231-366-8

Microsoft® PowerPoint® 97 At a Glance
Perspection, Inc.
U.S.A. **$16.95** ($22.95 Canada)
ISBN 1-57231-368-4

Microsoft® Access 97 At a Glance
Perspection, Inc.
U.S.A. **$16.95** ($22.95 Canada)
ISBN 1-57231-369-2

Microsoft® Office 97 At a Glance
Perspection, Inc.
U.S.A. **$16.95** ($22.95 Canada)
ISBN 1-57231-365-X

Microsoft® Windows® 95 At a Glance
Jerry Joyce and Marianne Moon
U.S.A. **$16.95** ($22.95 Canada)
ISBN 1-57231-370-6

Microsoft Press® products are available worldwide wherever quality computer books are sold. For more information, contact your book retailer, computer reseller, or local Microsoft Sales Office.

To locate your nearest source for Microsoft Press products, reach us at www.microsoft.com/mspress/, or call 1-800-MSPRESS in the U.S. (in Canada: 1-800-667-1115 or 416-293-8464).

To order Microsoft Press products, call 1-800-MSPRESS in the U.S. (in Canada: 1-800-667-1115 or 416-293-8464).

Prices and availability dates are subject to change.

Microsoft® Press